Communications
in Computer and Information Science   1250

Commenced Publication in 2007
Founding and Former Series Editors:
Simone Diniz Junqueira Barbosa, Phoebe Chen, Alfredo Cuzzocrea,
Xiaoyong Du, Orhun Kara, Ting Liu, Krishna M. Sivalingam,
Dominik Ślęzak, Takashi Washio, Xiaokang Yang, and Junsong Yuan

More information about this series at http://www.springer.com/series/7899

Marten van Sinderen · Leszek A. Maciaszek (Eds.)

Software Technologies

14th International Conference, ICSOFT 2019
Prague, Czech Republic, July 26–28, 2019
Revised Selected Papers

 Springer

Editors
Marten van Sinderen
Information Systems Group
University of Twente
Enschede, The Netherlands

Leszek A. Maciaszek
Institute of Business Informatics
Wrocław University of Economics
Wrocław, Poland

Macquarie University
Sydney, Australia

ISSN 1865-0929 ISSN 1865-0937 (electronic)
Communications in Computer and Information Science
ISBN 978-3-030-52990-1 ISBN 978-3-030-52991-8 (eBook)
https://doi.org/10.1007/978-3-030-52991-8

This Springer imprint is published by the registered company Springer Nature Switzerland AG
The registered company address is: Gewerbestrasse 11, 6330 Cham, Switzerland

Preface

The present book includes extended and revised versions of a set of selected papers from the 14th International Conference on Software Technologies (ICSOFT 2019), held in Prague, Czech Republic, from July 26–28, 2019.

ICSOFT 2019 received 116 paper submissions from 41 countries, of which 21 contributions (18%) were accepted and presented as full papers. After the conference, the authors of selected full papers were invited to submit a revised and extended version of their papers having at least 30% new material. In the end, 10 revised and extended papers have been included in this Springer book (i.e. 9% of the original 116 submissions).

The papers were selected by the event chairs and their selection was based on a number of criteria that included the classifications and comments provided by the Program Committee members, the session chairs' assessment, and the verification of the papers' revisions and extensions by the program and conference chairs.

The purpose of the ICSOFT conference is to bring together researchers, engineers, and practitioners interested in software technologies. The conference solicits papers and other contributions in themes ranging from software engineering and development via showcasing cutting-edge software systems and applications to addressing foundational innovative technologies for systems and applications of the future. The papers were presented in one of three conference areas: "Software Engineering and Systems Development," "Software Systems and Applications," and "Foundational and Trigger Technologies."

We would like to thank all the authors for their contributions and the reviewers for ensuring the quality of this publication.

July 2019

Marten van Sinderen
Leszek A. Maciaszek

Organization

Conference Chair

Leszek A. Maciaszek   Wrocław University of Economics, Poland,
and Macquarie University, Australia

Program Chair

Marten van Sinderen   University of Twente, The Netherlands

Program Committee

Jose Gonzalez	University of Seville, Spain
Waleed Alsabhan	KACST, UK
Peter Amthor	Technische Universität Ilmenau, Germany
Soumyadip Bandyopadhyay	BITS Pilani K K Birla Goa Campus and Hasso Plattner Institute, India
Davide Basile	University of Florence, Italy
Doina Bein	California State University, Fullerton, USA
Wolfgang Bein	University of Nevada, Las Vegas, USA
Fevzi Belli	Izmir Institute of Technology, Turkey
Yann Ben Maissa	INPT, Morocco
Jorge Bernardino	Polytechnic of Coimbra - ISEC, Portugal
Mario Berón	Universidad Nacional de San Luis, Argentina
Marcello Bersani	Politecnico di Milano, Italy
Dominik Bork	University of Vienna, Austria
Andrea Burattin	University of Innsbruck, Austria
Nelio Cacho	Federal University of Rio Grande do Norte, Brazil
Alejandro Calderón	University of Cádiz, Spain
Gerardo Canfora	University of Sannio, Italy
Cagatay Catal	Wageningen University, The Netherlands
Ana Cavalli	Telecom SudParis, France
Juan Chagüendo Benavides	Universidad Carlos III de Madrid, Spain
Alexandru Cicortas	West University Timisoara, Romania
Lidia López Cuesta	Universitat Politècnica de Catalunya, Spain
Sergiu Dascalu	University of Nevada, Reno, USA
Cléver Ricardo de Farias	University of São Paulo, Brazil
Martina De Sanctis	Gran Sasso Science Institute, Italy
Steven Demurjian	University of Connecticut, USA
Chiara Di Francescomarino	FBK-IRST, Italy
József Dombi	University of Szeged, Hungary
Gencer Erdogan	SINTEF, Norway

Santonu Sarkar   BITS Pilani Goa, India
Elad Schiller   Chalmers University of Technology, Sweden
Lionel Seinturier   University of Lille, France
Istvan Siket   Hungarian Academy of Science, Research Group
                                   on Artificial Intelligence, Hungary
Harvey Siy   University of Nebraska, Omaha, USA
Cosmin Spahiu   University of Craiova, Romania
Anca-Juliana Stoica   Uppsala University, Sweden
Hiroki Suguri   Miyagi University, Japan
Selma Suloglu   Rochester Institute of Technology, USA
Bedir Tekinerdogan   Wageningen University, The Netherlands
Claudine Toffolon   University of Maine, France
Joseph Trienekens   The Open University, The Netherlands
Michael Vassilakopoulos   University of Thessaly, Greece
Dessislava Vassileva   Sofia University, Bulgaria
László Vidács   University of Szeged, Hungary
Yan Wang   Google, USA
Dietmar Winkler   Vienna University of Technology, Austria
Andreas Winter   Carl von Ossietzky University Oldenburg, Germany
Jinhui Yao   Xerox Research, USA
Murat Yilmaz   Dublin City University, Ireland
Jingyu Zhang   Macquarie University, Australia
Zheying Zhang   Tampere University, Finland

Additional Reviewers

Victoria Döller   University of Vienna, Austria
Vimal Kunnummel   University of Vienna, Austria
Wissam Mallouli   Montimage, France
Damien Pollet   Inria, France
Frederik Reiche   KIT, Germany
Spyros Vosinakis   University of the Aegean, Greece

Invited Speakers

Manfred Reichert   Ulm University, Germany
Michael G. Hinchey   Lero, University of Limerick, Ireland
Hans-Georg Fill   University of Fribourg, Switzerland

Contents

Software Engineering and Systems Development

Equivalence Class Definition
for Automated Testing of Satellite
On-Board Image Processing

Ulrike Witteck[1]($\boxtimes$), Denis Grießbach[1]($\boxtimes$), and Paula Herber[2]($\boxtimes$)

[1] Institute of Optical Sensor Systems, German Aerospace Center (DLR),
Adlershof, Berlin, Germany
{ulrike.witteck,denis.griessbach}@dlr.de
[2] Embedded Systems Group, University of Münster, Münster, Germany
paula.herber@uni-muenster.de

Abstract. On-board image processing technologies in the satellite domain are subject to strict requirements with respect to reliability and accuracy in hard real-time. Due to the large input domain of such processing technologies it is impracticable or even impossible to execute all possible test cases.

As a solution we define a novel test approach that efficiently and systematically captures the input domain of satellite on-board image processing applications. We first partition each input parameter into equivalence classes. Based on these equivalence classes we define multidimensional coverage criteria to assess the coverage of a given test suite on the whole input domain. Finally, our test generation algorithm automatically inserts missing but relevant test cases into the given test suite such that our multidimensional coverage criteria are satisfied.

As a result we get a reasonably small test suite that covers the complete input domain. We demonstrate the effectiveness of our approach with experimental results from the ESA medium-class mission PLATO.

Keywords: Image processing · Software testing · Equivalence class partitioning · Satellite systems

1 Introduction

On-board image processing applications in the satellite domain are subject to strict requirements with respect to reliability and mathematical accuracy in hard real-time. The large input domain of such applications makes manual testing error-prone and time-consuming. To overcome that problem, we need a test approach that automatically and systematically generates test cases for such image processing applications. The major problem of the automated generation of test cases is the large amount of input parameters and their possible combinations. This leads to a high number of test cases which makes the systematic and efficient coverage of the complete input domain expensive.

© Springer Nature Switzerland AG 2020
M. van Sinderen and L. A. Maciaszek (Eds.): ICSOFT 2019, CCIS 1250, pp. 3–25, 2020.
https://doi.org/10.1007/978-3-030-52991-8_1

Automated test approaches for different domains, for example, for automotive and railway applications, are presented in [2, 7]. The authors investigate applications with huge input domains and complex functional behavior. However, their focus is on event-driven, reactive real-time systems and the approaches are not tailored to the domain of on-board image processing applications.

In this paper we present an extended version of our test approach given in [14]. This approach systematically selects test cases from the huge input domain given in image processing applications. Our objective is to achieve a high coverage of the input domain using a reasonably small test suite. To achieve that goal we adopt the equivalence class partition testing method. This method partitions a given domain into disjoint sub-domains called equivalence classes [13]. Only some test values are used as representatives from each class. That reduces the number of required test cases [1], but still systematically covers the respective domain. We use that method to partition each input parameter of the on-board image processing application into equivalence classes. Furthermore, we define multidimensional coverage criteria that combines individual coverage criteria for each input parameter. Finally, we specify a test generation algorithm that uses our multidimensional coverage criteria to automatically assess given test suites with respect to their coverage on the whole input domain. Moreover, the algorithm removes redundant test cases and inserts missing but relevant test cases. As a result we get a reasonably small test suite that covers the complete input domain of satellite on-board image processing applications.

To investigate the efficiency of our test approach using equivalence class definitions, we use the Fine Guidance System (FGS) algorithm of the European Space Agency (ESA) mission PLAnetary Transits and Oscillation of stars (PLATO) as a case study [14]. The FGS algorithm is a satellite on-board image processing algorithm to calculate the high-precision attitude of the spacecraft by comparing tracked star positions with known star positions from a star catalog. Recent studies have shown that some of the input parameters as presented in [14] can be partitioned more beneficial. In this paper we therefore present redefined equivalence classes for two input parameters: object position and sub-pixel position on the image plane. Moreover, we use an improved test criterion to investigate the effectiveness of our test approach. The experimental results show the effectiveness of our partitioning approach in terms of an increased error detection capability.

This paper is structured as follows: In Sect. 2, we briefly introduce equivalence class partition testing and give an overview of the ESA PLATO mission including the FGS algorithm. In Sect. 3, we outline related work about equivalence class testing for real-time systems. In Sect. 4, we present our redefined equivalence classes as well as the automated test generation algorithm for satellite on-board image processing applications. In Sect. 5, we present our experimental results and compare them with the results presented in [14]. We conclude with a summary in Sect. 6.

2   Preliminaries

We introduce the general concept of equivalence class partition testing and give an overview of the PLATO mission and its mission-critical FGS algorithm to understand the remainder of this paper.

2.1   Equivalence Class Partition Testing

To make testing more efficient and less time consuming, it is preferable to examine as many test cases as necessary to satisfy specified test criteria. However, the selection of the necessary test cases from a huge input domain is a major problem when testing an application [11].

Equivalence class partition testing offers a possible solution to this problem. It is a commonly used approach in practice. The technique partitions a given input domain or output domain into disjoint sub-domains, the equivalence classes. The method partitions the domain in such a way, that all elements in an equivalence class are expected to provoke the same system behavior according to a specification. Equivalence classes represent subsets of parameter values that completely cover the input or output domain. For the purpose of software testing, it is therefore sufficient to test some representative values of each equivalence class. The selection of test cases from equivalence classes can be made according to various criteria: using border values, testing special values or randomly selecting test cases [1,7,11].

The increased partitioning effort is a drawback of using equivalence class partition testing compared to random testing. In many cases, several definitions of the domain partitioning are applicable. This is mainly because the tester assumes that test cases of the same equivalence class have the same system behavior. However, the approach removes redundant test cases but retains the completeness of the tests. Hence, the approach reduces the test effort compared to exhaustive testing [1].

2.2   Context: PLATO Mission

PLATO is an ESA mission in the long-term space scientific program "Cosmic Vision" [5]. The German Aerospace Center (DLR) manages the international consortium for developing the payload and scientific operation of the project [3].

The main goal of the PLATO mission is the detection and characterization of Earth-like exoplanets orbiting in the habitable zone of solar-type stars. It achieves its scientific objectives by long uninterrupted ultra-high precision photometric monitoring of large samples of bright stars. This requires a large Field of View (FoV) as well as a low noise level. To achieve a high pupil size and the required FOV the instrument contains 26 telescopes for star observation. 24 normal cameras monitor stars fainter than magnitude 8 at a cycle of 25 s. Two fast cameras observe stars brighter than magnitude 8 at a cycle of 2.5 s. The size of a fast camera FoV is $38.7° \times 38.7°$. The cameras are equipped with four Charge Coupled Devices (CCD) in the focal plane, each with 4510×4510 pixels.

Each fast camera comes with a data processing unit running the FGS algorithm. It calculates attitude data with an accuracy of milliarcseconds from the image data. This data is supplied to the spacecraft attitude and orbit control system. The FGS is regarded as being a mission-critical component which implies an extensive test procedure.

Many spacecraft missions use a FGS to obtain accurate measurements of the spacecraft orientation. We use the PLATO FGS algorithm as a case study to investigate the efficiency of our test approach. The attitude calculation of a telescope is based on measured star positions on the CCD compared to their reference directions in a star catalog. Figure 1 gives an overview of the FGS algorithm [6].

The autonomous attitude tracking is initialized with an initial attitude given by the space craft. For each pre-selected guide star, an initial sub-window position is calculated by means of the camera model, which transforms from sky coordinates to pixel coordinates and vice versa [6]. Guide stars are predefined stars in a star catalog that satisfy given criteria. For example, the star magnitude is within a certain range, the star has very low contamination, etc. The FGS algorithm calculates centroids after reading 6×6 pixel sub-window every 2.5 s from the full CCD image.

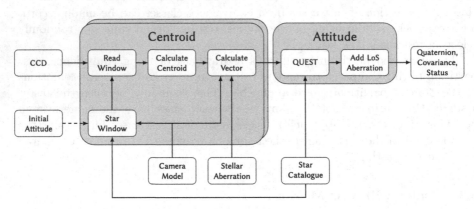

Fig. 1. Overview of the FGS algorithm [6].

A linear center of mass calculation estimates the initial centroid position. To get a more precise solution, the algorithm separately estimates each centroid using a Gaussian Point Spread Function (PSF) observation model. The PSF describes the distribution of the star light over the CCD pixels. Equation 1 shows the Gaussian PSF observation model $h(i, j)$ of a single pixel [6].

$$h = \frac{I_m}{2\pi\sigma^2} \int\limits_{i}^{i+1} e^{-\frac{(u-u_c)^2}{2\sigma^2}} du \int\limits_{j}^{j+1} e^{-\frac{(v-v_c)^2}{2\sigma^2}} dv + D + \xi \tag{1}$$

The FGS algorithm uses the measured pixel intensities to determine the centroid position $(u_c, v_c)^T$, intensity I_m, image background D and PSF width σ. A non-linear least square fitting method iteratively refines the parameters of the PSF model. The FGS algorithm calculates the correction by means of the QR-decomposition [6]. In the next step, the pixel coordinates of the calculated centroid position are transformed into star direction vectors in the camera boresight reference frame. The x- and y-axis of the detector and the optical axis of the camera describe the boresight reference frame.

Finally, the FGS algorithm calculates an attitude, including covariance, from at least two star directions in the boresight reference frame and the corresponding reference vectors from a star catalog [14].

3   Related Work

Equivalence class partition testing "is probably the most widely described, and one of the most widely practiced, software testing techniques" [8] Various studies investigated equivalence class partition testing strategies for different domains, for example, railway, automotive, avionics, etc. [7]. We present some previously published work on equivalence class partition testing for real-time systems.

In the automotive domain, DaimlerChrysler Research developed a test approach, called Time Partition Testing (TPT), to test the continuous behavior of control systems. Bringmann and Krämer [2] explained the principle of the TPT approach using an exterior headlight controller as an example. In most cases, automotive embedded control systems are based on complex functional behavior and large input domains. To increase the test efficiency the TPT approach systematically selects test cases revealing redundant or missing test scenarios. Using a graphical state machine notation, the TPT approach partitions a test scenario into stream-processing components. Each component defines the behavior of output variables depending on the behavior of input variables up to a certain point in time, specified by a temporal predicate. Test cases define variations in the state machine to test various functional aspects of the system under test.

The study shows that state machines are suitable to partition the temporal behavior of input and output variables in order to model, compare and select test cases. The modeled test cases test the complex functional requirements of control systems. A huge input domain and complex functional behavior are also characteristics of the system class we investigate in this paper. However, the behavior of systems from this class is not dependent on the arrival time of input values. Hence, the TPT approach is not applicable to the system class that we consider [14].

In [7], the authors presented a model-based black-box equivalence class partition testing strategy used in the railway domain. The approach automatically generates finite and complete test suites for safety-critical reactive systems in relation to fault models. Huang and Peleska investigated the approach using the Ceiling Speed Monitor of the European Train Control System as an example for systems with potentially infinite input domain but finite output domain and internal variables. Their approach models the reactive behavior of such systems by means of deterministic state transition systems. Moreover, the approach partitions the state space into a finite number of equivalence classes such that all states in a class provide the same output traces for the same non-empty input trace. Based on these classes, they generates a complete test suite in the following sense: First, at least one test in the suite fails if an application that violates a given specification is tested. Second, each test in the suite passes for all applications that satisfy the specification. Huang and Peleska investigated models whose behavior can be represented by state transition systems. However, we have no state transition system description of our considered satellite application. Hence, we present an approach that does not need such a description [14].

4 Equivalence Class Partitioning for Automated Test Generation

Satellite on-board image processing applications require various input parameters such as position of an object in the image, its brightness, sub-pixel position, its shape to distinguish different objects, etc. This leads to a huge input domain which makes testing expensive. Especially manual tests are error-prone and time-consuming. Thus, a test approach is needed that automatically and systematically generates test cases for such applications. However, a major challenge for automated test generation is the very large number of possible input parameter combinations. This potential enormous amount of test cases makes it hard to efficiently capture the complete input domain.

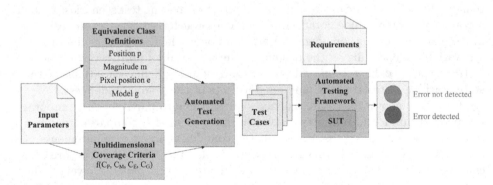

Fig. 2. Overview of the partitioning approach [14].

To overcome that problem, we define a partitioning approach that systematically selects test cases from the huge input domain of satellite on-board image processing applications. Moreover, our test approach assesses and enhances a given test suite. To evaluate the efficiency of our test approach, we investigate a case study, namely the PLATO FGS algorithm as described in Sect. 2.2.

Since satellite on-board image processing algorithms are subject to extremely strict requirements with respect to reliability and mathematical accuracy, such algorithms require extensive testing.

Figure 2 depicts an overview of our proposed partitioning approach. Our key idea is to define equivalence classes on input parameters that are typically used by satellite on-board image processing applications, namely position, magnitude, sub-pixel position, and distribution model. In this paper we present updated equivalence class definitions to partition the individual parameters. Recent studies have shown that some of the equivalence class definitions presented in [14] can be redefined more effectively. In a second step, we define multidimensional coverage criteria based on a combination of the individual criteria for each input parameter. After that, we define a test generation algorithm that automatically selects test cases that completely cover the whole input domain according to our multidimensional coverage criteria.

Our test objective is to automatically detect errors in the on-board image processing application code. To achieve this, our test generation algorithm selects a test case for each equivalence class combination from a given test suite as representatives. This reduces the number of redundant test cases. Furthermore, our algorithm generates new test cases for missing but relevant input combinations to reach a complete coverage of the input domain. The result is a reasonably small test suite that covers the whole input domain of the image processing application with respect to our multidimensional coverage criteria. The selected test cases serve as input for our automated testing framework. Moreover, we insert requirements for the automated evaluation of the image processing application results. If the test cases do not meet the requirements, an error is detected [14].

The following sections describe the mentioned steps of the partitioning approach in more detail, applying our new equivalence class definitions. We use the PLATO FGS algorithm as a case study.

4.1 Assumptions and Limitations

In the following, we consider systems whose input are objects in an image. In the case study, the observed objects are stars with magnitudes between 5.5 to 7.0, uniformly distributed in the image [6].

We consider four parameters that affect the mathematical accuracy of the FGS algorithm: the guide star position, its magnitude, sub-pixel position, and PSF shape. The evaluation of the test is based on the precision of the centroid position calculated by the FGS centroid algorithm as described in Sect. 2.2. The input of the centroid calculation is a single star image. Hence, we define a test star as a test case for the automated test generation.

4.2 Input Parameter Partitioning

The star signal is spread over all pixels in the sub-image. Hence, each pixel includes information about the star. However, 90% of the energy is within 2×2

pixel around the centroid. Moreover, each pixel contains noise, which in combination with the signal determines its Signal-to-Noise Ratio (SNR). The centroid calculation needs at least 5 linear independent equations to estimate the 5 unknown parameters of the pixel observation (cf. Eq. (1)).

The FGS input star parameters named in Sect. 4.1 affect the mathematical precision and accuracy of the centroid estimation. Hence, we define the input domain as a set of input parameters I. The set includes the position on the Focal Plane Assembly (FPA) $\mathcal{P}$, the magnitude $\mathcal{M}$, the sub-pixel position $\mathcal{E}$ and the PSF shape $\mathcal{G}$. The tester specifies start values to calculate the borders of the equivalence classes. This makes our approach more flexible and parameters can also be excluded from the analysis [14].

In this section we describe how the quality of the centroid calculation depends on these parameters and present our partitioning concepts for each input parameter in I.

Position on the FPA. Among others, the distribution of the star signal depends on the star position on the FPA. Due to optical aberrations of the telescope, the PSF shape of the star is wider in the FPA corner than close to the center. If the other input parameters contain reasonably good, constant values then a small PSF leads to a low number of pixels with a high SNR. In case of a wide PSF, more pixel contain a signal but the SNR is low. Both cases can be sufficient for an accurate parameter estimation [14].

In [14], our idea is to partition the FPA into equally sized, circular areas. Recent studies have shown, that the PSF changes not only with the distance to the FPA center but also with the polar angle. In the study each class of parameter $\mathcal{P}$ contains two stars per class of parameter $\mathcal{E}$. The stars have a constant medium magnitude as well as worst-case non-Gaussian PSF. Figure 3 depicts the residual noise of stars per circular FPA area. The figure shows that the residual noise is lower if the star is positioned near the FPA corner or near the FPA border. Moreover, the figure illustrates that the equivalence class borders have been well chosen since the residual noise of the stars is changed between neighboring classes.

Figure 4 shows that the residual noise also depends on the polar angle of the stars. The figure depicts the residual noise of stars per polar angle area. Figure 4 shows that the residual noise is different for each class. However, we consider only stars in the image area of the CCDs. That means, for some polar angle areas particular circular areas can not be covered by a star. Therefore, these polar angle areas contain fewer stars than others. Moreover, the stars in these polar angle areas are located near the FPA center. Hence, the residual noise for that area is low. However, the polar angle area between $90°$ and $135°$ contains less stars but the residual noise is high. This indicates, that this area is not suitable to select guide stars for the PLATO mission from there.

Bases on the study, we update our equivalence class definition of the input parameter $\mathcal{P}$ and additionally partition the polar angle in equally sized circular sectors.

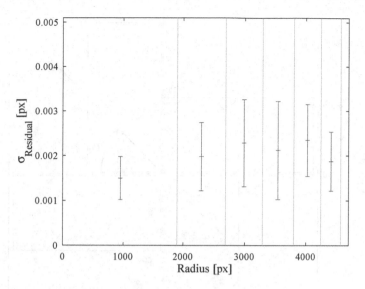

Fig. 3. Residual noise per radius of circular FPA areas.

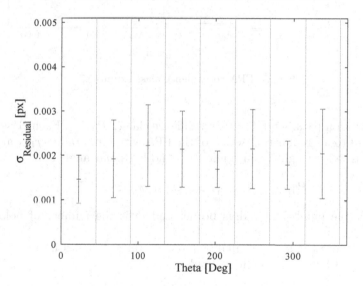

Fig. 4. Residual noise per polar angle of circular FPA areas.

The updated equivalence class definition is illustrated in Fig. 5. The rectangles represent the image area of the fast cameras CCDs and each circular ring sector corresponds to one equivalence class. The tester specifies the initial radius r_0 and the angle of the circular vectors θ_0.

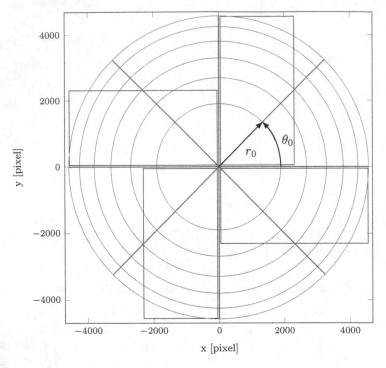

Fig. 5. FPA equivalence class example.

We partition parameter $\mathcal{P}$ into equivalence classes $P_{(r_i,\theta_j)}$. Each class $P_{(r_i,\theta_j)}$ corresponds to a circular ring sector of the FPA with inner radius r_{i-1} and outer radius r_i as well as right polar angle θ_{j-1} and left polar angle θ_j.

$$\mathcal{P} = P_{(r_0,\theta_0)} \cup P_{(r_0,\theta_1)} \cup ... \cup P_{(r_0,\theta_m)} \cup ... \cup P_{(r_n,\theta_m)} \tag{2}$$

where n is the number of radius border and m is the number of polar angle border.

Let S denote the set of available stars. A star $s \in S$ lies in an equivalence class $P_{(r_i,\theta_j)}$ if following condition holds:

$$r_{i-1} \leq p(s) < r_i, \text{ with } p(s) = \sqrt{x_s{}^2 + y_s{}^2} \tag{3}$$

and

$$\theta_{j-1} \leq t(s) < \theta_j, \text{ with } t(s) = \arctan\frac{x_s}{y_s} \tag{4}$$

where (x_s, y_s) is the position of star s on the FPA, $p(s)$ is the distance of star s to the FPA center and $t(s)$ is the polar angle of star s.

Sub-pixel Position. In addition to the position on the FPA, the sub-pixel position of the star also affects the SNR in a pixel. If the centroid is positioned in the center of the pixel, most star flux is accumulated in a few pixels with a high SNR. In contrast, more pixels have a sufficient SNR if the centroid is on the pixel border or corner. In this case, the star information is distributed more evenly over several pixels. The other pixels have a low SNR. But due to movement, the centroid may move to neighbor pixels. This leads to variations in the pixel illumination and the apparent centroid position [14].

In [14], we divide input parameter $\mathcal{E}$ into 9 sub-areas, whereas each area corresponds to one equivalence class. In this paper, we join the corner areas, the vertical border areas, the horizontal border areas, and the center area of the pixel to one equivalence class each. The 4, equally sized equivalence classes are shown in Fig. 7. Areas with the same pattern belong to the same equivalence class.

Figure 6 depicts the mean value and standard deviation of the residuals for stars in the respective pixel area. The stars are located in the same class of parameter $\mathcal{P}$ as well as have a constant medium magnitude and a worst-case non-Gaussian PSF. The figure shows that the residual noise is higher for stars positioned in a pixel corner than in the pixel center. The residual noise of stars in the horizontal border classes or vertical border classes is lower than the residual noise in the corner classes but higher compared to the center class. It is therefore beneficial to join the equivalence classes of input parameter $\mathcal{E}$ defined in [14].

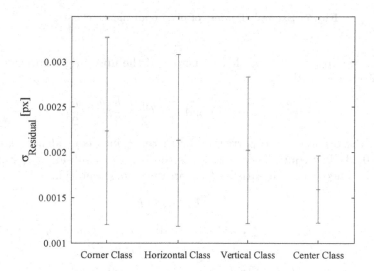

Fig. 6. Residual noise per pixel class.

The tester specifies the ratio r of the central area of the pixel to the pixel area, for example, $1/2$, $3/5$, etc. If a is the pixel size, then the length of the edge of the central area results from Eq. (5).

$$b = a\sqrt{r} \qquad (5)$$

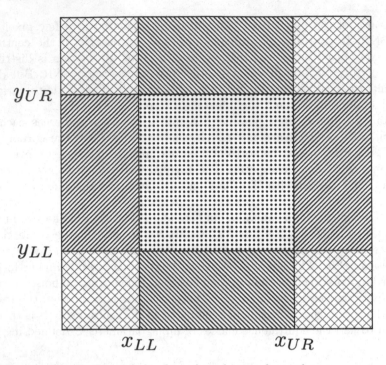

Fig. 7. Example borders of pixel equivalence classes.

With that, we obtain the lower left corner l and the upper right corner u of the central pixel area, with

$$l = (\frac{a}{2} - \frac{b}{2}, \frac{a}{2} - \frac{b}{2}) \text{ and } u = (\frac{a}{2} + \frac{b}{2}, \frac{a}{2} + \frac{b}{2}) \tag{6}$$

Based on these corners, we partition parameter $\mathcal{E}$ into equivalence classes E_i with $i = 0...3$. The equivalence class E_i is the i-th pixel sub-area. A star s lies in an equivalence class if it satisfies the corresponding condition.

$$\mathcal{E} = E_0 \cup E_1 \cup ... \cup E_4 \tag{7}$$

$E_0 : (0 \leq e_x(s) < x_l \ \lor \ x_u \leq e_x(s) < a) \land (0 \leq e_y(s) < y_l \ \lor \ y_u \leq e_y(s) < a)$
$E_1 : (0 \leq e_x(s) < x_l \ \lor \ x_l \leq e_x(s) < x_u) \land \ y_l \leq e_y(s) < y_u$
$E_2 : x_l \leq e_x(s) < x_u \ \land \ (0 \leq e_y(s) < y_l \ \lor \ y_l \leq e_y(s) < y_u)$
$E_3 : x_l \leq e_x(s) < x_u \ \land \ y_l \leq e_y(s) < y_u$

$$\tag{8}$$

$e_x(s)$ and $e_y(s)$ return the x-coordinate and y-coordinate of s in the pixel respectively.

Magnitude. The measured star flux (photo-electrons per second) depends on the magnitude. The accumulated number of photo-electrons per pixel denotes the

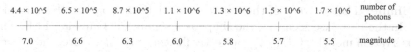

Fig. 8. Example partitioning of magnitude range [14].

illumination of a pixel. Equation (9) shows the relation between the magnitude m and the corresponding flux F_m in e^-/s.

$$F_m = F_0 TQA * 10^{-0.4*m} \tag{9}$$

with magnitude m, reference flux F_0 of a star with $m = 0$, transmission efficiency T of the optical system, quantum efficiency Q of the detector, and effective light-collecting area A. As the equation shows, the star flux is non-linear to the magnitude of the star. A low magnitude corresponds to a high number of photo-electrons, that leads to a higher SNR per pixel.

A useful partitioning of magnitude values into equivalence classes is not obvious. Our idea is to partition the star flux range into $I_{\mathcal{M}} \in \mathbb{N}$ equidistant parts that represent the equivalence classes. We define Eq. (10) to obtain the upper limit of a sub-range.

$$F_{m_j} = F_{7.0} + j \frac{F_{5.5} - F_{7.0}}{I_{\mathcal{M}}} \tag{10}$$

F_{m_j} is the flux of magnitude m_j and $j = 1...I_{\mathcal{M}}$ represents the j-th equivalence class of parameter $\mathcal{M}$. $F_{5.5}$ and $F_{7.0}$ correspond to the numbers of photons for magnitude 5.5 and 7.0. First, we calculate the flux values $F_{5.5}$ and $F_{7.0}$ by using Eq. (9). Then, we partition the flux range into equidistant sub-ranges. We use Eq. (11) to recalculate the magnitude m_j from the calculated flux limit F_{m_j} of the flux sub-range j.

$$m = -2.5 \, log \left(\frac{F_m}{F_0 TQA} \right) \tag{11}$$

From a formal point of view, we partition the parameter $\mathcal{M}$ into equivalence classes M_l.

$$\mathcal{M} = M_{7.0} \cup ... \cup M_{l_j} \cup ... \cup M_{5.5} \tag{12}$$

with $l_j \in \mathbb{R}$ and $5.5 \leq l_j \leq 7.0$. Each equivalence class M_{l_j} is a magnitude sub-range with upper limit l_j. Each available star s lies in equivalence M_{l_j} if it satisfies the condition in Eq. (13).

$$l_{j-1} \leq m(s) < l_j \tag{13}$$

where $m(s)$ denotes the observed magnitude of star s and l_j with $j = 1...I_{\mathcal{M}}$ is the upper limit of the j-th magnitude sub-range. The tester specifies the number of equivalence classes $I_{\mathcal{M}} \in \mathbb{N}$ of the parameter $\mathcal{M}$. Figure 8 illustrates an example partitioning of the magnitude range [14].

PSF Shape. The accuracy of the centroid calculation also depends on the PSF shape. In the best case scenario, the shape is a symmetric Gaussian-PSF. Then, the observation model (cf. Eq. (1)) perfectly fits the star. Therefore, the accuracy of the centroid calculation is high. In reality, the PSF shape is non-Gaussian. In that case, the observation model is less accurate and movements lead to stronger variations in the expected centroid positions [14].

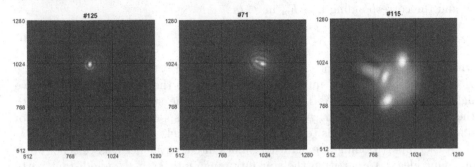

Fig. 9. Examples of different low quality stars [14].

We partition the input parameter $\mathcal{G}$ in two equivalence classes G_G and G_{NG} since two PSF shapes are distinctive. If a star has a Gaussian-PSF shape it is in class G_G otherwise it is in class G_{NG}.

Figure 9 shows some example stars with non-Gaussian-PSF shape that are less suitable as guide stars. These stars lead to inaccurate estimation results. What the three stars have in common is that their intensity is concentrated on a pixel edge. For all stars, the magnitude and FPA position are sufficiently good. However, a small variation due to movement leads to big changes of the illumination. Since the Gaussian-PSF observation model does not fit the PSF shape perfectly, the centroid estimation is less accurate.

4.3   Multidimensional Coverage Criteria

This section presents our definition of multidimensional coverage criteria on the input domain $I = \{\mathcal{P}, \mathcal{M}, \mathcal{E}, \mathcal{G}\}$ [14]. While individual parameter values might provide a good centroid estimation, a combination of parameters may change the quality of the results. To measure the coverage of a test suite with respect to input parameter combinations we define multidimensional coverage criteria on the input domain. If the measured coverage of a test suite is not complete, our automated test generation algorithm automatically inserts test cases for missing combinations.

The individual coverage of an input parameter denotes the ratio of equivalence classes that are covered by at least one test case from a given test suite to the number of equivalence classes of this input parameter. Equations (14)–(17) show this definition for the input parameters $\mathcal{P}, \mathcal{M}, \mathcal{E}$ and $\mathcal{G}$.

$$C_{\mathcal{P}} = \frac{\#\ covered\ elements\ of\ \mathcal{P}}{|\mathcal{P}|} \tag{14}$$

$$C_{\mathcal{M}} = \frac{\#\ covered\ elements\ of\ \mathcal{M}}{|\mathcal{M}|} \tag{15}$$

$$C_{\mathcal{E}} = \frac{\#\ covered\ elements\ of\ \mathcal{E}}{|\mathcal{E}|} \tag{16}$$

$$C_{\mathcal{G}} = \frac{\#\ covered\ elements\ of\ \mathcal{G}}{|\mathcal{G}|} \tag{17}$$

The Cartesian product of the equivalence classes of the input parameters $\mathcal{P}$, $\mathcal{M}$, $\mathcal{E}$ and $\mathcal{G}$ is the coverage domain for our multidimensional coverage criteria. Hence, an input combination is a tuple of equivalence classes (P_i, M_j, E_k, G_l), where $P_i \in \mathcal{P}$, $M_j \in \mathcal{M}$, $E_k \in \mathcal{E}$ and $G_l \in \mathcal{G}$ [14]. Furthermore, a test case is a star represented by a tuple of parameter values $((p,t), m, e, g) \in (P_i, M_j, E_k, G_l)$. The following example test cases clarify these definitions.

Example 1

$$((1969.4, 322.5), 6.5, (0.3, 0.2), G) \in (P_{(2687,360)} \times M_{6.6} \times E_2 \times G_G)$$

The test star position is in the FPA area with outer radius 2687 and outer polar angle 225°. The star belongs to equivalence class $M_{6.6}$ because its magnitude value is between 6.3 and 6.6. The star center is located in the lower-middle pixel sub-area. That corresponds to the horizontal pixel areas and therefore to equivalence class E_2. The star is part of equivalence class G_G, because it has a Gaussian-PSF shape.

Example 2

$$((2551.9, 357.3), 6.5, (0.9, 0.8), G) \in (P_{(2687,360)} \times M_{6.6} \times E_0 \times G_G)$$

The test star is similar to the star in the first example, but it is positioned nearby the upper right pixel border and therefore belongs to equivalence class E_0.

Our multidimensional coverage criterion is fully satisfied if the test cases in a test suite cover all possible input combinations at least once. The number of required covered input combinations for a complete coverage is $|\mathcal{P} \times \mathcal{M} \times \mathcal{E} \times \mathcal{G}|$. In the remaining sections, we denote a test suite that completely covers the input domain with respect to our multidimensional coverage criteria as a complete test suite. The multidimensional coverage C results from the ratio of input combinations covered by at least one test case to the total number of input combinations.

$$C = \frac{\#\ covered\ input\ combinations}{|\mathcal{P} \times \mathcal{M} \times \mathcal{E} \times \mathcal{G}|} \tag{18}$$

Our test approach calculates the individual and multidimensional coverage of a given test suite using Algorithm 1. The input parameters $\mathcal{P}$, $\mathcal{M}$, $\mathcal{E}$, and $\mathcal{G}$ contain $I_{\mathcal{P}}$, $I_{\mathcal{M}}$, $I_{\mathcal{E}}$, $I_{\mathcal{G}}$ equivalence classes respectively [14].

For each test case in the given test suite, the algorithm computes the input parameter index i_P, i_M, i_E, i_G of the corresponding equivalence class from $\mathcal{P}$, $\mathcal{M}$, $\mathcal{E}$ and $\mathcal{G}$. The algorithm adds the indices to the sets $C_{\mathcal{P}}$, $C_{\mathcal{M}}$, $C_{\mathcal{E}}$ and $C_{\mathcal{G}}$ respectively. Moreover, it inserts the tuple (i_P, i_M, i_E, i_G) into the set C that contains all covered input combinations. As the algorithm uses the union operator to add the tuples to the set, each tuple is included in the set only once. The algorithm applies Eqs. (14)–(18) to compute the individual and multidimensional coverage.

Input: Test suite TS
Output: Multidimensional coverage Cov of TS

1 $C_{\mathcal{P}} = C_{\mathcal{M}} = C_{\mathcal{E}} = C_{\mathcal{G}} = C = \emptyset$;
2 **foreach** tc *with* $((p, t), m, e, g) \in TS$ **do**
3 $\quad i_P = getPosECId(p, t)$;
4 $\quad C_{\mathcal{P}} \leftarrow C_{\mathcal{P}} \cup i_P$;
5 $\quad i_M = getMagECId(m)$;
6 $\quad C_{\mathcal{M}} \leftarrow C_{\mathcal{M}} \cup i_M$;
7 $\quad i_E = getPixECId(e)$;
8 $\quad C_{\mathcal{E}} \leftarrow C_{\mathcal{E}} \cup i_E$;
9 $\quad i_G = getModECId(g)$;
10 $\quad C_{\mathcal{G}} \leftarrow C_{\mathcal{G}} \cup i_G$;
11 $\quad C \leftarrow C \cup (i_P, i_M, i_E, i_G)$;
12 **end**
13 $Cov_{\mathcal{G}} \;= |C_{\mathcal{P}}|/I_{\mathcal{P}}$;
14 $Cov_{\mathcal{M}} = |C_{\mathcal{M}}|/I_{\mathcal{M}}$;
15 $Cov_{\mathcal{E}} \;= |C_{\mathcal{E}}|/I_{\mathcal{E}}$;
16 $Cov_{\mathcal{G}} \;= |C_{\mathcal{G}}|/I_{\mathcal{G}}$;
17 $Cov \;\;= |C|/(I_{\mathcal{P}} \cdot I_{\mathcal{M}} \cdot I_{\mathcal{E}} \cdot I_{\mathcal{G}})$

Algorithm 1. Coverage calculation [14].

Our partitioning approach uses individual and multidimensional coverage criteria to assess the quality of test suites with respect to their coverage on the input space of a satellite on-board image processing application [14].

4.4 Automated Test Generation

We present a test generation algorithm to automatically and systematically generate a test suite that completely covers the input domain according to our multidimensional coverage criteria. The complete test generation algorithm uses Algorithm 1 to assess a given test suite and systematically generates missing test cases based on this result.

Algorithm 2 generates set W that contains all input combinations not covered by the given test suite. For each input combination in W, the algorithm uses the procedure `generateTC` to generate a test case by randomly selecting values from the equivalence classes of the missing combinations. The algorithm adds the newly generated test case to the test suite. In this way, it efficiently inserts missing but relevant test cases into the test suite. This increases the multidimensional coverage and therefore the error detection capability of the given test suite. As a result we get a complete but reasonably small test suite.

If the set of covered input combinations C is empty, then the set of uncovered input combinations W is equal to the universe of possible input combinations U. Therefore, Algorithm 2 can be used to generate a new test suite that completely satisfies the multidimensional coverage criteria. From this test suite our automated testing framework only selects one test case per input combination. This efficiently reduces the number of redundant test cases for the test execution [14].

Input: Input combination universe U, covered input combination set C, test
     suite TS
Output: Complete test suite TS

1 Cov = computeMultidimCoverage(TS);
2 **if** $Cov < 1$ **then**
3     $W \leftarrow U \setminus C$;
4   **foreach** $w \in W$ **do**
5   tc = generateTC(w);
6        $TS \leftarrow TS \cup tc$;
7   **end**
8 **end**

Algorithm 2. Generate complete test suite [14].

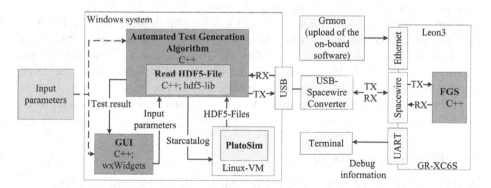

Fig. 10. Test setup [14].

5   Evaluation

We evaluate the applicability and error detection capability of our proposed test approach for satellite on-board image processing applications. For this purpose, we use the FGS algorithm of the ESA PLATO mission as case study and run the algorithms with various test suites.

5.1   Implementation

We have implemented the proposed partitioning and test generation algorithm in C++ based on the model-view-controller pattern. We allow the tester to specify input parameters with or without graphical user interface (GUI). Figure 10 shows the block diagram of our test setup. As the figure depicts, our test environment runs on a Windows system. Our automated test generation algorithm reads the star data of the test suite inserted by the tester. For missing test cases, our test generation algorithm returns a star catalog to simulate the star data. The catalog is a text file that includes right ascension, declination, and magnitude of stars that should be simulated. We manually insert the catalog into the PLATO simulator PlatoSim [9]. PlatoSim writes the simulated star data to HDF5 files [12]. Each file contains an image sequence of several time steps of a star in a hierarchical file format. Since PlatoSim is not developed for Windows systems, the simulator runs in a Linux virtual machine.

Figure 10 depicts, that we connect the Windows system via a SpaceWire USB brick to a GR-XC6S FPGA development board [10] running at 50 MHz. SpaceWire is a data-handling network for spacecraft defined in [4]. For that, our test environment uses the C SpaceWire USB API Library for the SpaceWire USB brick. A prototype of the FGS algorithm, written in C++, runs on the evaluation board. We load the software with the Leon debug monitor GRMON onto this board. Via a UART interface we receive debug information in a terminal. For example, stack size, hardware information, etc.

Our objective is to evaluate our approach for the development and test of the FGS algorithm implementation. Moreover, our goal is to test execution time and mathematical accuracy of the FGS algorithm under realistic conditions. For example, a calculation on the development board is slower than the same calculation on a Windows system. Therefore, we run the application under test on the target hardware and keep the test system in the software development cycle [14].

5.2   Experimental Results

In this section, we present the experimental results for generating a test suite using our redefined equivalence class definitions for testing the PLATO FGS algorithm.

Since the equivalence class borders used for the recent studies were been well chosen, as shown in Fig. 3, Fig. 4 and Fig. 6, we specify following start parameters for the experiment:

- Initial radius r_0 of FPA partitioning: 1900 pixel
- Initial polar angle θ_0 of FPA partitioning: 45°
- Number of magnitude sub-ranges: 6
- Ratio r of central sub-area to pixel area: 0.25

These start parameters lead to 48 equivalence classes of input parameter $\mathcal{P}$, 6 equivalence classes of parameter $\mathcal{M}$ and 4 equivalence classes of parameter $\mathcal{E}$. Input parameter $\mathcal{G}$ consists of two equivalence classes (G_G and G_{NG}). In the following we only consider equivalence classes of input parameter $\mathcal{P}$ that cover the image area of the CCDs. Therefore we use 36 classes of parameter $\mathcal{P}$. Thus, our automated testing framework needs 1728 test cases to completely cover the whole input domain of the FGS algorithm. That is twice the number of test cases used in [14]. The reason is that we refine the partitioning of input parameter $\mathcal{P}$.

To evaluate our approach, we investigate the error detection capability of a randomly generated test suite as well as a test suite generated by our algorithm. The randomly generated test suite contains 902 evenly distributed stars. The second test suite was generated by our automated test generation application using Algorithm 2 presented in Sect. 4.4. The test suite contains one test case for each input combination. Therefore it is complete with respect to our multi-dimensional coverage criteria and we call it complete test suite. Table 1 shows the coverage of the test suites for each input parameter as well as the achieved multidimensional coverage.

Table 1 shows that the utilization of the equivalence class partitioning method reduces the random test suite by hundreds of redundant test cases. Since there are no unnecessary executions of redundant test cases, the method increases the efficiency of the test process. The random test suite achieves a high individual

Table 1. Coverage values of the test suites.

	Random	Complete
Test stars	902	1728
Covered input combinations	256	1728
$C_{\mathcal{P}}$ [%]	100.0	100.0
$C_{\mathcal{M}}$ [%]	16.7	100.0
$C_{\mathcal{E}}$ [%]	100.0	100.0
$C_{\mathcal{G}}$ [%]	100.0	100.0
Multidimensional coverage [%]	14.8	100.0

Table 2. Output for a sample test case.

i_G	i_P	i_M	i_E	$StarId$	$deviation_x$ [px]	$deviation_y$ [px]	$result$
1	33	1	4	1017	112734.8	1097.8	Error detected
0	11	2	0	892	1.3×10^{-5}	4.4×10^{-5}	Error detected

coverage of three input parameters. However, due to the low individual coverage of input parameter $\mathcal{M}$, the multidimensional coverage of the test suite is low. Furthermore, Table 1 exhibits that the complete test suite covers the whole input domain of the FGS algorithm.

To assess the partitioning approach, we have automatically inserted some errors into the PLATO FGS algorithm code. These injected errors belong to three classes: missing assignment, wrong assignment and wrong condition. For each test execution, we have injected a single error at a different position in the code. Our objective is to check if the complete test suite achieves a higher error detection capability than the random test suite.

In each experiment, our test application sent 1000 packets, with one exposure each, per selected test star to the evaluation board running the FGS algorithm, and evaluated the calculated centroids. After that, our test application calculated the residual between the resulting centroid positions and a given position calculated by PlatoSim for each exposure. In this paper, we use another test criterion than in [14]: if the standard deviation of the residuals is greater than a reference value, the test detects the error. Table 2 shows the output for two test cases that detect a wrong assignment error. The high deviation between the standard deviation of the residuals and the reference values reveals an error in the centroid calculation.

During the experiments, we have injected three missing assignment errors, three wrong assignment errors, and three wrong condition errors. Table 3 summarizes the experimental results for both test suites.

Table 3 shows that both test suites do not reveal all injected errors with respect to the given test criterion. All test cases in the random test suite, as well as all test cases in the complete test suite, detects all missing assignment errors. In addition, both test suites detect two wrong assignment errors. But the percentage of test cases that detect this error is different. In the first case, 31% of the test cases in the complete test suite and 16% of the test cases in the random test suite detect the wrong assignment error. In the second case, 31% of the test cases in the complete test suite and 19% of the test cases in the random test suite detect the error. This means, some test cases are more capable to find errors than others. The percentage of error detecting test cases in the complete test suite is about 1.8 times higher than the percentage of error detecting test cases in the random test suite. Hence, the error detection capability of the complete test suite

Table 3. Test suites evaluation results.

	Random	Complete
Test cases	256	1728
Detected errors	5	5
Undetected errors	4	4
Error detection capability [%]	55.6	55.6

is higher. For randomly generated test cases it is not sure that it contains the necessary test cases to detect a special error. Furthermore, our test criterion only considers the centroid position not the other output parameters of the centroid calculation. These should also be taken into account in later experiments.

However, not all injected errors are suitable to investigate the error detection capability of a test suite because they lead to erroneous results for each input data. Thus, it is necessary to insert hard-to-find errors that only affects special input combinations. Otherwise one test cases is sufficient to detect an error.

Compared to the results presented in [14] the error detection capability of the complete test suite is increased. But also the random generated test suites reaches a higher error detection capability than presented in [14]. The reason for this is the improved test criterion.

Our partitioning approach reduces the number of relevant test cases. Therefore, applying the approach increases the test efficiency. The results show that the error detection capability of the test suite that completely satisfies our multidimensional coverage criteria is higher than the capability of the random test suite. The complete test suite includes more test cases that detect special errors than the random test suite. Furthermore, the experiment shows that the new test criteria leads to a higher error detection capability for both test suites compared to the results presented in [14].

6   Conclusion

Due to the large number of input parameters of satellite on-board image processing applications and their combinations an enormous amount of test cases is possible. Hence, it is infeasible to capture the complete input domain and execute test cases exhaustively. We have developed a test approach for this specific domain that automatically and systematically generates test suites that completely covers the input domain. Our approach is based on the well-known equivalence class partition testing method.

In this paper, we have redefined some of the equivalence class definitions presented in [14]. To assess test suites with respect to its coverage of the input domain, we have also presented individual coverage criteria for each input parameter as well as multidimensional coverage criteria to measure the number of covered input parameter combinations. Finally, we have specified an automated test generation algorithm that systematically generates missing test cases with respect to our multidimensional coverage criteria. As a result, our approach is able to fully automatically generate test suites that are reasonably small but complete with respect to our multidimensional coverage criteria. The tester specifies the size of our equivalence classes. This makes our approach adjustable to available test times and also to other image processing applications. Moreover, it allows to exclude an input parameter from the analysis by having only one class.

We have investigated the effectiveness of our proposed test approach on the FGS algorithm as mission critical component for the PLATO mission. In the experiments, our automated test generation algorithm generates a test suite that is complete with respect to our multidimensional coverage criteria. To demonstrate the effectiveness of our test approach with redefined equivalence class borders, we have compared the error detection capability of a randomly generated test suite and the generated complete test suite as well as with the complete test suite given in [14]. The use of our equivalence classes of the input parameters reduces the number of redundant test cases in the randomly generated test suite by 71.6%.

During the experiments, we have successively injected 9 errors in the FGS algorithm code to investigate the error detection capability of both test suites. In this paper, we have specified an improved test criterion: a test case detects an error if the standard deviation of the residual between the calculated centroid position and a given position is bigger than a reference value. We have observed that the changed test criterion leads to different test results compared to the results presented in [14]. In general, the error detection capability of the complete test suite as well as of the random test suite has increased. Both test suites detects all missing assignment errors and two wrong assignment errors. However, percentage of error detecting test cases in the complete test suite is about 1.8 times higher than for the random test suite. Thus, the error detection capability of the complete test suite is higher than the error detection capability of the random test suite. But both test suites do not detect all injected errors because the test criterion considers only the centroid position and not the other output parameters of the centroid calculation.

The error detection capability of both test suites is nearly the same, because not all injected errors are suitable to show the error detection capability of a test suite. The injected errors lead to erroneous results for each input data. Therefore, it is necessary to inject hard-to-find errors into the code that only affects specific input combinations.

However, the experiments showed that a systematic test using our proposed partitioning approach increases the error detection capability of a given test suite. This makes the partitioning approach efficient and effective. In addition, it facilitates automated generation, execution, and evaluation of test cases.

So far, we have injected errors in the application code. But in space, many missions suffer from cosmic radiation that flips bits in binary code or cause hot pixels in input images. We plan to investigate the efficiency of our approach by injecting errors in input data or in the binary code of the application in future work. Finally, we have evaluated our approach with a single application. Later on, we plan to investigate the flexibility of our approach for other applications, for example, blob feature extraction in the robotics domain [14].

References

1. Bhat, A., Quadri, S.: Equivalence class partitioning and boundary value analysis-a review. In: International Conference on on Computing for Sustainable Global Development (INDIACom), pp. 1557–1562. IEEE (2015)

2. Bringmann, E., Krämer, A.: Systematic testing of the continuous behavior of automotive systems. In: International Workshop on Software Engineering for Automotive Systems, pp. 13–20. ACM (2006)
3. DLR: Grünes Licht für europäisches Weltraumteleskop PLATO (2017). http://www.dlr.de/dlr/desktopdefault.aspx/tabid-10081/151_read-22858/#/gallery/27241
4. ECSS Executive Secretariat: Space engineering, spaceWire - links, nodes, routers and networks (2008)
5. ESA: ESA's 'Cosmic Vision' (2012). http://www.esa.int/Our_Activities/Space_Science/ESA_s_Cosmic_Vision
6. Grießbach, D.: Fine guidance system performance report. Technical report PLATO-DLR-PL-RP-0003, Deutsches Zentrum für Luft- und Raumfahrt (DLR) (2019)
7. Huang, W., Peleska, J.: Complete model-based equivalence class testing. Int. J. Softw. Tools Technol. Transf. **18**(3), 265–283 (2014). https://doi.org/10.1007/s10009-014-0356-8
8. Kaner, C.: Teaching domain testing: a status report. In: Conference on Software Engineering Education and Training, pp. 112–117. IEEE (2004)
9. Marcos-Arenal, P., et al.: The PLATO simulator: modelling of high-precision high-cadence space-based imaging. Astron. Astrophys. **566**, A92 (2014)
10. Pender electronic desiGN GmbH: Gr-xc6s-product_sheet (2011)
11. Liggesmeyer, P.: Software-Qualität: Testen, Analysieren und Verifizieren von Software, 2nd edn. Spektrum Akademischer Verlag, Heidelberg (2009)
12. The HDF Group: HDF5, 05 April 2018. https://portal.hdfgroup.org/display/HDF5/HDF5
13. Varshney, S., Mehrotra, M.: Automated software test data generation for data flow dependencies using genetic algorithm. Int. J. Adv. Res. Comput. Sci. Softw. Eng. **4**(2), 472–479 (2014)
14. Witteck, U., Grießbach, D., Herber, P.: Test input partitioning for automated testing of satellite on-board image processing algorithms. In: Proceedings of the 14th International Conference on Software Technologies - Volume 1: ICSOFT, pp. 15–26. SciTePress, INSTICC (2019). https://doi.org/10.5220/0007807400150026

What We Know About Software Architecture Styles in Continuous Delivery and DevOps?

Maya Daneva[✉] and Robin Bolscher

University of Twente, 7522NH Enschede, The Netherlands
m.daneva@utwente.nl, r.bolscher@student.utwente.nl

Abstract. This paper takes a software architect's perspective to DevOps/CD and attempts to provide a consolidated view on the architecture styles for which empirical publications indicate to be suitable in the context of DevOps and CD. Following techniques from the evidence-based software engineering paradigm, we set out to answer a number of research questions pertaining to (1) the architecture characteristics important in DevOps/CD projects according to published literature, (2) the architectural styles found to work well in this context, (3) the application domains in which architecture characteristics and styles were evaluated, and (4) the empirical method being used by researchers on this topic. We applied a research protocol grounded on well-established systematic literature review guidelines, and evaluated sources published between 2009 and 2019. Our results indicate that (a) 17 software architecture characteristics are beneficial for CD and DevOps adoption, (b) micro-services are a dominant architectural style in this context, and (c) large-scale organizational contexts are the most studied, and (d) qualitative approaches (case study based) are the most applied research method.

Keywords: Software architecture · Continuous delivery · Continuous integration · DevOps · Deployability · Micro-services · Systematic literature review

1 Introduction

Today, many businesses in the IT industry are embarking on DevOps and Continuous Delivery (CD). This interest in DevOps/CD is traceable to organizations' motivation to increase their abilities to deliver software fast and predictably well. The growing adoption of the DevOps and CD concepts is however not free of problems. For example, a 2017 systematic mapping study of literature [14] on CD challenges reports 40 problems discussed in scientific publications. The present article follows up on one of these problems, namely the use of unsuitable architecture in CD (and in DevOps) contexts. We felt intrigued to know what so far has been published on the qualities of suitable architectures for DevOps/CD. Our motivation to consolidate the published knowledge on this topic is based on the observation that although DevOps and CD have been employed massively for more than 5 years and much guidance has been published on how to implement these concepts well, little has been done so far to elaborate on the linkage between DevOps/CD and architecture. Yet, as Bass states [15],

© Springer Nature Switzerland AG 2020
M. van Sinderen and L. A. Maciaszek (Eds.): ICSOFT 2019, CCIS 1250, pp. 26–39, 2020.
https://doi.org/10.1007/978-3-030-52991-8_2

the DevOps practices have implications for the software architects in the DevOps-adopting organizations.

This research aims at consolidating the published experiences regarding the architecture styles' fit and misfit to DevOps and CD context. If such a consolidated view of the published knowledge exists, researchers would know those areas that have enjoyed much research efforts and those that are under-researched. Moreover, if a map of the published empirical evidence is provided to software architecture practitioners, they could possibly be able to consider it when making architecture design decisions in DevOps and CD contexts.

Using the techniques of the evidence-based software engineering paradigm, we designed a systematic review protocol in order to identify and evaluate the empirical evidence published on this topic. Our research took two stages: in *stage 1*, we investigated the software architecture challenges experienced in DevOps/CD-adopting organizations. In *stage 2*, we focus on the architecture styles that support the DevOps/CD implementation. The results of *stage 1* have been reported at the ICSOF 2019 conference [16]. The results of *stage 2* are now reported in the present paper. Although the two research stages are complementary and grounded on the same review protocol [16] and, in turn, analyze the same pool of selected literature sources, in contrast to the ICSOFT 2019 conference paper [16], this paper treats different research questions and therefore reports new findings.

The paper is structured as follows. Section 2 provides definitions of the terms used in our research. Section 3 presents the purpose of this work. Section 4 presents our research questions and the research method used. Section 5 presents the results of our SLR. Section 6 discusses the results. Section 7 is on the possible risks of passing bias into our study. Section 8 is on related work. Section 9 summarizes our findings and discusses some implications for research and practice.

2   Definitions of Terms

For clarity, before elaborating on the scope and the research questions of this SLR, we present the definitions of the concepts that we use [16]. Software architecture of a system is the set of structures needed to reason about the system, which comprise software elements, relations among them, and properties of both [17]. Continuous Delivery (CD) is a software engineering discipline in which the software is kept in such a state that in principle, it could be released to its users at any time [17]. The discipline is achieved through optimization, automatization and utilization of the build, deploy, test and release process. Furthermore, DevOps is a set of practices intended to reduce the time between committing a change to a system and the change being placed into 'normal' production, while ensuring high quality [15]. For the purpose of this work, we borrow Wood's definition of 'production' [4]: this is "any environment which is being used to perform valuable work" in an organization. As one could see from the definitions, CD and DevOps have overlapping goals. Both concepts serve companies to take full (end-to-end) advantage of Agile and Lean [14]. Since the two concepts are so similar, the effect they have on software architecture is expected to be very similar as well. This is why these two concepts are both included in our SLR.

3 Purpose

The purpose of this SLR is to identify and analyze the relationship between DevOps/CD and software architecture by using published empirical evidence regarding the architecture styles that support the implementation of CD and DevOps. For this purpose, we followed three areas of interest:

(1) characteristics of architecture that are important in DevOps/CD context,
(2) application areas in which these characteristics were identified or evaluated,
(3) empirical research method that was used by the authors of the published studies on this topic.

The first area concerns the non-functional requirements that, if met, render a software architecture beneficial for systems implemented by using DevOps/CD practices. The second area of interest concerns the contexts in which these non-functional requirements are deemed important according to published literature. We assume that not every application domain has been subjected to active research and, in turn, our knowledge of the non-functional requirements that a software architecture meets to support the implementation of DevOps/CD, may be fragmented or skewed. This assumption is justified by the observation that in many empirical studies on other software engineering phenomena, some application domains are more researched than others. Finally, the third area of interest concerns the research-methodological foundation of the published research studies, which would allow us to evaluate the realism of the published findings and their generalizability [18]. The results in each of these three areas are analyzed, focusing on how frequently our findings appeared in the selected set of papers and how they are framed in each paper. We tried to identify any inconsistencies in the results so that we can provide further knowledge gaps and lines for future research.

4 Research Questions and Method

Based on the purpose of our literature study, we set out to answer three Research Questions (RQs):

> *RQ1: What software architecture characteristics have been deemed important for enabling DevOps and CD, according to published literature?*
> *RQ2: What applications areas have been reported in published literature concerning the important architectural characteristics found in the answer to RQ1?*
> *RQ3: What research methods have been used in the published empirical papers used to answer RQ1 and RQ2?*

To answer these RQs, we planned and executed a SLR, adopting the guidelines of Kitchenham et al. [19]. These were complemented with the guideline of Kuhrmann et al. [20]. We adapted these guidelines to this specific research as elaborated in our review protocol (Fig. 1).

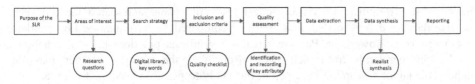

Fig. 1. Our research protocol.

For the purpose of our collection of possibly relevant articles, we explored the Scopus digital library by focusing on following string:

("software architecture" AND ("continuous delivery" OR "continuous deployment" OR "devops" OR "dev-ops" OR "dev ops")).

The search was carried out on May 14, 2019. It was applied to the Title, Abstract and Keyword sections of the Scopus digital library. Performing the search resulted in 39 papers from Scopus over a time span of 9 years (2009–2019). Our study selection process followed the inclusion and exclusion criteria listed below.

Inclusion Criteria

1. The paper treats DevOps/CD aspects as its core topic and discusses software architecture in this context;
2. The takes a practical point of view on the problems and/or solutions discussed (e.g. it is a case study or expert/practitioner experiences and opinions).

Exclusion Criteria

1. The paper presents no link to DevOps, CD or similar practices;
2. The paper is published before Jan 1, 2015;
3. The paper is purely theoretical;
4. The paper is a duplicate of a paper that was already found in Scopus;
5. The paper is not written in English.
6. The paper summarizes a workshop, a conference or another scientific event.

We would like to note that our process of the articles' selection was iterative and happened in multiple phases. The first application of the above list of criteria to titles and abstracts of the 39 papers resulted in a set of 23 papers that we deemed to fall in scope of this SLR. This reduction (from 39 to 23) was due to many duplicates. In the second iteration, we have read the 23 papers in detail and re-applied the inclusion/exclusion criteria. This ended up with 13 papers which we used in the data extraction and data synthesis stages of this SLR. The papers formed the following list of references: [1–13].

Once the paper selection was over, we focused on data extraction. This included carefully reading the whole text of each paper and keeping notes on the following pieces of information: countries of the affiliations of the authors, type of affiliation (industry or academic institution), explicit mentioning of software architecture characteristics, contextual settings in which the DevOps/CD concepts were implemented, application domain, explicit mention of research methodological sources and research method used, treatment of validity questions while using a research method. The precise data have been coded, analyzed and compared by two authors. For the data synthesis, we followed the Pawson's realistic synthesis practices [21]. The authors worked independently from each other so that they the senior researcher does not expose the junior researcher involved in this study to possible bias due to the fact that the senior researcher knew some of the authors of the selected papers. The two authors consolidated their results and found no discrepancies in their analysis of the papers.

5 Demographics, Themes and Trends

This section reports our findings. Before presenting our answers to our three RQs, we first report some demographic information on the papers in our analyzed set.

First, in our set of 13, we have six papers authored by individuals working in companies [1–4, 12, 13], three papers authored by collaborators from companies and universities [6, 7, 9] working in industry-university projects, and four papers authored by academic researchers [5, 8, 10, 11]. This distribution is unsurprising as we deliberately chose the presence of industrial experience as an inclusion criteria in our list (see Sect. 4 on the previous page).

Second, the affiliations of the authors of the selected papers are in seven different countries: Ireland, USA, United Kingdom, Germany, Austria, Switzerland, Sweden, Columbia, and Italy. This distribution suggests a diversity across geographic zones.

5.1 Software Architecture Characteristics and the Context in Which They Were Deemed Important (RQ1)

Our analysis of the 13 included papers resulted in a list of 17 software architecture characteristics that were important to the implementation of DevOps/CD according to the experiences of the authors in these papers [16]. These are listed in the second column of Table 1. In the third column, we present the references to those papers addressing each characteristic. The number of references clearly indicates those software architecture characteristics which have been treated most frequently in relation to CD/DevOps in scientific literature. These are: deployability (CH2), testability (CH11), automation (CH3), loosely coupled (CH6), modifiability (CH1).

The characteristics in Table 1 have been described in more detail as part of *stage 1* of our research, which has already been presented in the ICSOFT 2019 conference [16]. Here we relate these characteristics to the context in which the authors of the 13 selected papers experienced them as important. For this purpose, we looked at the type of industrial projects in which the reported experience happened and observations on the characteristics of software architecture were collected. We found that half of the papers reported the context of very large organizations, for example, Deutsche Bank [3] – a leading German bank, Fujitsu [6] – a global IT consultancy, Ericsson [9] – a large telecommunication company, plus a large Swedish automotive company [11], and some large software process consultancy firms [1, 4].

We also looked at the architectural styles that matched these contexts. Eight out of our 13 selected papers indicated that the architectural style fitting DevOps/CD implementation is the one of micro-services. Micro-services are a set of small services that can be developed, tested, deployed, scaled, operated and upgraded independently, allowing organizations to gain agility, reduce complexity and scale their applications in the cloud in a more efficient way. Besides that, micro-services are very popular, they are being used and promoted by industry leaders such as Amazon, Netflix and LinkedIn [7]. Shahin et al. describe micro-services as the first architectural style to be preferred for CD practice, by designing fine-grained applications as a set of small services [5]. Three papers [9–11] state explicitly some specific benefits of employing the micro-services architecture concept. Micro-services are said to be helpful in increasing modularity and isolating changes and as a consequence increasing deployment frequency [13]. The experience report by Berger et al. [11], where the authors implemented CD practices in a team developing software for self-driving cars, reported how a loosely coupled micro-service architecture helped them move towards CD. Chen et al. argue that micro-service architectures feature many of the CD/DevOps enabling characteristics (CH2, CH7, CH8) and are (in combination with DevOps) the "key to success" of large-scale platforms [12].

Three other papers [5, 6, 8] explicitly state some downsides of the micro-services architecture. E.g. tracing errors and finding root causes of production issues traveling through multiple system components [8], resulting in increasingly complex monitoring (IS10) and logging (IS9) [5]. Plus, at the inception stage of a project a micro-services architecture might be less productive due to the required effort for creating the separate services and the necessary changes in the organizational structure, eventually as the project matures the efficiency of the micro-services architecture surpasses that of the monolithic architecture though [6].

Other authors [7, 8, 10] treat the suitability of the concept of micro-services in a particular context. Pahl et al. [10] state that the idea of micro-services has been discussed as a suitable candidate for flexible service-based system composition in the cloud in the context of deployment and management automation.

Furthermore, Schermann et al. [8] look at micro-services from a continuous experimentation perspective which is based on CD. These authors state that "continuous experimentation is especially enabled by architectures that foster independently deployable services, such as micro-services-based architectures".

Micro-services emerged as a lightweight subset of the Service-Oriented Architecture (SOA), it avoids the problems of monolithic applications by taking advantage of some of the SOA benefits [7]. Pahl et al. [10] note that loose coupling, modularity, layering, and composability are guiding principles of service-oriented architectures.

The last architectural style is vertical layering. It is mentioned by Shahin et al. [5] and refers to removing team dependencies by splitting software components into vertical layers (instead of horizontal layers, e.g. presentation, business and persistence). It can be argued if this is an architectural style on its own, as it is also a characteristic of micro-services and SOAs in general.

Table 1. Software architecture characteristics supporting CD/DevOps [16].

ID	Software architecture characteristics	Reference
CH1	Agility/Modifiability	[1, 2, 12]
CH2	Deployability	[2, 5, 12, 13]
CH3	Automation	[11–13]
CH4	Traceability	[11, 13]
CH5	Stateless components	[11]
CH6	Loosely coupled	[1, 10, 11]
CH7	Production versioning	[12]
CH8	Rollback	[12]
CH9	Availability	[12]
CH10	Performance	[12]
CH11	Testability	[2, 5]
CH12	Security	[2]
CH13	Loggability	[2, 5]
CH14	Monitorability	[2]
CH15	Modularity	[5, 10]
CH16	Virtualization	[10]
CH17	Less reusability	[5]

5.2 Application Domains (RQ2)

The experiences in our set of selected papers reported observations from a variety of domains, namely: banking, automotive, telecommunication, bookmaking, software and IT consulting. The example of a case study from a leading German bank [3] is representative for a major trend happening in the banking sector, namely the embarking on the concept 'Banking-as-a-Service' (BaaS). Transitioning to BaaS helps big banks reinvent themselves as assemblers of financial management solutions, tailored to meet specific customer needs. To succeed in this transition, banks increasingly more "componentize" their business architecture and underlying solution architectures of the systems they operate. The software architecture style they consider important to their future is micro-services [28] as it allows financial institutions to layer their technology offerings like building blocks rather than monolithic "systemware".

Furthermore, the experience described by Berger et al. [11], reflects a recent trend in the automotive sector adopting micro-services architectures. For example, car makers including Ford, Mercedes-Benz, and VW are actively adapting microservices/container architecture principles in developing Internet-of-Things enabled apps for their vehicles. Traditionally, in this sector, most automotive software architectures can be considered component based; in many cases, these components are however so tightly interconnected that the architectures should be considered monolithic. Companies realized that these monolithic architectures are will become a burden in the future and many embark to micro-service architecture to secure flexibility in the future.

Next, the experience reported by Chen [2] is about more than 20 CD projects observed PaddyPower, an Irish a multi-billion euro betting and gaming company, operating Ireland's largest telephone betting service. The author derived lessons learned on the roadblocks to CD and emphasized the role of micro-services in countering the effects of these roadblocks.

The report of Stahl and Bosch [9] focuses on the context of large network operators, many of which are transitioning to DevOps/CD (e.g. Ericsson, Swisscom). These authors report on their proposal for a continuous integration and delivery architecture framework and its large-scale empirical evaluation at Ericsson.

Finally, a number of papers address the specific context of software process improvement consultancy and IT firms (e.g. Endava [4], Fujitsu [6], Amazon Web Services [7]). For example, Woods (Endava [4]) puts forward the use of a number of architecture artefacts that one can re-thing for use in DevOps/CD contexts: release models, configuration management models, administrative models and support models. The approach that employs such models can be considered an architecture approach in itself.

5.3 Research Methods Being Used (RQ3)

Regarding the application of research methods in the publications that formed our set for analysis in this SLR, we found that only four out of the 13 papers explicitly stated the methodological origins of their selected method (see Table 2 below).

Table 2. Use of research methods in the 13 selected papers.

Ref.	Explicitness of research process	Research method	Experience report paper
[1]	Implicit	Case study	Yes
[2]	Implicit	Case study	Yes
[3]	Implicit	Case study	n/a
[4]	Implicit	Case study	Yes
[5]	Explicit	Interview-based study	n/a
[6]	Implicit	Case study	n/a
[7]	Explicit	Case study	n/a
[8]	Explicit	Mixed method: survey + interviews	n/a
[9]	Explicit	Mixed method: SLR + interviews + group workshops	n/a
[10]	Implicit	Case study	n/a
[11]	Implicit	Case study	n/a
[12]	Implicit	Case study	Yes
[13]	Implicit	Case study	n/a

These four articles [5, 7–9] leveraged the qualitative interview techniques for the purpose of their investigation. In two papers, the qualitative interviews formed a part of a mixed-method process, e.g. Stahl and Bosch [9] complemented the interviews with group workshops, while Schermann et al. [8] used a survey together with interview. The remaining nine papers in the set of 13 only tacitly assumed the use of a case study. In fact, the authors provided rich details about the context of their organizations; there are descriptions either of project cases (e.g. [12]) or of case organizations (e.g. [2–4]). Moreover, we found four papers in the category of "experience reports"; this type of papers report on the application of a concept, method, or framework in one or several interesting industrial contexts, including the lessons-learned.

Regarding the ways in which the papers approach validity threats, we observe that threats have been explicitly discussed only by those authors that explicitly documented their research process.

6   Reflection on the Results

This section provides our reflection on our findings. First, we found 17 software architecture characteristics and as we could see from the findings regarding RQ2, these characteristics were deemed important in the context of large organizations transitioning to CD/DevOps. One can assume that these organizations maintain a large number of systems (some of which legacy systems) that are monolithic in nature. In an application landscape of monolithic systems it is then unsurprising that modifiability and agility are the most desired architecture characteristics. It is also not surprising that our SLR indicated the micro-services architecture style as the style considered the most suitable for this context.

Second, we found that the experiences published cover a broad range of application domains and companies operating in diverse business sectors. Also, from a broad range of countries located in Asia, America and Europe. This in itself has a positive implication: it allows us to think that the observations shared by the authors of the 13 papers are generalizable across application domains, business sectors and geographic zones.

Third, the finding that the case study approach was the one being used by most authors (see Table 2) matches the intuitive assumption that case studies are best in studied situations where the phenomenon of interest can be analyzed only in its real-world context (and can not be re-created in academic lab settings). However, many of the authors only implicitly mentioned the research method employed, which is at odds with the good practices and guidelines for reporting empirical software engineering research. This observation could be partly explained by the fact that many of the papers were published in practitioners' venues, such as the IEEE Software magazine, or on the practitioners' tracks of international scientific conferences. In both types of venues much more importance is placed on lessons learned and utility of the lessons learned for organizations than on the elaborate descriptions of the research method used.

7   Reflection on Bias in This SLR

In carrying out a SLR, it is also important to reflect on the criticality of researchers' own pre-knowledge and actions in reducing bias. As Archer et al. [22] state, knowledge in a scientific field is generated, developed, and interpreted by humans and relies on the methods employed for this purpose. We reflect on four types of bias that are critical for SLRs: sampling bias, selection bias, and within-study bias, as described by Felson [23], plus expectancy bias as described by Cooper [24].

Sampling bias (including retrieval bias and publication bias) is concerned with the failure to capture all relevant studies' findings on the aspects of interest [23]. Retrieval bias refers to the risk that the key words in our search string might not be chosen well enough, which in turn means that a number of highly relevant papers would not be hit while executing the search string. We countered this risk by implementing the guidelines of Kuhrman et al. [20] in regard to this issue. In fact, we experimented with a variety of search strings and compared their results in Scopus. Next, publication bias is concerned with to the tendency of conferences and journals to publish empirical research results that challenge or change existing knowledge, while studies that confirm previous results are less frequently published [25]. This issue is apparent in new and emerging areas of the software engineering discipline, where published research commonly seeks to be original through proposing new definitions or developing new approaches (e.g. CD and DevOps), hardly ever replicating previous studies. To counter this challenge, some methodologists (e.g. Tranfield et al. [26]), recommend researchers consider both published and unpublished studies. However, in our protocol, we decided to use peer-reviewed literature only, which means grey literature was not included. Moreover, in our report on *stage 1* of our research [16], we noted that we compared our already reported findings (in [16]) against themes discussed in practitioners' online venues and we found no discussion theme that contradicts our findings.

Second, selection bias is concerned with the inaccurate design or application of the inclusion/exclusion criteria. To counter this bias, we followed the guidelines of Kuhrman et al. [20] in regard to the design of our criteria. We note also that this bias can be caused in situations in which a researcher is the author of a paper on the topic of the SLR. However, in case of this review, none of the authors has a publication on the topic of software architecture and CD/DevOps.

Third, within-study bias is concerned with the risk of variability in the data extraction procedures used by both researchers. We think however that this risk is minimal because the data extraction was simple and based on a form in which all the information was recorded in a systematic way.

Finally, expectancy bias is concerned with the synthesis of the information of the 13 primary study in this SLR. One reason for the occurrence of this bias is that researchers may have differing perspectives that influence the interpretation of study findings. During study synthesis, researchers may also be biased in seeking information that conforms to their expectations and may overlook or disregard perplexing information [24]. We countered this bias by having both researchers analyze all 13 papers in our set. This was possible because the number of papers was small. Each researcher reviewed each paper individually. After this, the researchers compared their analytical results. No disagreements happened in this process.

8 Related Systematic Literature Reviews

There are five literature studies that are related to our work. First, the 2014 study of Erich et al. [29] treats the question of how DevOps influences the performance of information system development and information system operation. This study looked at the evidence indicating specific benefits of DevOps. Unlike the SLR of Erich et al. [29], our research focused solely on the relationship between software architecture and DevOps.

The second SLR (2016) is on the practices of DevOps [33]. The authors of this SLR look into DevOps definitions and practices, while comparing DevOps with other software development method. This work explicitly states the practice of designing architecture as one belonging to DevOps.

The third review is the systematic mapping study of Rodrigues et al. [14] on the phenomenon of CD. These authors found that "CD demands a software architecture in which the product and its underlying infrastructure continuously evolve and adapt to changing requirements" (p. 15, [14]). This means that the underlying architecture should be flexible so that it can accommodate rapid feedback. This, in tur, points to architecture style that is modular and loosely coupled. Our findings agree with the findings of these authors. Our results however complement the findings in [14] by adding a list of architecture characteristics which are not among those mentioned in this mapping study [14].

The fourth study is the 2019 SLR of Céspedes et al. on the effects of DevOps on software product quality [31]. This SLR revealed a strong effect of the adoption of DevOps practices on reliability and maintainability of software products. The practices associated with DevOps, such as the minimum viable product, deployment automation, test automation, cloud computing and team cooperation, show a relationship with the improvement in software product quality. Our list of characteristics (Table 2) partly overlaps with those in this study [31]. In fact, modifiability (CH1 in Table 1) is a dimension of maintainability of a software architecture [32].

The fifth review is the mapping study of Di Francesco et al. [30] on the phenomenon of architecting with micro-services. As part of these authors' analysis, the study yielded a list of architecture quality attributes that were treated in studies on micro-service architecture. Performance, maintainability, and functional suitability were found as the most studied attributes. Although these attributes were the focus of researchers working on micro-services, our SLR did not find them as the most frequently mentioned architecture characteristics from DevOps/CD perspective (see Table 1). This difference could be explained with the fact that many researchers investigated the architecting-with-micro-cervices practice in contexts in which large organizations transition from monolithic to micro-services architecture without necessarily employing DevOps and CD.

9 Summary and Implications

Using 13 publications on software architecture in DevOps/CD, this SLR indicates that:

(1) there are 17 software architecture characteristics which are beneficial for CD and DevOps adoption according, according to published literature;
(2) micro-services are recommended architectural style in this context, and
(3) large-scale organizational contexts are the most studied, and
(4) qualitative approaches (case study based) are the most applied research method.

Our review has some implications for researchers. As we found that most knowledge comes from large organizational settings in which there are many systems with monolithic architecture, it may be interesting for researchers to focus on greenfield projects in DevOps/CD. What are the architecture styles that DevOps/CD teams adopt in case of developing new systems that did not exist before? This seems a worthwhile topic for exploratory research in the future.

Another question related to the context of start-ups. While DevOps seems a logical choice for many startups in the IT and software marketplace, practitioners warn (e.g. in [27]) that the micro-service architecture may not always be the best choice in the startup context. Understanding how startup companies embracing DevOps choose their architecture styles is an industry-relevant line for research in the future.

Finally, research on the topic of interest in this SLR so far has been qualitative in nature taking into account the real-world contexts in which architecture characteristics were deemed most beneficial for DevOps/CD. However, only four of our 13 analyzed papers were explicit on the research method used. This poses a threat to the validity of the reported lessons learned by practitioners and possible candidates for good practices. From research and knowledge generation perspective, these lessons learned and candidate good practices could serve as lists of hypotheses that researchers could test in other settings in order to generate empirical evidence to draw more specific conclusions. Only then, we could make some well-substantiated claims about the software architecture characteristics beneficial for the implementation of DevOps/CD.

Our SLR has some practical implications. First, it brings good news to large organizations regarding the fit of the micro-service architecture style to DevOps/CD. Our included papers presented working examples of a broad range of industry sectors and countries, which allows us to conclude the viability of the micro-service architecture as an option to consider.

Second, software architects who may be interested in developing some architecture guidelines in their organizations using DevOps/CD might consider our list of characteristics as one possible starting point along with other considerations, such as current IT project portfolio and proportion of green-field projects in it.

References

1. Sturtevant, D.: Modular architectures make you agile in the long run. IEEE Softw. **35**(1), 104–108 (2017)

2. Chen, L.P.: Towards architecting for continuous delivery. In: Bass, L., Lago, P., Kruchten, P. (eds.) 12th Working IEEE/IFIP Conference on Software Architecture, pp. 131–134 (2015)

3. Erder, M., Pureur, P.: Continuous Architecture: Sustainable Architecture in an Agile and Cloud-Centric World, pp. 1–303. Morgan Kaufmann, Burlington (2015)

4. Woods, E.: Operational: The forgotten architectural view. IEEE Softw. **33**(3), 20–23 (2016)

5. Shahin, M., Babar, M.A., Zhu, L.: The intersection of continuous deployment and architecting process: Practitioners' perspectives (2016)

6. Elberzhager, F., Arif, T., Naab, M., Süß, I., Koban, S.: From agile development to DevOps: Going towards faster releases at high quality – experiences from an industrial context. In: Winkler, D., Biffl, S., Bergsmann, J. (eds.) SWQD 2017. LNBIP, vol. 269, pp. 33–44. Springer, Cham (2017). https://doi.org/10.1007/978-3-319-49421-0_3

7. Villamizar, M., et al.: Evaluating the monolithic and the microservice architecture pattern to deploy web applications in the cloud. In: 10th Computing Colombian Conference (10CCC) (2015)

8. Schermann, G., et al.: We're doing it live: a multi-method empirical study on continuous experimentation. Inf. Softw. Technol. **99**(7), 41–57 (2018)

9. Ståhl, D., Bosch, J.: Cinders: The continuous integration and delivery architecture framework. Inf. Softw. Technol. **83**(3), 76–93 (2017)

10. Pahl, C., Jamshidi, P., Zimmermann, O.: Architectural principles for cloud software. ACM Trans. Internet Technol. **18**(2), 1–23 (2018)

11. Berger, C., et al.: Containerized development and microservices for self-driving vehicles: Experiences & best practices. In: 2017 IEEE International Conference on Software Architecture Workshops, pp. 7–12 (2017)

12. Chen, H.M., et al.: Architectural support for DevOps in a neo-metropolis BDaaS platform. In: 2015 IEEE 34th Symposium on Reliable Distributed Systems Workshop, pp. 25–30 (2015)

13. Bass, L.: The software architect and DevOps. IEEE Softw. **35**(1), 8–10 (2017)

14. Rodríguez, P., et al.: Continuous deployment of software intensive products and services: a systematic mapping study. J. Syst. Softw. **123**, 263–291 (2017)

15. Bass, L., Weber, I., Zhu, L.: DevOps: A Software Architect's Perspective. Addison-Wesley, Boston (2015)

16. Bolscher, R., Daneva, M.: Designing software architecture to support continuous delivery and DevOps: a systematic literature review. In: ICSOFT 2019, pp. 27–39 (2019)

17. Humble, J., Farley, D.: Continuous Delivery: Reliable Software Releases through Build, Test, and Deployment Automation. Pearson Education, London (2010)

18. Wieringa, R., Daneva, M.: Six strategies for generalizing software engineering theories. Sci. Comput. Program. **101**, 136–152 (2015)

19. Kitchenham, B.: Guidelines for performing systematic literature reviews in software engineering. Keele University, UK (2007)

20. Kuhrmann, M., Méndez Fernández, D., Daneva, M.: On the pragmatic design of literature studies in software engineering: An experience-based guideline. Emp. Softw. Eng. **22**(6), 2852–2891 (2017)

21. Pawson, R.: The Promise of a Realist Synthesis, Working Paper No.4, ESRC Evidence Network, Centre for Evidence Based Policy and Practice (2001). http://www.evidencenetwork.org/Documents/wp4.pdf

22. Archer, M., Bhaskar, R., Collier, A., Lawson, T., Norrie, A.: Critical Realism: Essential Readings. Routledge, London (1998)

23. Felson, D.T.: Bias in meta-analytic research. J. Clin. Epidemiol. **45**(8), 885–892 (1992)

24. Cooper, D.H.M.: Research Synthesis and Meta-Analysis: A Step-by-Step Approach. Sage Publications Inc., Los Angeles (2010)

25. Littell, J.H., Corcoran, J., Pillai, V.: Systematic Reviews and Meta-Analysis. Oxford University Press, Oxford (2008)
26. Tranfield, D., Denyer, D., Smart, P.: Towards a methodology for developing evidence-informed management knowledge by means of systematic review. Br. J. Manag. **14**(3), 207–222 (2003)
27. https://adevait.com/software/why-most-startups-dont-need-microservices-yet
28. Bucchiarone, A., et al.: From monolithic to microservices: an experience report from the banking domain. IEEE Softw. **35**(3), 50–55 (2018)
29. Erich, F., Amrit, C., Daneva, M.: A mapping study on cooperation between information system development and operations. In: Jedlitschka, A., Kuvaja, P., Kuhrmann, M., Männistö, T., Münch, J., Raatikainen, M. (eds.) PROFES 2014. LNCS, vol. 8892, pp. 277–280. Springer, Cham (2014). https://doi.org/10.1007/978-3-319-13835-0_21
30. Di Francesco, P., Lago, P., Malavolta, I.: Architecting with microservices: a systematic mapping study. J. Syst. Softw. **150**, 77–97 (2019)
31. Céspedes, D., Angeleri, P., Melendez, K., Dávila, A.: Software product quality in DevOps contexts: A systematic literature review. In: Mejia, J., Muñoz, M., Rocha, Á., Calvo-Manzano, J.A. (eds.) CIMPS 2019. AISC, vol. 1071, pp. 51–64. Springer, Cham (2020). https://doi.org/10.1007/978-3-030-33547-2_5
32. Bengtsson, P., Lassing, N., Bosch, J., van Vliet, H.: Architecture-level modifiability analysis (ALMA). J. Syst. Softw. **69**(1–2), 129–147 (2004)
33. Jabbari, R., Bin Ali, N., Petersen, K., Tanveer, B.: What is DevOps?: a systematic mapping study on definitions and practices. In: XP Workshops 2016, p. 12 (2016)

Analysing the Performance of Mobile Cross-platform Development Approaches Using UI Interaction Scenarios

Stefan Huber[1(✉)], Lukas Demetz[1](iD), and Michael Felderer[2]

[1] University of Applied Sciences Kufstein, Andreas Hofer-Straße 7,
6330 Kufstein, Austria
{stefan.huber,lukas.demetz}@fh-kufstein.ac.at
[2] Department of Computer Science, University of Innsbruck,
Technikerstraße 21a, 6020 Innsbruck, Austria
michael.felderer@uibk.ac.at

Abstract. For developing mobile apps, developers can choose between a native development approach, in which a unique code base needs to be maintained for each supported mobile platform, and mobile cross-platform development (MCPD) approaches. MCPD approaches allow building and deploying mobile apps for several mobile platforms from one single code base. As MCPD approaches build on top of different technologies, in this paper, we analyze the performance of MCPD approaches based on UI interactions. We developed one app natively, and two using MCPD approaches. Using automated tests, we measured CPU usage, memory consumption and rendered frames of these apps when executing UI interaction scenarios consisting of three selected UI interactions (i.e., opening/closing a navigation drawer, screen transition, and virtual scrolling). The study confirms results of previous studies showing that, compared to natively developed apps, apps developed using MCPD approaches put a higher load on mobile devices regarding CPU usage, main memory and GPU memory consumption.

Keywords: Android · Ionic/Capacitor · Mobile cross-platform development · Performance analysis · React native

1 Introduction

Mobile apps are projected to generate revenues of nearly $ 953 billion worldwide by the end of 2023 [17]. When developing mobile apps, developers can exploit, on the one hand, a native development approach. This requires developers to build and maintain a unique code base for each mobile platform they want to support. As Google Android and Apple iOS dominate the market for mobile apps [16], developers need to maintain at least two code bases when they want to address the majority of mobile users. On the other hand, there exists a plethora of mobile cross-platform development (MCPD) approaches. The advantage of

© Springer Nature Switzerland AG 2020
M. van Sinderen and L. A. Maciaszek (Eds.): ICSOFT 2019, CCIS 1250, pp. 40–57, 2020.
https://doi.org/10.1007/978-3-030-52991-8_3

these approaches is that mobile apps can be easily deployed for several mobile platforms from one single code base.

To be able to deploy the same code base to multiple platforms, these approaches use different techniques [12]. React Native, for instance, pursues an interpretive approach, in which JavaScript is used to render native user interface (UI) components [3]. Others, such as Ionic/Capacitor, render the app as a website created using standard web technologies (e.g., HTML, CSS, JavaScript) within a native WebView component.

The underlying techniques used by MCPD approaches impose different requirements on mobile devices. As they render the user interface differently, they put a higher load on mobile devices, especially when compared to a native implementation [5,20]. Research so far focused mainly on programmatic performance of compute-intensive apps developed using MCPD approaches, for instance, run-time differences of sorting algorithms [1]. Typical UI interactions (e.g., swipe gestures) were not considered in performance analyzes. Most mobile apps are, however, interactive, that is, users interact heavily with the app via the user interface [18]. Thus, as UI interactions are an important aspect of mobile app usage, they should not be neglected in performance analyzes.

In a previous research [10], we investigated performance differences between native implementations and apps developed using MCPD approaches when executing one selected UI interaction. The results show substantial performance differences regarding CPU usage and memory consumption. In this present research, we continue this stream of research and test a series of UI interaction scenarios consisting in total of three UI interactions. Thus, to further investigate possible performance differences on mobile devices when performing UI interactions, the aim of this paper is to answer the following research question, *How do mobile cross-platform development approaches differ with respect to performance and load on mobile devices when performing typical UI interaction scenarios?*

In doing so, we present a quantitative performance analysis of three typical UI interactions: opening and closing of a navigation drawer, screen transitions between two different screens, and continuous swiping through a virtual scrollable list. The analysis is based on a native mobile app used as a baseline, and two apps developed using React Native and using Ionic/Capacitor. All three apps implement the same three UI interactions. The study confirms results of previous studies showing that, compared to natively developed apps, apps developed using MCPD approaches put a higher load on mobile devices regarding CPU usage, main memory and GPU memory consumption. The results indicate that the load on the mobile device (CPU consumption, main memory and GPU memory usage) of the two apps developed using MCPD approaches is substantially higher compared to the native app. We also show that the better the mobile device, the lower is the additional load on resources. Our results confirm results of previous studies and extend the body of knowledge by testing UI interactions. Mobile app developers can use these results as guidance for selecting MCPD approaches.

This paper begins by presenting research related to this study (Sect. 2). We start by discussing different MCPD approaches (Sect. 2.1). We continue by highlighting related research regarding performance measurement (Sect. 2.2) and resource usage (Sect. 2.3). Section 3 outlines the applied research method. We begin by presenting the tested implementation (i.e., the mobile app) along with implementation details for each MCPD approach, the test case, and the measurement. We will then go on to present the results of this measurement in Sect. 4. These results as well as limitation of this paper are discussed in Sect. 5. The last section (Sect. 6) concludes this paper and provides possible avenues for future research.

2   Background

This section presents literature related to this study. We start with defining mobile cross platform development and provide a general overview of MCPD approaches (Sect. 2.1). Afterwards, we present literature analyzing the performance of such approaches. They fall under the two broad categories user-perceived performance (Sect. 2.2) and resource usage (Sect. 2.3).

2.1   Mobile Cross-platform Development Approaches

Mobile cross-platform development approaches follow a write one run anywhere approach [7]. In doing so, they help developers to create and maintain one code base and to deploy this single code base to multiple mobile platforms, such as Google Android and Apple iOS. To be useful, MCPD approaches should meet several criteria, such as, multiple platform support, security, and access to built-in features [5]. Literature presents a plethora of such approaches which can be distinguished. The approaches make use of different technologies to allow the write once run anywhere approach. Base on the technologies used, multiple taxonomies can be distinguished. For instance, [15] argues for a new taxonomy using the six categories endemic apps, web apps, hybrid web apps, hybrid bridged apps, system language apps, and foreign language apps. In contrast, [3] present the five categories hybrid, interpreted, cross-compiled, model-driven, and progressive web apps. As this taxonomy is widely used, we shortly present these categories in the following.

Hybrid Approaches use web technologies (e.g., HTML, CSS and JavaScript) to implement the user interfaces and behavior. That is, a developer develops a website, which is then displayed in a WebView component (i.e., a web browser) embedded inside a native UI component [11]. Apache Cordova, formerly Adobe PhoneGap, and Ionic Capacitor leverage this approach.

Interpreted Approaches build on top of JavaScript. In contrast to the hybrid approach, developers do not build a website, but use JavaScript to render platform native UI components [6,7]. Examples for this category are Facebook React Native and Appcelerator Titanium.

Cross-compiled Approaches use a common programming language to develop a mobile app. This source code is then compiled into native code that can be executed on a mobile platform [4]. Microsoft Xamarin is a prominent example for this type of MCPD approaches.

Model-driven Approaches use the idea of domain specific languages. For this, such approaches provides generators that translate the app written in a domain specific language into native code that can be executed on a mobile platform [8]. An example for this category is MD^2.

Progressive Web Apps are web apps that are hosted on and served by a web server. Progressive web apps provide more sophisticated functions (e.g., offline availability) than standard web apps. The web app itself is developed using standard web technologies, such as HTML, CSS and JavaScript [3]. Web frameworks such as Ionic or Onsen UI offer progressive web app capabilities.

2.2 User-Perceived Performance

Previous research already investigated the user-perceived performance of apps developed using MCPD approaches and provides varying results. Andrade et al. [2], for instance, conducted a real-world experiment, with 60 employees of a company in the Brazilian public sector. A native and a hybrid app were developed and used by the employees for two weeks each. Only 13.33% of users noted a performance difference between the two approaches. Xanthopoulos and Xinogalos [21], for instance, rated different mobile cross-platform development approaches based on the user-perceived performance as low, medium or high. The classification was based on the authors experience and information published on the web. Mercado et al. [13] selected 60 mobile apps and investigated the apps' user complaints in app markets. The apps were created either natively or with MCPD approaches. Using natural language processing methods, the authors conclude that user complain more frequently about performance issues of apps developed using MCPD approaches than about native apps.

2.3 Resource Usage Measurements

Previous research on the usage of resources (e.g., CPU, memory) of MCPD approaches show more consistent results. Ajayi et al. [1] analyzed performance of algorithms, such as quicksort, implemented natively with Android and using a hybrid approach. The results show that the native app uses less CPU and memory resources than the hybrid app. Willocx et al. [19] measured several performance properties of two MCPD implementations and compared them to native implementations of iOS and Android devices. Besides metrics such as launch time, pause and resume time, time between page transitions, memory and CPU usage was measured. The authors repeated their measurements in [20] with 10 different MCPD approaches including measurements for Windows Phones. Overall, their findings show that the hybrid approaches are highest in resource consumption independent of the mobile platforms. Non-hybrid based approaches have a significant lower resource consumption, however, still higher than native implementations. Dalmasso et al. [5] used the two MCPD approaches Titanium and PhoneGap to create apps for Android. The authors measured memory, CPU and battery usage. Their findings indicate that the JavaScript framework used inside the WebView component has a high impact on memory and CPU consumption.

The results of user-perceived performance studies provide a good indication that apps developed with MCPD approaches are inferior in terms of performance in comparison to native apps. The studies on resource usage validate these findings quantitatively. Although all measurements give good indications on differences of the approaches, it is unclear under which concrete UI interactions the results are created. Previous research mainly focused on performance differences of rather computing intensive mobile apps developed using MCPD approaches. Mobile apps rather focus on interacting with users through the UI and not on complex computations [18]. Thus, when analyzing performance and resource consumption of mobile apps, UI interactions should not be left out. To close this research gap, we continue our previous research [10] in this study and analyze the performance of mobile apps developed using MCPD approaches when executing typical UI interactions. More concretely, we focus on the UI interactions opening and closing of a navigation drawer, screen transitions between two screens, and continuous swiping through a virtual scrollable list.

3   Research Method

For assessing the performance of typical UI interaction scenarios, three functionally identical Android apps, based on different development approaches, were realized. Repeatable test cases for each user interaction were created. This allowed us to interact with the apps fully automated. During the operation, CPU usage, main memory usage, GPU memory usage and frame rendering were monitored and later analyzed.

3.1   Selection of Approaches

Besides the native development approach, we selected the two MCPD approaches Ionic/Capacitor and React Native for performance analysis. These MCPD approaches allow reusing web development skills for developing mobile apps. Additionally, they enable transferring existing code bases (e.g., web application developed in JavaScript) into mobile apps. Besides, both approaches are supported by large developer communities (e.g., visible on GitHub and Stack Exchange). Many successful apps found in app markets are developed with these approaches. As a result, we selected these two approaches.

3.2   UI Interaction Scenarios

For the performance analysis, three distinct UI interaction scenarios were envisioned, which are frequently found in mobile apps. These are opening and closing a navigation drawer, screen transitioning and virtual scrolling. The UI interactions are supported by all the development approaches and are testable using an automated script. Additionally, the scenarios are not computing intensive meaning that no complex computations need to be done. The focus is on interacting with the user.

All UI interaction scenarios are part of a basic contact app. The app consists of two screens. The main screen is a list of contact entries, which can be scrolled. An additional screen provides a form for adding new contact entries. At startup of the app 500 demo contact entries with name and phone number are generated.

Opening/Closing a Navigation Drawer. A navigation drawer is a common UI component for displaying a dynamic menu. The drawer can be opened with a left-to-right swipe from the edge of the display to the center.

In Fig. 1 the native implementation of the navigation drawer scenario is presented. The left side shows the initial state and by swiping from left-to-right the resulting state on the right is produced. For the performance analysis, the drawer is opened by a respective swipe. After a two second pause, the drawer is closed with a touch event on the outside of the drawer.

Fig. 1. Navigation drawer opening/closing UI interaction (native implementation).

Screen Transitioning. Most apps have more than one screen, thus, transitions between screens are basic UI interactions within apps.

Figure 2 presents the native implementation of the screen transition scenario. The left side shows the initial state and by clicking on the action on the top-right corner a screen transition is started. The result of the transition is shown on the right side, which shows a new screen with a form for entering new data. By clicking the back button on the top-left corner, the initial state is loaded again. For the performance analysis, a screen transition is initiated from the initial screen to the form screen. After two seconds, the back button is clicked to return to the initial screen.

Virtual Scrolling. Virtual scrollable lists are common UI components found in mobile apps. Smartphones have only limited screen space available. Thus, only a small part of data presented inside a list is visible for a user. All hidden entries do not need to be processed and rendered before being visible. The scrolling feature is simulated and new entries in the list are created at runtime while scrolling down or up a list.

In Fig. 3 the native implementation of the virtual scrolling scenario is presented. The left side shows the initial state and by swiping from bottom-to-top the resulting state on the right is produced. For the performance analysis, three consecutive bottom-to-top swipes were executed. Between each swipe a pause of two seconds was set.

Fig. 2. Screen transition UI interaction (native implementation).

3.3   Implementation Details

To answer our research question, we developed three instances of the contact app described in Sect. 3.2. One instance was developed using native Google Android development tools, two instances using MCPD approaches (React Native and Ionic/Capacitor). All three apps were packaged and signed for release on Google Android. Thus, any performance degradation caused by debugging build features could be eliminated to minimize the creation of incorrect results. Table 1 provides an overview of the three developed apps including version information. A more detailed description on the implementations is provided in the following.

Table 1. Overview of apps.

Approach	Version
Android native	Compiled Android API Level 28, Minimum Android API Level 23
React native	React Native 0.60.6
Ionic/Capacitor	Ionic 4.9.1, Capacitor Android 1.2.1

Fig. 3. Virtual scrolling UI interaction (native implementation).

Native Android. Offers all required UI components for realizing the envisioned app within the core framework. Thus, no additional libraries were used. For realizing a navigation drawer, we used Android's *DrawerLayout*. Each screen in the app was realized as an Android *Activity* and navigation between the screens is done with *Intents*. Virtual scrolling was implemented using the *RecyclerView* component. This component is the default approach for realizing a virtual scrollable list on Android. An *Adapter* component has to be implemented to provide an app specific binding to a data source. The adapter design pattern allows for dissolving any dependency between the data and the display logic. The demo data was generated on app start up and stored in memory. It was provided to the RecyclerView component through the adapter.

React Native: offers the *AndroidDrawerLayout* component for realizing a navigation drawer. For navigating between different screens of an app, React Native does not provide a default approach. Therefore, the external libraries *react-navigation* and *react-navigation-stack* were used. React Native offers the *FlatList* component. This UI component is an abstraction over the native implementations of virtual scrollable lists (e.g., RecyclerView on Android). Within the React app, the demo data was generated at app start up and stored in memory. The data was directly referenced by the FlatList for actual display.

Ionic/Capacitor: is a combination of the Ionic JavaScript web-framework and the Capacitor WebView wrapper. No additional libraries were needed to implement the envisioned app. The Ionic library aims to provide reusable UI components styled like Android or iOS native components. The navigation drawer was realized with the *ion-menu* component. For navigation between different screens, *ion-router* was used. Ionic offers the *ion-virtual-scroll* component, which is a virtual scrollable list implementation for the web. The UI component emulates virtual scrolling within a WebView or web browser. The demo data for the list was generated at start up and stored in memory. The data was directly referenced by ion-virtual-scroll for actual display. The app was packaged within a Capacitor wrapper, which is the default approach for Ionic apps.

3.4 Test Cases

To execute the three UI interaction scenarios with each of the developed apps, fully automated test cases were created. The exact same test case could be used to produce measurement results for each app on different devices. This allows a direct comparison of the results.

Each step of a test case execution is exactly timed. In the following, a detailed step by step description of the general test case execution is given. Each of the test cases can be executed repeatedly without any human intervention.

- Install the app on a connected Android device.
- Start the app by triggering an Android Intent on the connected device.

- Wait for 20 s. The different development approaches have different loading times, therefore a certain waiting time is required. The apps were always loaded before the 20 s of waiting time on the test device.
- Start vmstat with a total recording time of 30 s.
- Wait for 3 s.
- Start the execution of one of the UI interaction scenarios: navigation drawer opening/closing, screen transitioning, or virtual scrolling
- Wait for 5 s.
- Start the generation of gfxinfo results on the device.
- Wait for 15 s.
- Close the app and uninstall it from the device.
- Wait for 25 s.
- Download the measurement results (vmstat and gfxinfo) from the device.

The test procedures were created using the AndroidViewClient [14] library. This library enables the scripting of UI interactions with Python code. For all device management tasks the Android Debugging Bride (adb) was used. Each test case was executed 25 times per app and per device, which resulted in a total of 225 executions. The full test procedure is made available publicly within a git-repository[1].

3.5   Measurement Tools and Metrics

As Android is Linux-based, it offers many of Linux' command-line utilities. vmstat [9] is a Linux tool for executing continuous performance measurements. Amongst other measurements periodic recordings for CPU usage expressed in percent and freely available main memory expressed in bytes were gathered. The tool was started in parallel to the execution of the automated test cases as described in Sect. 3.4. The recording interval was set to one second and vmstat was running for 30 s, thus a time series of 30 measurements was produced for each test case execution.

CPU usage is a value expressed in percent which shows the utilization of the CPU and could be taken directly from the vmstat results. The main memory usage is a deduced metric based on the vmstat results for the freely available main memory expressed in bytes. The freely available memory is compared between the idle state of the test device and the active phase throughout the execution of the test cases. The memory increase from the idle state to the active state is then deduced as a value in percent.

Additionally, Android offers gfxinfo, a tool which aggregates information about frame rendering performance of an app. Amongst other measurements the percentage of janky frames and the usage of GPU memory expressed in megabytes were gathered. The percentage of janky frames gives an indication of the fluidness of the UI of an app. A janky frame is a frame that could not be rendered correctly and needs to be dropped in the rendering process.

---

[1] https://www.github.com/stefanhuber/ICSOFT-2019.

3.6   Test Devices

The test cases were executed on three different mobile devices running Google Android. The Android versions of the devices were updated to the maximum supported version of the manufacturers. In Table 2, details of the device specifications are listed.

Table 2. Mobile device specifications.

Device	CPU	RAM	Resolution	Display size	Android Version
LG Nexus 5	Quad-core 2.3 GHz	2 GB	1080 × 1920	4.95 in.	6.0.1
Samsung Galaxy S5	Quad-core 2.5 GHz	2 GB	1080 × 1920	5.1 in.	6.0.1
LG Nexus 5X	Hexa-core 4 × 1.4 GHz/2 × 1.8 GHz	2 GB	1080 × 1920	5.2 in	8.0

4   Results

This section is devoted to the results of this study. We present the results according to the four measured metrics namely CPU usage (Sect. 4.1), main memory usage (Sect. 4.2), janky frames (Sect. 4.3) and GPU memory usage (Sect. 4.4). The results were produced by executing the UI interaction scenarios 25 times per test device and implementation.

The results are presented in form of heat maps. The heat maps indicate higher values with a darker background color and lower values with a lighter background color. The whole spread of values inside each individual graphic is shown with a color bar below each graphic. The values for the heat maps are based on the statistical mean of the produced measurements, as described in Sect. 3.5

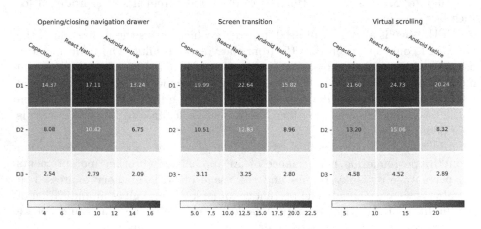

Fig. 4. Average CPU usage (%) for 3 interaction scenarios on 3 test devices. (D1 = Samsung Galaxy S5, D2 = LG Nexus 5, D3 = LG Nexus 5X).

4.1 CPU Usage

Figure 4 shows a comparison of average CPU usage in form of a heat map. It can be seen that the native development approach (right most column) has the lowest average CPU usage on all devices and for all scenarios. Apps developed with MCPD approaches always come with a overhead compared to native development.

Ionic/Capacitor (left most column of each heat map) requires between 7% (Virtual scrolling on the Samsung Galaxy S5) and 59% (Virtual scrolling on the LG Nexus 5) more CPU resources on average than a native implementation (right most column of each heat map). React Native (middle column of each heat map) requires between 16% (Screen transition on the LG Nexus 5X) and 81% (Virtual scrolling on the LG Nexus 5) more CPU resources on average.

React Native has for most scenarios a higher average load on CPU than Ionic/Capacitor. Only virtual scrolling on the LG Nexus 5X has a slightly lower average CPU load for the React Native implementation. For all other scenarios React Native requires between 5% (Screen transition on the LG Nexus 5X) to 29% (Opening/closing navigation drawer on the LG Nexus 5) more average CPU resources than the Ionic/Capacitor counterpart.

4.2 Main Memory Usage

Figure 5 shows a comparison of average memory increase from an idle state of the test device to the execution of the interaction scenario in form of a heat map.

In general the Android Native implementation (right most column) has clearly the lowest memory footprint. For all scenarios and test devices the memory increase lies between 1.8% and 8.2%. MCPD approaches have a substantial higher demand for main memory compared to a native implementation.

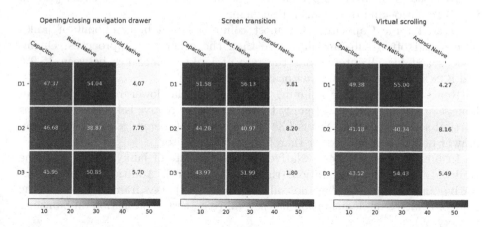

Fig. 5. Average memory increase (%) for 3 interaction scenarios on 3 test devices. (D1 = Samsung Galaxy S5, D2 = LG Nexus 5, D3 = LG Nexus 5X).

The memory requirement for Ionic/Capacitor implementations (left most column) rises between 41.2% and 51.6% compared to the idle state. For React Native (middle column) implementation the memory requirement is between 38.9% and 56.1%. React Native requires less memory on the LG Nexus 5 than Ionic/Capacitor for all tested scenarios. On the other two devices the contrary is the case and Ionic/Capacitor requires less memory than React Native.

4.3 Janky Frames

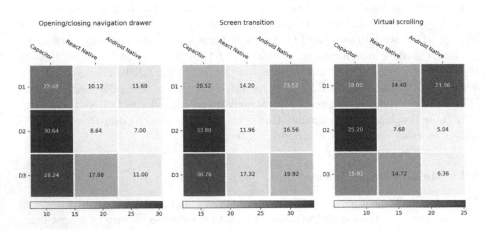

Fig. 6. Average janky frames (%) for 3 interaction scenarios on 3 test devices. (D1 = Samsung Galaxy S5, D2 = LG Nexus 5, D3 = LG Nexus 5X).

Figure 6 shows the average percentage of janky frames in the rendering process for all scenarios and devices as a heat map.

Overall Ionic/Capacitor (left most column) has a high amount of janky frames and often substantially more than the other two approaches. On all devices and for all interactions the rate of janky frames lies between 15.9% and 33.8% for the Ionic/Capacitor implementations.

React Native (middle column) has a substantial lower rate of jank than Ionic/Capacitor. The rate of janky frames for React Native is between 1.1 times (virtual scrolling on LG Nexus 5X) and 3.5 times (opening/closing navigation drawer on LG Nexus 5) lower than for Ionic/Capacitor.

In 5 cases out of 9 React Native has a lower rate of janky frames than the Android Native implementation (right most column). Additionally, the React Native implementation has no values over 18% janky frames, however the Android Native implementation has several (e.g., screen transition on Samsung Galaxy S5).

4.4   GPU Memory Usage

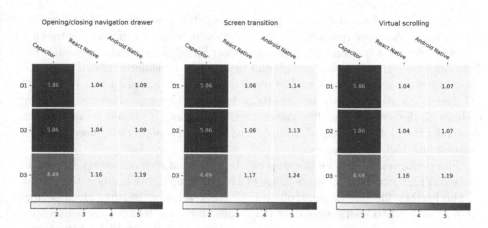

Fig. 7. Average GPU memory usage (%) for 3 interaction scenarios on 3 test devices. (D1 = Samsung Galaxy S5, D2 = LG Nexus 5, D3 = LG Nexus 5X).

Figure 7 shows a comparison of GPU memory usage of the test devices in form of a heat map.

Clearly, the Ionic/Capacitor implementation (left most column) has the highest demand for GPU memory. React Native (middle column) and Android Native (right most column) have an almost identical demand, although for React Native the demand is marginally lower.

In general, Ionic/Capacitor requires between 3.8 times (screen transition on LG Nexus 5X) and 5.5 times (virtual scrolling Samsung Galaxy S5) more GPU memory than React Native or Android Native.

5   Discussion

In this study, a systematic examination of performance differences of typical UI interaction scenarios based on different app implementations was performed. As metrics CPU usage, main memory usage, janky frames and GPU memory usage were selected. The results show the difference between Android Native implementations and MCPD implementations and thus provide some guidance to mobile app developers in selecting a suitable MCPD approach.

In terms of UI fluidity (indicated by the amount of janky frames) React Native and Android Native are comparable. For instance, for screen transitions the amount of janky frames is even lower for React Native than for Android Native on all tested devices. This means, these two approaches provide a more fluid user interaction and thus a higher user-perceived performance. This comes, however, at the cost of a higher load on CPU and main memory for React Native. Ionic/Capacitor has a similar high load on CPU and main memory compared to React Native although missing the benefit of a low janky frame rate and low GPU memory usage. Thus, Ionic/Capacitor is more prone to a user-perceived performance degradation.

The selection of a mobile development approach impacts the success of mobile app projects. As prior research has shown, users perceive a difference between a native implementation and an implementation based on MCPD approaches [2]. This difference is acceptable if high-end devices are considered [20]. This study also confirms this observation. The more advanced or high-end test device D3 LG Nexus 5X device has a substantially lower CPU usage than the Samsung Galaxy S5 device D1, a rather low-end mobile device. It should be noted that especially the global market of Android smartphones is highly dispersed between low-end and high-end devices.

The performance of a mobile app can be a competitive advantage in certain contexts. The increased resource usage of MCPD approaches has negative effects on the battery lifetime of smartphones [4]. Also, a lower user-perceived performance can lead to user complaints [13]. Thus, for apps which have a necessity for frequent user interactions, a native implementation should be considered. Users might switch to competing apps in favor of lower battery drainage or an increased user-perceived performance.

There is a development practice of mixing native development with MCPD approaches. For instance, frequently used parts of an app can be implemented natively to reduce resource consumption. Other parts of an app with lesser importance (e.g., settings menu) can be implemented with MCPD approaches. It should be noted, that additionally to the native code bases (e.g., one for Android and one for iOS) a third cross-platform code base needs to be maintained. This however contradicts with a major advantage of MCPD approaches to reduce maintenance and development costs. Therefore, this practice should be used carefully.

A number of caveats need to be noted regarding the present study. First, we only used an Android Native implementation to compare the performance results of the two MCPD approaches. A native implementation for Apple iOS was not tested. This is mainly because iOS is a more restricted operating system than Android and we faced restrictions on the automatic execution of UI interactions and low-level monitoring of CPU/memory usage. Our proposed approach is not transferable to analyze MCPD approaches on iOS.

We only considered two MCPD approaches, hybrid and interpreted. However, there are three other types of approaches [3]. To have an in depth analysis of MCPD approaches, all five categories of approaches should be included. This study confirms results of previous studies [5,20], which showed that MCPD approaches put a higher load on resources. The current body of literature is expanded as a systematic examination of performance with respect to UI interaction scenarios of different mobile development approaches was conducted. Additionally, the automated test of UI interaction scenarios show a novel approach of performance testing.

To ensure construct validity, the exact same automated test cases were used for examining the differences of each MCPD approach on different devices. Also, the metrics CPU usage, memory consumption and janky frames are commonly used for performance studies. To mitigate threats to internal validity, the test procedure was set up such that each individual test case was started by completely reinstalling the app on a clean slate. After the execution of a test case, the app was also completely removed from the test device. Furthermore, each app is packaged for release to mitigate any performance degradation caused by debugging build features. Regarding external validity and to increase the generalizability of our results, three different test devices and three different UI interaction scenarios were examined. Additionally, the research method is repeatable as automatic executions are used and the whole procedure is made available publicly within a git-repository.

6 Conclusion

This study is a continuation of a previous study [10] in which a performance analysis of three implementations (two MCPD approaches and one native approach) of three different UI interaction scenarios was conducted. We found that MCPD approaches put a higher load on CPU and main memory. Ionic/Capacitor puts also a higher load on GPU memory usage. These results are in line with results of previous studies. Nevertheless, in this study, we pursued a different approach to test the performance of mobile apps as we focus on interactions with the UI. Previous studies focused mainly on rather computing intensive apps.

In terms of UI fluidness (indicated by the rate of janky frames) React Native is comparable to Android Native. In our conclusion React Native can produce a similar user-perceived performance than the Android Native baseline, although at a higher load on CPU and main memory. Ionic/Capacitor has similar resource usage as React Native although missing the low rate of janky frames.

The use of MCPD approaches for app development has substantial consequences for CPU usage and memory consumption. Mobile app developers face a difficult decision on the choice of the development approaches as performance can be a competitive advantage. We conclude that a mixture of a native development approach with a MCPD approach within the same app is plausible. For frequently used parts of an app a native implementation can decrease the resource usage and increase the battery lifetime.

As we only tested two MCPD approaches, future work should extend this research by increasing the number of MCPD approaches for the performance analysis of typical UI interactions. Also, an iOS native implementation and iOS test devices should be included. This would provide a broader picture of the performance of MCPD approaches.

References

1. Ajayi, O.O., Omotayo, A.A., Orogun, A.O., Omomule, T.G., Orimoloye, S.M.: Performance evaluation of native and hybrid android applications. Perform. Eval. **7**(16), 1–9 (2018)
2. Andrade, P.R., Albuquerque, A.B., Frota, O.F., Silveira, R.V., da Silva, F.A.: Cross platform app: A comparative study. Int. J. Comput. Sci. Inf. Technol. **7**(1), 33–40 (2015). https://doi.org/10.5121/ijcsit.2015.7104
3. Biørn-Hansen, A., Grønli, T.M., Ghinea, G.: A survey and taxonomy of core concepts and research challenges in cross-platform mobile development. ACM Comput. Surv. (CSUR) **51**(5), 108 (2018)
4. Ciman, M., Gaggi, O.: An empirical analysis of energy consumption of cross-platform frameworks for mobile development. Pervasive Mob. Comput. **39**, 214–230 (2017). https://doi.org/10.1016/j.pmcj.2016.10.004
5. Dalmasso, I., Datta, S.K., Bonnet, C., Nikaein, N.: Survey, comparison and evaluation of cross platform mobile application development tools. In: 2013 9th International Wireless Communications and Mobile Computing Conference (IWCMC). IEEE, Jul 2013. https://doi.org/10.1109/iwcmc.2013.6583580
6. Dhillon, S., Mahmoud, Q.H.: An evaluation framework for cross-platform mobile application development tools. Softw. Pract. Exp. **45**(10), 1331–1357 (2015). https://doi.org/10.1002/spe.2286
7. El-Kassas, W.S., Abdullah, B.A., Yousef, A.H., Wahba, A.M.: Taxonomy ofcross-platform mobile applications development approaches. Ain Shams Eng. J. **8**(2), 163–190 (2017). https://doi.org/10.1016/j.asej.2015.08.004
8. Heitkötter, H., Majchrzak, T.A.: Cross-platform development of business apps with MD². In: vom Brocke, J., Hekkala, R., Ram, S., Rossi, M. (eds.) DESRIST 2013. LNCS, vol. 7939, pp. 405–411. Springer, Heidelberg (2013). https://doi.org/10.1007/978-3-642-38827-9_29
9. Henry, W., Fabian, F.: Man page for vmstat. https://www.unix.com/man-page/linux/8/vmstat/ (2009). Accessed 11 Feb 2019
10. Huber, S., Demetz, L.: Performance analysis of mobile cross-platform development approaches based on typical ui interactions. In: Proceedings of the 14th International Conference on Software Technologies (ICSOFT 2019), pp. 40–48. SCITEPRESS - Science and Technology Publications, Lda, Prague, Czech Republic (2019). https://doi.org/10.5220/0007838000400048
11. Latif, M., Lakhrissi, Y., Nfaoui, E.H., Es-Sbai, N.: Cross platform approach for mobile application development: A survey. In: 2016 International Conference on Information Technology for Organizations Development (IT4OD), IEEE, Mar 2016. https://doi.org/10.1109/it4od.2016.7479278
12. Majchrzak, T.A., Biørn-Hansen, A., Grønli, T.M.: Comprehensive analysis of innovative cross-platform app development frameworks. In: Proceedings of the 50th Hawaii International Conference on System Sciences (2017). https://doi.org/10.24251/HICSS.2017.745
13. Mercado, I.T., Munaiah, N., Meneely, A.: The impact of cross-platform development approaches for mobile applications from the user's perspective. In: Proceedings of the International Workshop on App Market Analytics, pp. 43–49. ACM (2016)
14. Milano, D.T.: AndroidViewClient. https://github.com/dtmilano/AndroidViewClient (2019). Accessed 04 Nov 2019

15. Nunkesser, R.: Beyond web/native/hybrid: a new taxonomy for mobile app development. In: MOBILESoft 2018: 5th IEEE/ACM International Conference on Mobile Software Engineering and Systems, pp. 214–218. ACM, New York; Gothenburg, Sweden, May 2018. https://doi.org/10.1145/3197231.3197260
16. Statista: Global smartphone sales by operating system from 2009 to 2017 (in millions). https://www.statista.com/statistics/263445/global-smartphone-sales-by-operating-system-since-2009/ (2018). Accessed 11 Feb 2019
17. Statista: Worldwide mobile app revenues in 2014 to 2023 (in billion U.S. dollars). https://www.statista.com/statistics/269025/worldwide-mobile-app-revenue-forecast/ (2019). Accessed 12 Nov 2019
18. Vallerio, K.S., Zhong, L., Jha, N.K.: Energy-efficient graphical user interface design. IEEE Trans. Mob. Comput. **5**(7), 846–859 (2006)
19. Willocx, M., Vossaert, J., Naessens, V.: A quantitative assessment of performance in mobile app development tools. In: 2015 IEEE International Conference on Mobile Services, pp. 454–461. IEEE (2015)
20. Willocx, M., Vossaert, J., Naessens, V.: Comparing performance parameters of mobile app development strategies. In: 2016 IEEE/ACM International Conference on Mobile Software Engineering and Systems (MOBILESoft), pp. 38–47. IEEE (2016)
21. Xanthopoulos, S., Xinogalos, S.: A comparative analysis of cross-platform development approaches for mobile applications. In: Proceedings of the 6th Balkan Conference in Informatics on - BCI 2013. ACM Press (2013). https://doi.org/10.1145/2490257.2490292

Quantitative Analysis of Mutant Equivalence

Amani Ayad[1], Imen Marsit[2], Sara Tawfig[3], Ji Meng Loh[4], Mohamed Nazih Omri[2],
and Ali Mili[4(✉)] ⓘD

[1] SUNY, Farmingdale, NY, USA
ayada@farmingdale.edu
[2] University of Sousse, Sousse, Tunisia
imen.marsit@gmail.com, mohamednazih.omri@fsm.rnu.tn
[3] SUST, Khartoum, Sudan
stawfig2006@gmail.com
[4] NJIT, Newark, NJ, USA
{loh,mili}@njit.edu

Abstract. Program mutation is the process of generating syntactic variations of
a base program and analyzing them by comparison with the base; this process is
meaningful only to the extent that the mutants are semantically distinct from the
base program, but that is not always the case. Two programs may be syntactically
distinct yet semantically equivalent. The problem of identifying and weeding out
equivalent mutants has eluded researchers for a long time. In this chapter we
argue that researchers ought to abandon the overly ambitious goal of determining
whether a program and its mutant are equivalent, and focus instead on the more
modest, but sufficient, goal of estimating the number of equivalent mutants that a
program is prone to generate.

Keywords: Mutation testing · Software metrics · Equivalent mutants ·
Redundant mutants · Mutation score

1 Mutation Equivalence: The Bane of Mutation Testing

Program mutation consists in taking a base program and applying a range of elementary
syntactic modifications thereto to generate variants thereof, called *mutants*. Mutants are
used for a variety of purposes, the most common of which is the generation and validation of test data suites: because mutations are deemed to be adequate representations
of faults [2, 16, 23], a test data suite can be assessed by its ability to distinguish mutants
from the base program. The trouble with this approach is that many mutants may be
semantically equivalent to the base program, despite being syntactically distinct. Hence
if a test data suite fails to distinguish a mutant from the base program (aka: to *kill* the
mutant), it may be because the mutant is semantically equivalent to the base program,
not because there is anything wrong with the suite.

   As a result a great deal of research has been devoted to the problem of identifying and weeding out equivalent mutants from a set of generated program mutants

This research is partially supported by NSF under grant DGE 1565478.

M. van Sinderen and L. A. Maciaszek (Eds.): ICSOFT 2019, CCIS 1250, pp. 58–80, 2020.
https://doi.org/10.1007/978-3-030-52991-8_4

[1,2,8,10–18,23–26,28,30,31]. Despite several decades of research, the problem of equivalent mutants remains largely unsolved [27]. We argue that a major reason why this problem has eluded researchers for so long is that its goal has been set too high, and unnecessarily so. Determining whether two programs (a base program and a mutant, in this case) are semantically equivalent is known to be undecidable [7]. This theoretical result notwithstanding, the task of determining whether two programs are semantically equivalent is virtually insurmountable in practice. Researchers have resorted to two approximate solutions in practice:

- Either inferring global program equivalence from local equivalence of affected source code; this yields sufficient but unnecessary conditions of equivalence. Two programs may well be semantically distinct at a local level yet still globally equivalent, due to masking.
- Or inferring semantic equivalence from global functional or behavioral envelopes; this yields necessary but insufficient conditions of equivalence. Two programs may exhibit similarity in their functional or behavioral envelopes yet still be semantically distinct.

Whereas the task of determining whether a program and a mutant are equivalent is complex, costly, tedious, and error-prone, we have to remember that in practice this task must be conducted not a for a single mutant, but for a larger set of mutants; hence identifying and weeding out equivalent mutants in a set of size N is $O(N)$ times an already high cost. Also, once we have identified those mutants that are not equivalent to the base program P, we must then worry about whether these mutants are equivalent to each other; analyzing mutual equivalence among N mutants (which are known to be distinct from P, but may be equivalent to each other) is $O(N^2)$ times the already high cost of testing whether two programs are semantically equivalent.

Testing for equivalence of N mutants against a base program is not only costly; it is also unnecessary. We argue that for most intents and purposes, it is not necessary to identify individually all the mutants of P that are equivalent to P; it suffices to estimate their number. Fortunately, estimating their number can be done efficiently, by analyzing the source code of P and the mutant generation policy that is applied to P, which we define specifically by the set of mutation operators that are deployed on P. For a given program P and mutant generation policy, we let the *Ratio of Equivalent Mutants* (abbrev: *REM*) be the fraction of generated mutants that are equivalent to P. We argue that this parameter can be estimated by analyzing P under the selected mutant generation policy, and we find that knowing the *REM* of a program enables us to answer many important questions pertaining to the mutation behavior of P, including the degree to which non-equivalent mutants of P are in turn equivalent to each other.

This paper extends and builds on the results of [6] by discussing the details of the estimation of a program's *REM*, and by discussing the validation of the assumptions and results that we are obtaining by estimating and using the *REM*. In Sect. 2 we present the motivation of a quantitative approach to the analysis of mutation equivalence and in Sect. 3 we introduce a number of metrics that we believe, on the basis of analytical arguments, to be statistically correlated to the *REM* of a program. In Sect. 4 we discuss the design of a Java (pseudo) compiler that we derived using compiler generation technology to scan Java code and compute the metrics discussed in Sect. 3. In Sects. 5

and 6 we discuss means that we have developed to, respectively, estimate the *REM* of a program, and use it to analyse the mutation attributes of the program. We conclude in Sect. 7 by summarizing our findings, evaluating them, and exploring venues for further research.

2   A Quantitative Approach

The issue of mutant equivalence has a bearing on many aspects of mutation testing; we review these below.

– *Equivalence between a Base Program and a Mutant.* When we generate, say 100 mutants of some program P, and we want to check whether some test data T can detect (kill) all the mutants, we ought to consider only those mutants that are not equivalent to P; indeed the mutants that are semantically equivalent to P cannot be detected (killed) regardless of how adequate test data set T is. In this paper we define a function we call *REM* (Ratio of Equivalent Mutants) to capture the ratio of equivalent mutants that a program P is prone to generate, for a given mutant generation policy.

– *Mutant Redundancy: Equivalence between Mutants.* Let us assume that out of the 100 mutants we have generated, we have determined that 80 are not equivalent to P; let us further assume that test data set T is able to detect (kill) all 80 mutants. What this tells us about T depends to a large extent on how many of these 80 mutants are equivalent to each other: If test T has killed 80 mutants, it is important to tell whether it has killed 80 distinct mutants, or just killed the same mutant (albeit in different syntactic forms) 80 times. Hence it is important to know how many equivalence classes the set of 80 mutants has, modulo the relation of semantic equivalence. In this paper we define a function we call *NEC* (Number of Equivalence Classes) to capture the number of equivalence classes of the set of mutants modulo semantic equivalence (excluding the equivalence class of P); and we show how we can estimate NEC.

– *Mutation score.* Imagine that we run the 100 mutants we have generated on test data T, and we find that 60 mutants are detected (killed) and 40 are not; it is common to take 0.6 (= 60/100) as the *mutation score* of T. We argue that this metric is flawed, for two reasons: first, the mutation score ought to be based not on the total number of generated mutants, but rather on those that are estimated to be non-equivalent to P ($(1 - REM) \times 100$, in this case); second, the mutation score ought not count the number of individual mutants detected (for the reasons cited above), but rather the number of equivalence classes covered by the detected mutants. Indeed, whenever one mutant is detected by test data T, all the mutants in the same class are also detected; at an extreme case, if all 80 mutants form a single equivalence class, and test data T detects one of them, it automatically detects all 80; to say in such a situation that T detected 80 mutants is misleading; it is more meaningful to say that T detected one equivalence class. Hence we argue that the mutation score should be defined in terms of equivalence classes, not in terms of individual mutants; in this paper, we introduce a metric to this effect, which we call *EMS* (Equivalence-based Mutation Score).

As we shall see in this paper, NEC is defined in terms of REM, and EMS is defined in terms of NEC; hence REM plays a pivotal in this study. To gain some insight into how to estimate REM, we ask two related questions:

- What makes a program prone to generate equivalent mutants?
- Given a base program P and a mutant M, what may cause the mutant to be equivalent to the base program?

To answer the first question, we make the following observation: A program that is prone to generate equivalent mutants is a program that can continue performing the same function despite the presence and sensitization of mutations in its source code. Now, mutations are supposed to simulate faults in programs; if we replace "*mutations*" by "*faults*" in the above statement we find that a program that is prone to generate equivalent mutants is a program that can continue perfoming the same function despite the presence and sensitization of faults in its source code. This is exactly the characterization of fault tolerant programs, and we know too well what attribute makes programs fault tolerant: it is redundancy. Hence if we can quantify the redundancy of a program, we can use the redundancy metrics to predict the REM of a program.

To answer the second question, we consider the following circumstances that may cause a mutant to be equivalent to a base program (using the terminology of Laprie et al. [4, 19–21]).

- *The mutation is not a fault*, i.e. it never generates a state that is different from the original program; this arises in trivial circumstances such as when the mutation applies to dead code, but may also arise in more common cases, such as, e.g. changing $<$ onto $\leq$ when the operands being compared are never equal (e.g. an array of unique identifiers).
- *The mutation is a fault, but it causes no error*; i.e. it does cause the generation of a different state, but the state it generates is correct (as correct as the state generated by the base program). As an example, imagine that the mutation causes a list of items to be visited in a different order from the original program, but the order is irrelevant (example; if the program is performing a commutative associative operation on the elements of the list. As another example, consider the situation of a sorting algorithm where the mutation operator reverses all the comparison operators, likely causing the mutant to sort the array in reverse order from the base program, but the array is getting sorted merely to extract its median.
- *The mutation is a fault, it does cause errors, but the errors do not cause failure.* In other words the mutation causes the generation of an erroneous state, but the error is subsequently masked by downstream code. This arises routinely, as program functions are typically very non-injective.
- *The mutation is a fault, it does cause errors, the errors do cause failure, but the failure falls within the tolerance of the equivalence oracle.* If the equivalence oracle does not test for comprehensive equality between the final state of P and the final state of M, it is conceivable that M and P are considered equivalent while their final states are distinct. This arises for example if the oracle that tests for equivalence does not check for identity of all the variables, only important program variables, and the mutation affects secondary auxiliary variables; this may also arise if the mutation affects local/ limited scope program variables after their value has been referenced.

3   Redundancy Metrics

In this section, we review some metrics which, we feel, may be statistically related to the REM of a program; these metrics reflect various forms of program redundancy, and they are related with the circumstances we cite above for a mutant to be equivalent to a base program. These metrics are defined by means of Shannon's entropy function [29]; we use the notations $H(X)$, $H(X|Y)$ and $H(X, Y)$ to denote, respectively, the entropy of random variable X, the conditional entropy of X given Y, and the joint entropy of random variables X and Y; we assume that the reader is familiar with these concepts, their interpretations, and their properties [9]. For each metric, we briefly present its definition, its interpretation, how we calculate it, and why we believe that it is correlated to (because it affects) the REM of a program; in Sect. 4 we discuss how we automate the calculation of these metrics for Java code. For illustrative examples of how these metrics are computed (by hand), see [5]

Because the REM is a ratio that ranges between 0 and 1, we resolve to define all our metrics as values between 0 and 1, so as to facilitate the derivation of a regression model. For the sake of simplicity, we compute all entropies under the assumption of equal probability.

3.1   State Redundancy

What We Want to Represent: When we declare variables in a program, we do so for the purpose of representing the states of the program; for a variety of reasons, it is very common to find that the range of values that program variables may take is much larger than the range of values that actual/ feasible program states may take. We want *state redundancy* to reflect the gap between the entropy of the declared state and that of the actual state of the program.

How We Define It: If we let S be the declared state of the program, and σ be the actual state of the program, then the state redundancy of the program can be measured by the difference between their respective entropies; to normalize it (so that it ranges between 0.0 and 1.0) we divide it by the entropy of the declared state. Recognizing that the entropy of the actual state decreases (hence the redundancy increases) as the execution of the program proceeds from the initial state to the final state, we define, in fact two different measures of state redundancy, one for each state.

Definition 1 *(Due to [6]). Given a program P whose declared state (defined by its variable declarations) is S, we let σ_I and σ_F be its initial and final actual states, we define its* initial state redundancy *and its* final state redundancy *as, respectively:*

$$SR_I = \frac{H(S) - H(\sigma_I)}{H(S)},$$

$$SR_F = \frac{H(S) - H(\sigma_F)}{H(S)}.$$

How We Calculate It: To compute $H(S)$ we use a table (due to [6]) that maps each data type to its width in bits,

Table 1. Entropy of declared state (due to [6]).

Data type	Entropy (bits)
bool	1
char	1
int	32
float	64

Why We Feel It Is Correlated to the REM of a Program: State redundancy reflects the amount of duplication of the information maintained by the program, or the amount of extra bits of information that are part of the declared state; the more duplicated bits or unused bits are lying around in the program state, the greater the likelihood that a mutation affects bits that are not subsequently referenced in the execution of the program (hence do not affect its outcome).

3.2 Non Injectvity

What We Want to Represent: A function f is said to be *injective* if and only if it maps different inputs onto different outputs, i.e. $x \neq x' \Rightarrow f(x) \neq f(x')$. A function is non-injective if it violates this property; it is all the more non-injective that it maps a larger set of distinct inputs onto a common output.

How We Define It: For the purposes of this metric, we view a program as mapping initial states onto final states. One way to quantify non-injectivity is to use the conditional entropy of the initial state given the final state: this entropy reflecte the uncertainty we have about the initial state if we know the final state; this entropy increases as more initial states are mapped to the same final state; to normalize it, we divide it by the entropy of the initial state.

Definition 2 *(Due to [6]). Given a program P on space S, the* non-injectivity *of P is denoted by NI and defined by:*

$$NI = \frac{H(\sigma_I | \sigma_F)}{H(\sigma_I)},$$

where σ_I and σ_F are, respectively, the initial actual state and the final actual state of P.

Because σ_F is a function of σ_I, the conditional entropy can be simplified [9], yielding the following formula:

$$NI = \frac{H(\sigma_I) - H(\sigma_F)}{H(\sigma_I)}.$$

In [3], Androutsopoulos et al. introduce a similar metric, called *squeeziness*, which they find to be correlated to the probability that an error arising at some location in a program fails to propagate to the output.

How We Calculate It: We have already discussed how to compute the entropies of the initial state and final state of a program.

Why We Feel It Is Correlated to the REM of a Program: One of the main sources of mutant equivalence is the ability of programs to mask errors that have infected the state, by mapping the erroneous state onto the same final state as the correct state. This happens all the more frequently that the function of the program is more non-injective; hence non-injectivity measures exactly the capability of the program to mask errors caused by the sensitization of mutations.

3.3   Functional Redundancy

What We Want to Represent: Not all programs can be faithfully modeled as mappings from initial states to final states, as we do in Sect. 3.2; sometimes a more faithful model of a program may be a heterogeneous function from some input space X to some output space Y. Programs exchange information with their environment through a wide range of channels: they receive input information (X) through read statements, message passing, passed by-value parameters, access to global variables, etc; and they send output information (Y) through write statements, passed by-reference parameters, return statements, access to global variables, etc. We want a metric that reflects non-injectivity (hence the potential for masking errors) for this model of computation.

How We Define It: We let X be the random variable that represents all the input information used by the program, and we let Y be the random variable that represents all the output information that is delivered by P.

Definition 3 *(Due to [6]). Given a program P that takes input X and returns output Y, the* functional redundancy *of P is denoted by FR and defined by:*

$$FR = \frac{H(X|Y)}{H(X)}.$$

Because Y is a function of X, we know [9] that the conditional entropy ($H(X|Y)$) can be written as ($H(X) - H(Y)$). Also, the entropy of Y is less than or equal to the entropy of X, and both are non-negative, hence FR ranges between 0 and 1 (we assume, of course, that $H(X) \neq 0$).

How We Calculate It: The entropy of X is the sum of the entropies of all the input channels and the entropy of Y is the sum of the entropies of all the output channels.

Why We Feel It Is Correlated to the REM of a Program: Functional redundancy, like non-injectivity, reflects the program's ability to mask errors caused by mutations; whereas non-injectivity models the program as a homogeneous function on its state space, functional redundancy models it as a heterogeneous mapping from an input space to an output space.

All the metrics we have discussed so far pertain to the base program; we refer to them as the program's *intrinsic metrics*. The metric we present in the next section deals not with the base program, but rather with the oracle that is used to rule on equivalence.

3.4 Non Determinacy

What We Want to Represent: Whether two programs (in particular, a program and a mutant thereof) are equivalent or not may depend on how thoroughly we check their behavior. For example, it is possible that out of three program variables, two represent the intended function of the programs and the third is merely an auxiliary variable. In such a case, the oracle of equivalence ought to check that the relevant variables have the same value, but ignore the auxiliary variable.

From this discussion we infer that the equivalence between a base program P and a mutant M may depend on what oracle is used to compare the output of P with the output of M, and we are interested to define a metric that reflects the degree of non-determinacy of the selected oracle.

We are given a program P on space S and a mutant M on the same space, and we consider an oracle $\Omega()$ on S defined by an equivalence relation on S. We want the *non-determinacy* of $\Omega()$ to reflect how much uncertainty we have about the output of M for a given input if we know the output of P for the same input.

Definition 4 *(Due to [6]). Given a program P and a mutant M on space S, and given an oracle $\Omega()$ defined as an equivalence relation on S, we let S_P and S_M be the random variables that represent the final states of P and M for a common input. The non-determinacy of $\Omega()$ is denoted by ND and defined by:*

$$ND = \frac{H(S_P|S_M)}{H(S_P)}.$$

Given that $\Omega()$ defines an equivalence class over S, this metric reflects the amount of uncertainty we have about an element of S if all we know is the equivalence of this element by relation $\Omega()$.

How We Calculate It: The conditional entropy $H(S_P|S_M)$ is really the entropy of the equivalence classes of S modulo the equivalence relation defined by $\Omega()$. It represents the amount of uncertainty we have about an element of S if all we know is its equivalence class; if $\Omega()$ is the identity relation then all equivalence classes are singletons and $ND = 0$; else it is the base 2 logarithm of the size of equivalence classes. As an example, we consider space S defined by three variables, say x, y, z of type integer, and we show in the following table a number of possible oracles with their respective non-determinacies. For all these oracles, $H(S_P) = 3 \times 32 = 96$; the only term that changes is $H(S_P|S_M)$ (Table 2).

Table 2. Non determinacy of sample oracles (due to [6]).

$\Omega()$	$H(S_P|S_M)$	ND
$(x_P = x_M) \wedge (y_P = y_M) \wedge (z_P = z_M)$	0	0
$(x_P = x_M) \wedge (y_P = y_M)$	32	0.33
$(x_P = x_M)$	64	0.66
True	96	1.0

Why We Feel It Is Correlated to the REM of a Program: Of course, the weaker the oracle that tests for equivalence, the more mutants will be found to be equivalent to the base program.

3.5 A Posteriori Justification

In Sect. 2, we had asked two questions: First, what attribute makes a program prone to generate equivalent mutants; second, under what circumstances can a mutant behave in a way that is equivalent to a base program. The metrics we introduced in Sect. 3 answer the first question, since they capture different aspects of redundancy. In Table 3, we discuss why we feel that the selected metrics answer the second question, in the sense that they reflect the likelihood of occurrence of each circumstance that we had identified.

Table 3. Metrics vs circumstances of equivalence (due to [6]).

Metrics	Circumstances of equivalence
SR_I	Mutation not a fault
SR_F	Mutation is a fault Causes no error
FR, NI	Mutation is a fault Causes errors Errors masked
ND	Mutation is a fault Causes errors Errors propagate Failure undetected

4   A Java Compiler

In order to automate the calculation of these redundancy metrics, and ensure that our calculations are applied uniformly, we use compiler generation technology (*ANTLR*, http://www.antlr.org/) to parse Java code and derive these metrics for individual methods in Java classes. For each method, we must estimate the following quantities:

- The entropy of the declared space, $H(S)$.
- The entropy of the initial actual space, $H(\sigma_I)$.
- The entropy of the final actual space, $H(\sigma_F)$.
- The entropy of the input space, $H(X)$.
- The entropy of the output space, $H(Y)$.

The entropies of the declared space, the input space, and output space are fairly straightforward; they consist in identifying the relevant variables and adding their respective entropies, depending on their data type, as per Table 1.

4.1 Entropy of the Initial State

For the entropy of the initial actual space, we are bound to rely on input from the source code, as we have no other means to probe the intent of the programmer (re: how they use declared variables to represent the actual program state). To this effect, we introduce a special purpose assert statement, which the engineer may use to specify the precondition of the method whose REM we want to compute. We propose the following statement

```
preassert(<precondition>)
```

whose semantic definition is exactly the same as a normal assert statement, but this statement is used specifically to analyze the entropy of the initial actual state. When the method has an exception call at the beginning as a guard for the method call, then it is straightforward to have a `preassert()` statement immediately after the exception statement, with the negation of the condition that triggers the exception. The entropy of the initial actual state is computed as:

$$H(\sigma_I) = H(S) - \Delta H,$$

where ΔH is the reduction in entropy represented by the assertion of the `preassert()` statement. This quantity is defined inductively according to the structure of the assertion, as shown summarily below:

- $\Delta H(A \wedge B) = \Delta H(A) + \Delta H(B)$.
- $\Delta H(A \vee B) = max(\Delta H(A), \Delta H(B))$.
- $\Delta H(X == Y)$, where X and Y are expressions of the same type, equals the entropy of the common type. For example, if x and y are integer variables, then $\Delta H(x + 1 == y - 1)$ is 32 bits.
- $\Delta H(X < Y) = \Delta H(X <= Y) = \Delta H(X > Y) = \Delta H(X >= Y) = 1$ bit. So for example $\Delta H(x + 1 > 0) = 1$ bit, since this equality reduces the range of possible values of x by half, whose log_2 is then reduced by 1.

This is not a perfect solution, but it is adequate for our purposes.

4.2 Entropy of the Final State

For the entropy of the final actual space, we have to keep track of dependencies that the program creates between its variables. We do so using a Boolean matrix (called D, for Dependency), which is initialised to the identity (T on the diagonal, F outside, to mean that initially each variable depends only on itself); whenever we encounter an assignment statement, of the form (x=E(y,z,u,w)), we replace the row of x in D with the logical OR of the rows of all the variables that appear in expression E; if no variable appears in expression E (x is assigned a constant value), then the row that corresponds to x is filled with F's. At the end of the program we add (i.e. take the logical OR) of all the rows of the matrix; this yields a vector that indicates which program variables affect the value of the final state of the program. The sum of the entropies of the selected variables is the entropy of the final actual state.

For illustration, we consider a program with, say, four integer variables, and we assume that it has no `preassert()` statement, hence we get:

$H(S) = 128$ bits.

$\Delta H = 0$, hence $H(\sigma_I) = H(S) = 128$ bits.

To compute the entropy of its final actual state, we scan its source code:

```
int x, y, z, w;
x=y+z;
w=2*x+5*z+9;
z=y*5;
```

Figure 1 shows the evolution of the dependency matrix as the execution of this program proceeds. The Boolean vector V is obtained by adding (logically) all the rows of matrix D; it shows that the final state depends on the initial values of only two variables, namely y and z. Hence the entropy of the final actual state in this case is:

$$H(\sigma_F) = 2 \times 32 = 64 \; bits.$$

If the assignment statements are within an if-statement, then we perform the same operation as above, but we consider the variables that appear in the condition of the if-statement as part of the right hand-side of every assignment statement. Figure 2 shows the evolution of the dependency matrix for the following if-statement:

```
int x, y, z, w;
if (x>10)
   {x=y+z;
   w=2*x+5*z+9;
   z=y*5;}
```

According to the final vector V, the entropy of the final actual state is:

$$H(\sigma_F) = 3 \times 32 = 96 \; bits.$$

To analyze an if-then-else statement, we consider the two branches of the statement (then-branch, else-branch), process them the same way as we advocate above for the if-statement (i.e. consider that the variables that appear in the condition are part of the right hand side of every assignment), then we adopt for the matrix of the whole statement the branch matrix that yields the smallest entropy (hence the greatest redundancy). For illustration, we consisder the following program:

```
int x, y, z, w;
if (x>10)
   {x=y+z;
   w=2*x+5*z+9;
   z=y*5;}
else
   {x=x+2;
   y=2*y;
   z=10;
   w=y;}
```

int x, y, z, w;

D	x	y	z	w
x	T	F	F	F
y	F	T	F	F
z	F	F	T	F
w	F	F	F	T

x=y+z;

D	x	y	z	w
x	F	T	T	F
y	F	T	F	F
z	F	F	T	F
w	F	F	F	T

w=2*x+5*z+9;

D	x	y	z	w
x	F	T	T	F
y	F	T	F	F
z	F	F	T	F
w	F	T	T	F

z=5*y;

D	x	y	z	w
x	F	T	T	F
y	F	T	F	F
z	F	T	F	F
w	F	T	T	F

Summary

	x	y	z	w
V	F	T	T	F

Fig. 1. Evolution of the dependency matrix for assignments.

Figure 3 illustrates how we analyze this if-then-else statement; because the then-branch is the same as the previous example, we skip the line-by-line analysis of this branch, and focus on the else-branch instead. Note that for each assignment statement we assume that x appears in the right hand side of the statement, since it directs the int x, y, z, w;

D	x	y	z	w
x	T	F	F	F
y	F	T	F	F
z	F	F	T	F
w	F	F	F	T

if (x>10) {x=y+z;

D	x	y	z	w
x	T	T	T	F
y	F	T	F	F
z	F	F	T	F
w	F	F	F	T

w=2*x+5*z+9;

D	x	y	z	w
x	T	T	T	F
y	F	T	F	F
z	F	F	T	F
w	T	T	T	F

z=5*y;}

D	x	y	z	w
x	T	T	T	F
y	F	T	F	F
z	T	T	T	F
w	F	T	T	F

Summary

	x	y	z	w
V	T	T	T	F

Fig. 2. Evolution of the dependency matrix for conditionals.

execution of the whole branch. Also note that when we execute the statement z=10; the whole row of z becomes F, to which we add the row of x.

The entropy of the final state of the then-branch is 96 bits and the entropy of the else-branch is 64 bits; hence we adopt the matrix of the else-branch as the dependency of the whole statement. Whence we find:

```
int x, y, z, w;
if (x>10) {x=y+z; w=2*x+5*z+9; z=5*y;}
```

D	x	y	z	w
x	T	T	T	F
y	F	T	F	F
z	T	T	T	F
w	F	T	T	F

Summary, then branch

V_0	x	y	z	w
	T	T	T	F

```
else{
```

D	x	y	z	w
x	T	F	F	F
y	F	T	F	F
z	F	F	T	F
w	F	F	F	T

```
x=x+2;
```

D	x	y	z	w
x	T	F	F	F
y	F	T	F	F
z	F	F	T	F
w	F	F	F	T

```
y=2*y;
```

D	x	y	z	w
x	T	F	F	F
y	T	T	F	F
z	F	F	T	F
w	F	F	F	T

```
z=10;
```

D	x	y	z	w
x	T	F	F	F
y	T	T	F	F
z	T	F	F	F
w	F	F	F	T

```
w=y;}
```

D	x	y	z	w
x	T	F	F	F
y	T	T	F	F
z	T	F	F	F
w	T	T	F	F

Summary, else branch

V_1	x	y	z	w
	T	T	F	F

Summary, whole statement

V	x	y	z	w
	T	T	F	F

Fig. 3. Evolution of the dependency matrix for If-Then-Else.

$$H(\sigma_F) = 64\ bits.$$

While statements are treated the same way as if-statements: the variables that appear in the loop condition are treated as though they appear on the right hand side of every assignment statement of the loop body, and the dependency matrix of the whole loop is the matrix we obtain for the loop body under these conditions.

5 Estimating the REM

5.1 A Regression Model

In order to test our assumption that our redundancy metrics are statistically correlated with the *REM* of a program, we have conducted an empirical experiment, whereby we select a set of Java classes from the *Apache Common Mathematics Library* and run our Java compiler to compute the redundancy metrics of each method of each class. On the other hand, we apply a mutant generator to these classes using a uniform set of standard mutation operators, then we execute the base program and the mutants on benchmark test data sets, and record how many mutants are killed by the test. Simultaneously, we keep track of coverage metrics, and exclude from consideration any method whose line coverage falls below 90%. By keeping in our sample only those Java classes for which line coverage is high (in fact the vast majority reach 100% line coverage) we maximize the likelihood that mutants that are found to survive after undergoing the test are equivalent to the base program. Under this assumption, we use the ratio of surviving mutants of each method over the total number of mutants as an approximation of the *REM* of the method. Our data sample includes about two hundred methods, but when we exclude those whose size is below 20 LOC we end up with 66 methods; because we treat individual methods rather than whole classes, this condition excludes many small methods.

We peform a statistical regression using *REM* as the dependent variable and the intrinsic redundancy metrics (i.e. those metrics that pertain to the program, not the equivalence oracle) as the independent variables. We use a logistic model, i.e. a model such that $log(\frac{REM}{1-REM})$ is a linear combination of the independent variables. The metric that pertains to the equivalence oracle (ND) is not part of the regression analysis, but is integrated in the equation in such a way that if $ND = 0$ we obtain the regression formula involving the intrinsic metrics, and if $ND = 1$ (extreme case when the oracle tests trivially for **true** , i.e. all the mutants are found to be equivalent) we want the *REM* to be 1. The resulting formula is:

$$REM = ND + (1 - ND) \times (-3.27 + 1.35 \times SR_F + 1.26 \times FR).$$

With this equation in place, we can now have a tool that automatically computes the redundancy metrics, then derives the *REM* using this formula.

5.2 Mutation Policies

The statistical model we have developed in the previous section was based on a fixed mutant generation policy, which was used throughout the experimentation; hence this model can only be used so long as we are using this mutant generation policy. To make provisions for other mutant generation policies, we envision two possible venues:

- Either we select a number of standard mutant generation policies, which may bear special significance due to their use, or their properties [2, 16, 23]. Then we build a regression model for each selected policy; this may be a viable option, despite its limited scope, if it werent for the fact that we are already considering to derive a range of regression models even for a single policy, to take into account the many dimensions of variability between software products (in terms of language, paradigm, size, application domain, etc).
- Or we derive a regression model for each individual mutation operator, then find a formula that enables us to compute the *REM* that corresponds to a given mutation policy from the *REM*'s that correspond to its members. This matter is discussed in [22], where it is conjectured that when a policy includes N operators, whose *REM*'s are $REM_1, REM_2, \dots REM_N$, then the *REM* of the overall policy can be computed as:

$$REM = 1 - \prod_{i=1}^{N}(1 - REM_i).$$

This conjecture is based on limited empirical observation, and is currently under investigation for possible confirmation.

6 Uses of the REM

Whereas we resolved to analyze the *REM* of a program primarily for the purpose of estimating the number of equivalent mutants that the program is prone to produce, we find that in fact the *REM* can inform us a great deal about many relevant aspects of mutation testing; we review some of these in this section.

6.1 Mutant Equivalence

Given a set of M mutants of a base program P, and given a ratio of equivalent mutants REM, the number of equivalent mutants is estimated to be $M \times REM$. Hence we cannot expect any test data set T to kill more than $N = M \times (1 - REM)$ mutants (modulo the margin of error in the estimation of REM).

6.2 Mutant Redundancy

In [27], Papadakis et al. raise the problem of mutant redundancy as the issue where many mutants may be equivalent among themselves, hence do not provide test coverage commensurate with their number. If we have sixty mutants divided into twelve classes where each class contains five equivalent mutants, then we have only twelve distinct mutants; and if some test data set T kills these sixty mutants, it should really get credit for twelve mutants (twelve casualties, so to speak), not sixty, since whenever it kills a mutant from one equivalence class, it automatically kills all the mutants of the same class. Of course, it is very difficult to determine, in a set of mutants, which mutants are equivalent and which are not; but again, the *REM* enables us to draw some quantitative data about the level of redundancy in a pool of mutants.

The *REM* of the base program is computed using a regression formula whose independent variables are the redundancy metrics extracted from the source code of the program. Since the mutants are generated from the base program by means of elementary syntactic changes, it is reasonable to consider that the mutants have the same redundancy metrics, therefore the same *REM* as the base program. If we interpret the *REM* as the probability that any two mutants are semantically equivalent, then we can estimate the number of equivalence classes by answering the following question: *Given a set of size N, and given that any two elements of this set have a probability* REM *to be in the same equivalence class modulo some relation EQ, what is the expected number of equivalence classes of this set modulo EQ?*

We denote this number by $NEC(N, REM)$, and we write it as follows:

$$NEC(N, REM) = \sum_{k=1}^{N} k \times p(N, REM, k),$$

where $p(N, REM, k)$ is the probability that a set of N elements where each pair has probability *REM* to be equivalent has k equivalence classes. This probability satisfies the following inductive conditions.

– *Basis of Induction.* We have two base conditions:
  - *One Equivalence Class.* $p(N, REM, 1) = REM^{N-1}$. This is the probability that all N elements are equivalent.
  - *As Many Equivalence Classes as Elements, or: All Equivalence Classes are Singletons.* $p(N, REM, N) = (1 - REM)^{\frac{N \times (N-1)}{2}}$. This is the probability that no two elements are equivalent: every two elements are not equivalent; there are $N \times (N - 1)$ pairs of distinct elements, but because equivalence is a symmetric relation, we divide this number by 2 ($M_i \neq M_j$ is the same event as $M_j \neq M_i$).
– *Inductive Step.* When we add one element to a set of $N - 1$ elements, two possibilities may arise: either this adds one to the number of equivalence classes (if the new element is equivalent to no current element of the set); or it maintains the number of equivalence classes (if the new element is equivalent to one of the existing equivalence classes). Since these two events are disjoint, the probability of the disjunction is the sum of the probabilities of each event. Hence:

$$p(N, REM, k) = p(N - 1, REM, k) \times (1 - (1 - REM)^k$$
$$+ p(N - 1, REM, k - 1) \times (1 - REM)^{k-1}.$$

The following recursive program (Due to [6]) computes the number of equivalence classes of a set of size N whose elements have probability REM of being equivalent.

```
#include <iostream>
#include "math.h"

using namespace std;

double p(int N, int k, double R);

int main ()
{
   float R=0.158;   int N=65;
   float mean = 0.0;   float ps=0.0;
   for (int k=1; k<=N; k++)
      {float prob=p(N,k,R); ps = ps+prob;
       mean = mean + k*prob;}
   cout<<"ps:"<<ps<<" mean:"<<mean<<endl;
}
double p(int N, int k, double R)
   {if (k==1) {return pow(R,N-1);}
    else
    if (N==k) {return pow(1-R,(k*(k-1))/2);}
    else {return p(N-1,k,R)*(1-pow(1-R,k))
                 +p(N-1,k-1,R)*pow(1-R,k-1);}}
```

Execution of this program with $N = 65$ and $REM = 0.158$ yields $NEC(N, REM) = 14.64$, i.e. our 65 mutants represent only about 15 different mutants; the remaining 50 are redundant.

6.3   Mutation Score, Revisited

The quantification of redundancy, discussed in the previous section, casts a shadow on the traditional way of measuring the mutation score of a test data set T: usually, if we execute a set of M mutants on some test data set T and we find that X mutants have been killed (i.e. shown to be different from the base program P), we assign to T the *mutation score* X/M. This metrics ignores the possibility that several of M mutants may be equivalent, and several of the X killed mutants may be equivalent. We argue that this metric can be improved and made more meaningful, in three ways:

- Because of the possibility that mutants may be equivalent to the base program P, the baseline ought to be the number of non-equivalent mutants, i.e. $N = (1 - REM) \times M$.
- Because of the possibility that those mutants that are not equivalent to P may be equivalent amongst themselves, we ought to focus not on the number of these mutants, bur rather on the number of equivalence classes modulo semantic equivalence. This is defined in the previous section as $NEC(N, REM)$.
- Because of the possibility that the X mutants killed by test data set T may be equivalent amongst themselves, we ought to give credit to T not for the cardinality of X, but rather for the number of equivalence classes that X may overlap. We refer to this number as $COV(N, K, X)$ (COV stands for: coverage), where

$K = NEC(N, REM)$ is the number of equivalence classes of the set of N mutants modulo equivalence.

To compute $COV(N, K, X)$, we designate by $C_1, C_2, ...C_K$ the K equivalence classes, we designate by f_i, for $(1 \leq i \leq K)$, the binary functions that take value 1 if and only if equivalence class C_i overlaps with (i.e. has a non-empty intersection with) set X, and value 0 otherwise. Then $COV(N, K, X) = E(\sum_{i=1} K f_i)$. If we assume that all classes are the same size and that elements of X are uniformly distributed over the set of mutants, then this can be written as:

$$cov(N, K, X) = K \times p(f_i = 1) = K \times (1 - p(f_i = 0)),$$

for an arbitrary i. For the first class to be considered, $p(f_1 = 0) = \frac{K-1}{K}^X$, since each element of X has a probability $\frac{K-1}{K}$ of not being in class C_1; for each subsequent element, the numerator and denominator each drops by 1. Hence we have the following formula:

$$COV(N, K, X) = K \times (1 - \frac{K-1}{K}^X \times \prod_{i=0}^{X-1} \frac{N - \frac{i}{K-1}}{N - i}).$$

The following program (due to [6]) computes this function, for $N = 65$, $K = 15$ and $X = 50$.

```
#include <iostream>
#include "math.h"
using namespace std;

double cov(int N, int K, int X);

int main ()
{
    int N=65; int K=15; int X=50;
    cout << "cov: " << cov(N,K,X)   << endl;
}

double cov(int N, int K, int X)
    {
      float prod=1;
      for (int i=0; i<K; i++)
        {prod = prod *
              (N-i/(float)(K-1))/(float)(N-i);}
      return K*(1-prod*pow((K-1)/(float)K,X));
    }
```

Execution of this program yields $COV(65, 15, 50) = 12.55$. We propose the following definition.

Definition 5 *Given a base program P and M mutants of P, and given a test data set T that has killed X mutants, the mutation score of T is the ratio of equivalence classes covered by X over the total number of equivalence classes amongst the mutants that are not equivalent to P.*

We denote the mutation score by $EMS(M, X)$. The following proposition gives an explicit formula of the mutation score.

Proposition 1 *Given a program P and M mutants of P, and given a test data set T that has killed X mutants, the mutation score of T is given by the following formula:*

$$EMS(M, X) = \frac{COV(N, NEC(N, REM), X)}{NEC(N, REM)},$$

where REM is the ratio of equivalent mutants of P and $N = M(1 - REM)$ is the number of mutants that are not equivalent to P.

In the example above, for $N = 65$, $REM = 0.158$, and $X = 50$ we find

$$EMS(77, 50) = \frac{12.55}{15} = 0.84.$$

6.4 Empirical Validation

We are currently conducting an empirical validation of these results pertaining to the use of the *REM* to analyze mutation testing. The focus of our validation is function $NEC(N, REM)$, as it plays a major role in our investigations. To this effect, we take a number of programs from standard benchmarks, generate mutants thereof, run tests to estimate their *REM*, use the formula of $NEC(N, REM)$ to estimate the number of equivalence classes among the N mutants that are not equivalent to the base program P. Then we try to compute this number empirically by testing the N mutants for equivalence with each other. Given that we estimate the program's *REM* and we test for the mutants' mutual equivalence by using the limited test data that comes with each software component, we realize that our calculations are prone to be imprecise: We rule that two programs are equivalent if and only if they produce the same output for the (small) test data set.

An alternative approach we are considering is to test the assumption on which the formula of $NEC(N, REM)$ is based, namely the assumption that P has the same *REM* as all the mutants generated from P. There are two ways to conduct this experiment:

- Given a base program P and N mutants M_1, M_2, M_3, ... M_N, we compute the *REM* of P by testing it against each of the N mutants, then we compute the *REM* of mutant M_i by permuting P and M_i, then testing M_i for equivalence to P and the remaining mutants.
- Given a base program P and N mutants M_1, M_2, M_3, ... M_N, we compute the *REM* of P by testing it against each of the N mutants, then we compute the *REM* of mutant M_i by applying the mutant generator to M_i as if it were a base program, then testing it for equivalence against its mutants using available mutation tools (e.g. *PiTest*).

Though the first option gives more meaningful results (as the mutants are unchanged from one *REM* estimate to the next), the second option is easier to automate. Our preliminary experimentation shows that P and the mutants have very similar *REM*'s, which is very encouraging.

7   Conclusion

7.1   Summary

In this paper, we argue that the determination of mutant equivalence and mutant redundancy by inspection and analysis of individual mutants is very expensive and error-prone, at the same time that it is in fact unnecessary, for most purposes. As a substitute, we propose to analyze the amount of redundancy that a program has, in various forms, and we find that this enables us to extract a number of mutation-related metrics at negligible cost. Central to this quantitative analysis is the concept of ratio of equivalent mutants, which measures the probability that any two mutants, or a mutant and the base program, are semantically equivalent. We discuss the generation of the *REM* of a program, by means of a Java (pseudo-) compiler that estimates the program's redundancy metrics, then derives an estimate of the *REM* using a regression model.

7.2   Assessment and Threats to Validity

Our study highlights something of a paradox: On one hand, we find that our analysis of the mutation attributes of a program depends critically on the precision with which we estimate the *REM*; on the other hand, we find it difficult to estimate the *REM* with great precision.

- The value of $NEC(N, REM)$ is much more sensitive to REM than it is to N; for larger values of REM, $NEC(N, REM)$ takes small values even for very large values of N. For example, for $REM = 0.15$ and $N = 3000$ we find $NEC = 38$; in other words, for an *REM* of 0.15 (not an uncommon value), we kill as many as 3000 mutants, only to find that we have actually killed a mere 38 distinct mutants. Hence any error that arises in the estimation of REM is likely to greatly affect the precision of $NEC(N, REM)$; this, in turn, affects the precision of $COV(N, K, X)$, and that of $EMS(M, X)$. This puts a heavy onus on us to double check the way the redundancy metrics are computed.
- The machinery we have put in place to compute the redundancy metrics is optimized for programs that handle static state spaces, which proceed by successive updates of program variables, thereby increasing program redundancy (by creating more and more relationships between program variables). But much of today's source code does not fit this simple pattern: it involves dynamic allocation and deallocation of memory, inter-object communication, data whose entropy is undefined or difficult to quantify, etc.

7.3   Prospects

Our plan for future research is a direct consequence of the assessment given in the previous subsection: We envision to review the definition and the calculation of redundancy metrics; then we envision to revisit the statistical models that we use to derive the *REM* from the redundancy metrics.

Also, we envision to proceed with an empirical validation of the functions introduced in this study, using thorough test data sets; finally, we envision to resolve the questions raised in Sect. 5.2 about how to integrate the mutant generation policy into our analysis.

Acknowledgements. This work is partially supported by a grant from NSF, number DGE1565478.

References

1. Adamopoulos, K., Harman, M., Hierons, R.M.: How to overcome the equivalent mutant problem and achieve tailored selective mutation using co-evolution. In: Deb, K. (ed.) GECCO 2004. LNCS, vol. 3103, pp. 1338–1349. Springer, Heidelberg (2004). https://doi.org/10.1007/978-3-540-24855-2_155
2. Andrews, J., Briand, L., Labiche, Y.: Is mutation an appropriate tool for testing experiments? In: Proceedings, ICSE (2005)
3. Androutsopoulos, K., Clark, D., Dan, H., Hierons, R.M., Harman, M.: An analysis of the relationship between conditional entropy and failed error propagation in software testing. In: Proceedings, ICSE 2014 (2014)
4. Avizienis, A., Laprie, J.C., Randell, B., Landwehr, C.E.: Basic concepts and taxonomy of dependable and secure computing. IEEE Trans. Dependable Secure Comput. **1**(1), 11–33 (2004)
5. Ayad, A., Marsit, I., Loh, J., Omri, M.N., Mili, A.: Quanatitative metrics for mutation testing. In: Proceedings, ICSOFT 2019, Prague, Czech Republic, July 2019
6. Ayad, A., Marsit, I., Mohamed Omri, N., Loh, J.M., Mili, A.: Using semantic metrics to predict mutation equivalence. In: van Sinderen, M., Maciaszek, L.A. (eds.) ICSOFT 2018. CCIS, vol. 1077, pp. 3–27. Springer, Cham (2019). https://doi.org/10.1007/978-3-030-29157-0_1
7. Budd, T.A., Angluin, D.: Two notions of correctness and their relation to testing. Acta Informatica **18**(1), 31–45 (1982)
8. Carvalho, L., Guimares, M., Fernandes, L., Hajjaji, M.A., Gheyi, R., Thuem, T.: Equivalent mutants in configurable systems: an empirical study. In: Proceedings, VAMOS 2018, Madrid, Spain (2018)
9. Csiszar, I., Koerner, J.: Information Theory: Coding Theorems for Discrete Memoryless Systems. Cambridge University Press, Cambridge (2011)
10. Delamaro, M.E., Maldonado, J.C., Vincenzi, A.M.R.: Proteum /im 2.0: an integrated mutation testing environment. In: Wong, W.E. (ed.) Mutation Testing for the New Century, vol. 24, pp. 91–101. Springer, Boston (2001). https://doi.org/10.1007/978-1-4757-5939-6_17
11. Gruen, B., Schuler, D., Zeller, A.: The impact of equivalent mutants. In: Proceedings, MUTATION 2009, Denver, CO, USA (2009)
12. Hierons, R., Harman, M., Danicic, S.: Using program slicing to assist in the detection of equivalent mutants. J. Softw. Test. Verif. Reliab. **9**(4), 233–262 (1999)
13. Inozemtseva, L., Holmes, R.: Coverage is not strongly correlated with test suite effectiveness. In: Procedings, 36th International Conference on Software Engineering. ACM Press (2014)
14. Just, R., Ernst, M., Fraser, G.: Using state infection conditions to detect equivalent mutants and speed up mutation analysis. In: Dagstuhl Seminar 13021: Symbolic Methods in Testing, Wadern, Germany (2013)
15. Just, R., Ernst, M., Fraser, G.: Efficient mutation analysis by propagating and partitioning infected execution states. In: Proceedings, ISSTA 2014, San Jose, CA, USA (2014)
16. Just, R., Jalali, D., Inozemtseva, L., Ernst, M., Holmes, R., Fraser, G.: Are mutants a valid substitute for real faults in software testing? In: Proceedings, FSE (2014)

17. Just, R., Ernst, M.D., Fraser, G.: Using state infection conditions to detect equivalent mutants and sped up mutation analysis. In: Proceedings, Dagstuhl Seminar 13021: Symbolic Methods in Testing (2013)
18. Kintis, M., Papadakis, M., Jia, Y., Malveris, N., Le Traon, Y., Harman, M.: Detecting trivial mutant equivalences via compiler optimizations. IEEE Trans. Softw. Eng. **44**(4), 308–333 (2018)
19. Laprie, J.C.: Dependability: Basic Concepts and Terminology: In English, French, German, Italian and Japanese. Springer, Heidelberg (1991). https://doi.org/10.1007/978-3-7091-9170-5
20. Laprie, J.C.: Dependability - its attributes, impairments and means. In: Randell, B., Laprie, J.C., Kopetz, H., Littlewood, B. (eds.) Predictably Dependable Computing Systems, pp. 1–19. Springer, Heidelberg (1995). https://doi.org/10.1007/978-3-642-79789-7_1
21. Laprie, J.C.: Dependable computing: concepts, challenges, directions. In: Proceedings, COMPSAC (2004)
22. Marsit, I., Omri, M.N., Loh, J.M., Mili, A.: Impact of mutation operators on mutant equivalence. In: Proceedings, ICSOFT 2018, pp. 55–66 (2018)
23. Namin, A.S., Kakarla, S.: The use of mutation in testing experiments and its sensitivity to external threats. In: Proceedings, ISSTA (2011)
24. Nica, S., Wotawa, F.: Using constraints for equivalent mutant detection. In: Andres, C., Llana, L. (eds.) Second Workshop on Formal methods in the Development of Software, pp. 1–8. EPTCS (2012). https://doi.org/10.420/EPTCS.86.1
25. Offut, A.J., Pan, J.: Automatically detecting equivalent mutants and infeasible paths. Softw. Test. Verif. Reliab. **7**(3), 165–192 (1997)
26. Papadakis, M., Delamaro, M., LeTraon, Y.: Mitigating the effects of equivalent mutants with mutant clasification strategies. Sci. Comput. Program. **95**(P3), 298–319 (2014)
27. Papadakis, M., Kintis, M., Zhang, J., Jia, Y., Traon, Y.L., Harman, M.: Mutation testing advances: an analysis and survey. In: Advances in Computers (2019)
28. Schuler, D., Zeller, A.: Covering and uncovering equivalent mutants. In: Proceedings, International Conference on Software Testing, Verification and Validation, pp. 45–54 (2010). https://doi.org/10.1109/ICST.2010.30
29. Shannon, C.: A mathematical theory of communication. Bell Syst. Tech. J. **27**(379–423), 623–656 (1948)
30. Wang, B., Xiong, Y., Shi, Y., Zhang, L., Hao, D.: Faster mutation analysis via equivalence modulo states. In: Proceedings, ISSTA 2017, Santa Barbara, CA, USA (2017)
31. Yao, X., Harman, M., Jia, Y.: A study of equivalent and stubborn mutation operators using human analysis of equivalence. In: Proceedings, ICSE (2014)

Distributed Frames: Pattern-Based Characterization of Functional Requirements for Distributed Systems

Roman Wirtz[✉], Maritta Heisel, and Marvin Wagner

University of Duisburg-Essen, Duisburg, Germany
roman.wirtz@uni-due.de

Abstract. In the connected world, the complexity of software-based systems increases. Many of those systems consist of different subsystems which are connected with each other via a network. The decomposition into those subsystems requires a detailed analysis and documentation of their functional requirements. Documenting and managing such requirements in a consistent manner is a challenge for software engineers. The requirements for each subsystem cannot be considered in isolation, but it is necessary to state the relations between the functional requirements, too. In previous work, we proposed a method that allows systematically identifying and documenting functional requirements for distributed systems. The method is model-based and makes use of Jackson's problem frames approach which defines patterns for reoccurring software development problems. We now extend his approach with patterns for problems specifically for distributed systems which we call Distributed Frames. Using a pattern description template, we provide different examples of such frames. To exemplify the application of those patterns, we show how they can be embedded into our requirements elicitation method.

Keywords: Requirements engineering · Distributed systems ·
Model-based · Functinonal requirements · Requirements analysis

1 Introduction

In the connected world, software-based systems are often realized as distributed systems. Tanenbaum defines a distributed system as a system whose components are located on different connected computers [15]. Those components communicate via messages to achieve a common goal.

The complexity of distributed systems confronts software engineers with new problems during the entire software development process. Especially in one of the earliest phases of software development, namely requirements engineering, it is a challenge for engineers to capture all aspects of a distributed system under development. Although the different components may be deployed independently of each other in different environments, the functionalities of the components highly depend on each other. Thus, it does not suffice to elicit and document

© Springer Nature Switzerland AG 2020
M. van Sinderen and L. A. Maciaszek (Eds.): ICSOFT 2019, CCIS 1250, pp. 81–107, 2020.
https://doi.org/10.1007/978-3-030-52991-8_5

requirements for each component independently. In addition, the connection between the components is often remote and, hence, is not reliable.

For further analysis, e.g. with regard to privacy or security, it is of essential importance to document the dependencies and interfaces between the subsystems in a consistent and systematic manner. For example, an attacker may inject malicious code on the client-side which will then affect stored data on the server-side.

Our aim is to assist software engineers in performing a detailed and systematic elicitation and documentation of functional requirements for distributed systems.

In previous work [18], we proposed a model-based method called *RE4DIST* (**R**equirements **E**ngineering for **DIST**ributed Systems). The method is based on Jackson's problem frames notation which we extended to model functional requirements for distributed systems. The extension allows making the connection between the subsystems and the relations between the corresponding requirements explicit. The method starts with the decomposition based on the system's context, and it ends up with a model of functional requirements to be fulfilled by the subsystem.

In the present paper, we follow Jackson's pattern-based approach and introduce so-called *Distributed Frames*. Each distributed frame is a pattern that describes a common problem class for a distributed system, i.e, specific types of its functional requirements. An instance of a frame describes a concrete instance of a functional requirement for a distributed system. The pattern-based approach allows making knowledge about requirements reusable. Furthermore, by instantiating the pattern, software engineers can document the elicited requirements in a consistent manner. To specify a distributed frame, we propose a template-based format. It describes the frame itself, textual patterns for the functional requirement, and typical examples for the frame's application context.

To exemplify the application of distributed frames, we extend our *RE4DIST* method with regard to the frames. The extension allows the elicitation and documentation of functional requirements by instantiating an appropriate frame.

The remainder of the paper is structured in the following way: In Sect. 2, we introduce a notation for Michael Jackson's problem frames and five basic frames. In Sect. 3, we present the underlying requirements model in form of an Ecore metamodel [14]. Section 4 contains the template for specifying distributed frames and some examples. We describe the extension of our method in Sect. 5, and using a small case study, we exemplify the application of the method in Sect. 6. We discuss related work in Sect. 7 and conclude the paper in Sect. 8 with a brief summary and an outlook on future research directions.

2   Problem Frames

We first introduce the notation for problem frames and problem diagrams, followed by the introduction of some basic frames.

2.1 Notation

To model functional requirements, we make use of the problem frames approach as introduced by Michael Jackson [10]. We consider two types of diagrams, context diagrams and problem diagrams, which both consist of domains, phenomena, and interfaces.

Machine domains (◻) represent the piece of software to be developed.

Problem domains represent entities of the real world. There are different types of these domains: biddable domains with an unpredictable behavior, e.g. persons (☺), causal domains(✿) with a predictable behavior, e.g. technical equipment, and lexical domains (▣) for data representation. A domain can take the role of a connection domain (�) which serves as a connection between two other domains.

Interfaces between domains consist of phenomena. There are (i) symbolic phenomena, representing some kind of information or a state, (ii) causal phenomena, representing commands, actions and the like, and (iii) events. Each phenomenon is controlled by exactly one domain and can be observed by other domains. A phenomenon controlled by one domain and observed by another is called a shared phenomenon between these two domains. Interfaces (solid lines) contain sets of shared phenomena. Such a set contains phenomena controlled by one domain, indicated by $D!\{...\}$, where D stands for an abbreviation of the controlling domain.

A context diagram describes where the problem, i.e. software to be developed, is located and which domains it concerns. It does not contain any requirements. We show an example of such a diagram in Fig. 1a. It contains four domains and the corresponding interfaces. There are *Software* ◻, *Equipment* ✿, *Information* ▣, and *Person* ☺.

A problem diagram is a projection of the context. It contains a functional requirement (represented by the symbol ▨) describing a specific functionality to be developed. A requirement is an optative statement that describes how the environment should behave when the software is installed.

Some phenomena are *referred to* by a requirement (dashed line to the controlling domain), and at least one phenomenon is *constrained* by a requirement (dashed line with arrowhead and italics). The domains and their phenomena that are *referred to* by a requirement are not influenced by the machine, whereas we build the machine to influence the *constrained* domain's phenomena in such a way that the requirement is fulfilled.

In Fig. 1b, we show a small example describing a functional requirement for updating some information which is a projection of the context given in Fig. 1a. A *Person* ☺ provides information to *Software* ◻ to be updated. We make use of a lexical domain *Information* ▣ to represent a database. The functional requirement *Update* ▨ refers to the phenomenon *updateInformation* and constrains the phenomenon *information*.

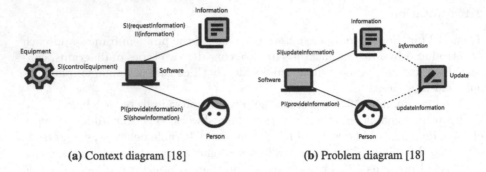

(a) Context diagram [18]   **(b)** Problem diagram [18]

Fig. 1. Examples.

Table 1. Basic problem frames.

Name	Domain types referred to	Domain types constrained
Required behavior	–	C ⚙
Commanded Behavior	B ⊙	C ⚙
Information display	C ⚙	C ⚙
Simple workpiece	B ⊙	L ▣
Transformation	L ▣	L ▣

*Legend: **C** - causal, **L** - lexical, **B** - biddable*

The icons we use in our diagrams differ from Jackson's notation. We adopted icons from Google's Material Design[1] to provide intuitive views for the diagrams [18].

2.2   Problem Frames

Jackson distinguishes between five problem frames which we will consider in the following sections for further analysis concerning distributed systems. In Table 1, we provide an overview for these frames.

Required Behavior. Some parts of the physical environment shall be controlled. The task is to build a machine that imposes that control.

Commanded Behavior. An operator can issue commands to control some part of the physical environment. The machine to be built shall receive the commands and shall impose the control accordingly.

Information Display. The machine shall obtain some information from the environment continuously and present it at the required place and in the required form.

Simple Workpieces. The task is to build a machine that allows users to process some information, e.g. to edit, delete, or copy it.

---

[1] Google Material - https://material.io (last access: March 15, 2019).

Transformation. The machine to be built shall take some machine-readable information as input and transform it into the required output.

In Sect. 4, we provide these frames for distributed systems.

3   Meta Model

To model functional requirements, we make use of Jackson's problem frames approach (cf. Sect. 2) for which we introduce a metamodel in the following. We extend that model with additional elements to capture specific aspects of distributed systems. For instantiating and maintaining the model, we developed a graphical editor. We decided to build that tool based on the *Eclipse Modeling Framework (EMF)* [14]. EMF is open source and offers a wide range of products for model-based development. For example, we use Eclipse Sirius[2] to provide a graphical editor for the application of our method.

3.1   Model Elements

Domains. A domain can be a connection domain, which is indicated by an appropriate attribute. We distinguish between *Machine* and *Problem Domains* as proposed by Jackson. Besides, we introduce the domain type *Distributed System*. A problem domain can be a *Causal Domain*, *Biddable Domain* or *Lexical Domain*. For expressing the relation between different machines, we introduce the domain type *Remote Machine*. The domain acts as a placeholder for a subsystem and therefore references exactly one machine domain. We show the relevant part of the model in Fig. 2.

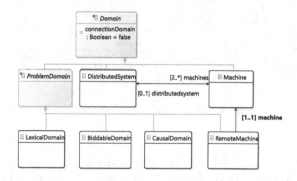

Fig. 2. Metamodel - domains.

Interfaces. In Fig. 3, we show the part of the model to describe interfaces. A *Domain Interface* connects at least two domains and contains a set of *Phenomena*. A phenomenon is controlled by exactly one domain. To describe the realization of interfaces in more detail, we adapt the so-called attack vector from the

---

[2] Eclipse Sirius - https://www.eclipse.org/sirius/ (last access: November 12, 2019).

Common Vulnerability Scoring System (CVSS) [6]. An attack vector predefines values to describe how an attacker accesses a vulnerable component. We introduce an *AccessVector* to describe how domains interact with each other. The vector distinguishes the following four values: *Network* describes remote connections through different networks, e.g. connections via the internet, *adjacent* stands for local network connections, *local* means access to domains not connected to the internet, e.g. some user interfaces, and *physical* describes physical connection to domains, e.g. sensors.

Fig. 3. Metamodel - interfaces.

Requirements. Figure 4 shows the part of the model to describe requirements. A *Requirement* is a special kind of *Statement*. It can be distributed, which means that it concerns more than one machine. Each statement has at least one *StatementReference* for at least one *Phenomenon*. A reference can either be a *ConstrainsReference* or a *RefersToReference*. For each requirement, we also make the machines explicit that are related to the specific requirement.

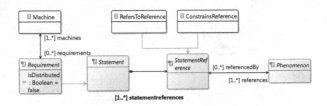

Fig. 4. Metamodel - requirements.

Diagrams. Within the model, it is possible to define different views on specific elements using diagrams (see Fig. 2). As mentioned in Sect. 2, Jackson distinguishes between context diagrams and problem diagrams. We introduce two new types of context diagrams. A *GlobalContextDiagram* describes the overall context of the distributed system. A *SubContextDiagram* is derived from it and describes the context for a specific subsystem (Fig. 5).

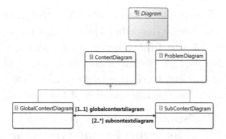

Fig. 5. Metamodel - diagrams.

4 Distributed Frames

In Sect. 2, we introduced five basic problem frames. In the context of our previous work, we now propose distributed frames which are a special kind of problem frames applicable for distributed systems. In contrast to a problem frame, a distributed frame does not only consider a single system but different subsystems. Each frame describes a pattern that allows the characterization of reoccurring problems in the context of functional requirements for distributed systems. We first introduce a description format for distributed frames followed by several examples of frames.

4.1 Description Format

We provide a template to specify distributed frames in a consistent way, for which we give an overview in Table 2. The template consists of some basic information and a frame description.

Table 2. Frame description format.

Basic Information	
Name	Short and descriptive name for the frame.
Description	Short informal description about the frame and the context for which it is applicable.
Known uses	List of typical examples where the pattern can be applied.
Frame Description	
Sender	
Frame Diagram	Diagram which contains the relevant domains and interfaces on the sender side.
Textual pattern	Textual pattern for the relevant part of the functional requirement on the sender side.
Receiver	
Frame Diagram	Diagram which contains the relevant domains and interfaces on the sender side.
Textual pattern	Textual pattern for the relevant part of the functional requirement on the receiver side.

Basic Information. We provide a short informal description that summarizes the distributed frame and briefly describes the context for which it is applicable. The textual description of the functional requirement to be satisfied by the distributed system is also part of that informal description. The requirement will later be decomposed for the involved subsystems. Last, we list typical examples of scenarios as known uses for the application of the frame.

Frame Desciption. We distinguish between the sender side and the receiver side. Since our approach is applicable for any type of distributed system, we do not use the notion of client/server side here. For each side, we provide a frame diagram using the notation as described in Sect. 2.1. A frame diagram contains the domain types, connecting interfaces, and requirement references for the frame. By instantiating the frame diagram in the concrete context, one can create a problem diagram. Besides the frame diagram, we propose a textual pattern that describes the functional requirement in natural language. ⟨...⟩ indicates a variable in the textual pattern that needs to be filled.

4.2   Frame Specifications

In the following, we give specifications for distributed frames. Table 3 provides an overview. It contains the name of the distributed frame (DF) and the constrained and referred to domain types on the sender and receiver side.

4.3   Basic Frames

In Sect. 2.2, we described five basic frames that have been defined by Jackson [10]. We specify those frames for distributed systems using our previously defined format.

Table 3. Distributed frames overview.

Name	Sender		Receiver	
	Domain types referred to	Domain types constrained	Domain types referred to	Domain types constrained
Basic Frames				
Required behavior (DF)	–	*RM* ⌨	*RM* ⌨	*C* ⚙
Commanded Behavior (DF)	*B* ☻	*RM* ⌨	*RM* ⌨	*C* ⚙
Information display (DF)	*C* ⚙	*RM* ⌨	*RM* ⌨	*C* ⚙
Simple workpiece (DF)	*B* ☻	*RM* ⌨	*RM* ⌨	*L* 🖹
Transformation (DF)	*L* 🖹	*RM* ⌨	*RM* ⌨	*L* 🖹
Additional Frames				
Query (DF)	*B* ☻	*RM* ⌨, *CON* ▣	*RM* ⌨, *L* 🖹	*RM* ⌨
Update (DF)	*B* ☻	*RM* ⌨, *CON* ▣	*RM* ⌨	*RM* ⌨, *L* 🖹

*Legend: **C** - causal, **L** - lexical, **B** - biddable, **RM** - remote machine*

Table 4. Frame description for *Required Behavior (DF)*.

Sender	Receiver
A control command ⟨C1⟩ can be sent to ⟨Submachine 2⟩.	The ⟨Controlled Domain⟩ is controlled with ⟨C2⟩ according to the command ⟨C1⟩ issued by ⟨Submachine 1⟩.

Required Behavior (DF)

Description. A subsystem can control domains of its physical environment. Another subsystem can issue commands to control those domains. The task is to build a distributed system in which the machine of one subsystem can control domains in the physical environment of another subsystem remotely.

Known Uses

- Smart home services are often deployed as a cloud application. Previously defined commands are sent from the cloud service to the customer's home to control the equipment.
- Traffic light controllers can be connected to send control commands, e.g. to prioritize a tram.

Frame Description. In Table 4, we show the frame description for the frame *Required Behavior (DF)*. There is a frame diagram for each sender and receiver side. The corresponding textual patterns are given below. In the frame diagrams we use abbreviations for the phenomena annotated at the interfaces. Y stands for symbolic phenomena, C for causal phenomena, and E stands for events (cf. Sect. 2).

Commanded Behavior (DF)

Description. A subsystem can control domains of its physical environment. Operators can issue commands via another subsystem to control those domains. The task is to build a distributed system in which an operator can control domains in the physical environment of another subsystem remotely.

Known Uses

- Smartphone applications can be used to control equipment, such as TVs or smart home equipment.

- Sound and light equipment for concerts can be configured remotely.
- Vehicles can be maintained remotely by the manufacturer.

Frame Desciption. In Table 5, we show the frame description for the frame *Commanded Behavior (DF)*.

Table 5. Frame description for *Commanded Behavior (DF)*.

Sender	Receiver
The ⟨Operator⟩ can cause the event ⟨E1⟩ to trigger ⟨C2⟩ of ⟨Submachine 2⟩.	The ⟨Controlled Domain⟩ is controlled with ⟨C2⟩ according to the command ⟨C1⟩ issued by ⟨Submachine 1⟩.

Information Display (DF)

Description. One subsystem continuously receives information from the physical environment. Another subsystem has some display in its environment. The task is to exchange the received information between the subsystems and to display them.

Known Uses

- A vehicle sends sensor data to the driver's smartphone where the data is displayed.
- Traffic monitors at train stations show the estimated arrival time of a train.

Frame Description. In Table 6, we show the frame description for the frame *Information Display (DF)*.

Table 6. Frame description for *Information Display (DF)*.

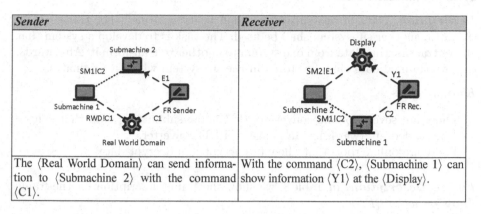

Sender	Receiver
The ⟨Real World Domain⟩ can send information to ⟨Submachine 2⟩ with the command ⟨C1⟩.	With the command ⟨C2⟩, ⟨Submachine 1⟩ can show information ⟨Y1⟩ at the ⟨Display⟩.

Simple Workpieces (DF)

Description. A user can use a subsystem to manipulate some data which is remotely accessible at another subsystem. The task is to transmit the commands to the subsystem where the data is available and to manipulate the data accordingly.

Known Uses

- Some technical equipment allows editing the configuration remotely.
- Using a web service, a user can edit his/her data.
- Collaboration tools allow data manipulation in the cloud.

Frame Description. In Table 7, we show the frame description for the frame *Simple Workpieces (DF)*.

Table 7. Frame description for *Simple Workpieces (DF)*.

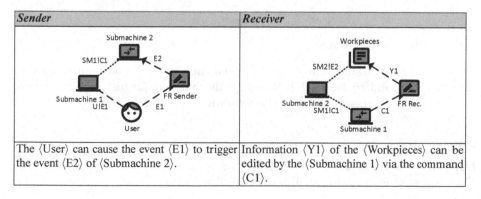

Sender	Receiver
The ⟨User⟩ can cause the event ⟨E1⟩ to trigger the event ⟨E2⟩ of ⟨Submachine 2⟩.	Information ⟨Y1⟩ of the ⟨Workpieces⟩ can be edited by the ⟨Submachine 1⟩ via the command ⟨C1⟩.

Transformation (DF)

Description. Data of one subsystem shall be transformed. For transforming the data, another subsystem shall be used. The task is to develop a system that allows transmitting data from one system to another to transform it. Afterwards, the transformed data shall be stored in the subsystem where it originates.

Known Uses

- There are several online converters that allow submitting data that can be downloaded afterward, i.e. an image to PDF converter.
- There are online tools that allow to encrypt and decrypt data.

Frame Description. In Table 8, we show the frame description for the frame *Transformation (DF)*.

Table 8. Frame description for *Transformation (DF)*.

Sender	Receiver
Some information ⟨Y1⟩ can be transmitted to ⟨Submachine 2⟩ while triggering the command ⟨C3⟩. The transformed information is stored at ⟨Outputs⟩ (⟨Y2⟩).	⟨Submachine 1⟩ can transform some information with the command ⟨C1⟩ which is returned afterwards.

4.4   Additional Frames

Besides the basic frames, we show the specifications of two additional frames, namely *Query* and *Update* [3,16]. We adapt those frames for distributed systems and provide their specifications in the following.

Query (DF)

Description. Users want to request data from a remotely accessible resource. The requested information shall be displayed to them.

Known Uses

- Requesting a website.
- Smartphone applications that retrieve information from an external resource.
- Reading data from network-attached storages (NAS).

Frame Description. In Table 9, we show the frame description for the frame *Query (DF)*.

Table 9. Frame description for *Query (DF)*.

Sender	Receiver
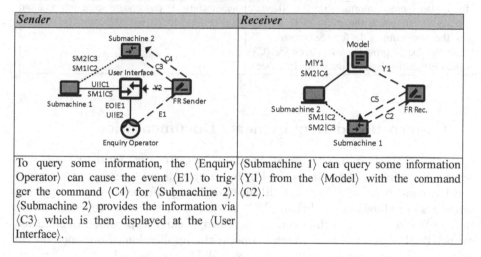	
To query some information, the ⟨Enquiry Operator⟩ can cause the event ⟨E1⟩ to trigger the command ⟨C4⟩ for ⟨Submachine 2⟩. ⟨Submachine 2⟩ provides the information via ⟨C3⟩ which is then displayed at the ⟨User Interface⟩.	⟨Submachine 1⟩ can query some information ⟨Y1⟩ from the ⟨Model⟩ with the command ⟨C2⟩.

Update (DF)

Description. Users want to manipulate data that is available at a remotely accessible resource. In contrast to the frame *Simple Workpiece (DF)*, there is feedback for the users.

Known Uses

- Websites where users can enter or edit some information to be stored.
- Uploading data to a NAS with a progress bar as feedback.

Frame Description. In Table 10, we show the frame description for the frame *Update (DF)*.

In the next section, we extend the *RE4DIST* method with our proposed frames.

Table 10. Frame description for *Update (DF)*.

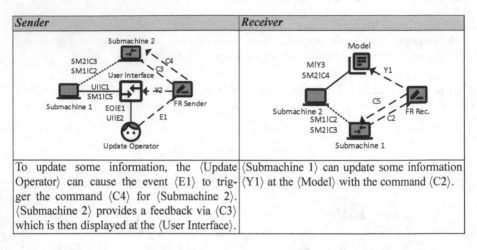

Sender	Receiver
To update some information, the ⟨Update Operator⟩ can cause the event ⟨E1⟩ to trigger the command ⟨C4⟩ for ⟨Submachine 2⟩. ⟨Submachine 2⟩ provides a feedback via ⟨C3⟩ which is then displayed at the ⟨User Interface⟩.	⟨Submachine 1⟩ can update some information ⟨Y1⟩ at the ⟨Model⟩ with the command ⟨C2⟩.

5   Pattern-Based Requirements Documentation

Our method to elicit and document functional requirements for distributed systems (DS) consists of six steps. In Fig. 6, we provide an overview of the steps and the corresponding input and output of each step. For each step, we present examples of validation conditions (VC) to ensure that errors occurring during the application of our method can be identified as early as possible. In addition, we briefly describe the tool which supports the application of our method. In Sect. 6, we provide a case study which exemplifies our method.

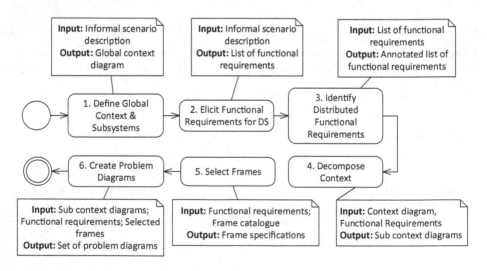

Fig. 6. Method overview.

5.1   Step 1: Define Global Context and Subsystems

The goal of the first step is to get an understanding of the global context in which the distributed system will operate. We consider an informal scenario description as the initial input. Based on this input, we identify problem domains in the context of the distributed system.

We document the results in a context diagram as described in Sect. 2. There is exactly one distributed system domain (represented by the symbol ⧉) in the context diagram which covers all subsystems that shall be developed. Since existing systems do not need to be developed, we describe them by means of causal domains. Using interfaces, we describe the communication between the distributed system and the environmental domains.

For the distributed system, we identify those subsystems that shall be developed. There are at least two subsystems. The subsystems do not necessarily differ from each other. For example, in a peer-to-peer system, the subsystems realized as peers can have the same functional requirements. We represent the subsystems as machine domains with aggregations to the distributed system in the context diagram.

Validation Conditions. Based on the description of the step, we define four validation conditions (VC).

VC1. There is exactly one distributed system in the global context diagram.
VC2. A distributed system consists of at least two subsystems.
VC3. All subsystems have been identified and have been documented in the context diagram.
VC4. All problem domains of the context have been identified, e.g. stakeholders and technical equipment.

Tool Support. As mentioned in Sect. 3, we make use of an Ecore model for our tool. To define the initial context and subsystems, we provide a graphical editor based on *Eclipse Sirius*[3]. The editor assists software engineers in creating the initial context diagram and ensures the semantic rules provided by the model.

Our tool supports the automatic validation of *VC1* and *VC2*. The other two conditions have to be validated manually, but we ask the user of the tool to confirm the validation before proceeding to the next step.

5.2   Step 2: Elicit Functional Requirements for DS

Based on the informal scenario description and the global context diagram, we identify the functional requirements that the distributed system shall satisfy. For each functional requirement, we define a unique name and a proper description of the expected functionality, and we document both textually.

---

[3] Eclipse Sirius - https://www.eclipse.org/sirius/ (last access: March 12, 2019).

Validation Conditions. For the second step of our method, we define two validation conditions.

VC5. Each functional requirement has a unique name and a valid description.
VC6. Each functional requirement has been identified and has been documented.

Tool Support. Our tool provides a table to list all functional requirements one by one. To this table, one can add new requirements using a wizard, and all requirements will be stored in the model to be reusable in further steps.

The first validation condition can partially be checked via the model, whereas the second one has to be confirmed by the user of our tool before proceeding to the next step.

5.3   Step 3: Identify Distributed Functional Requirements

Due to different environments in which the subsystems may be realized, e.g. a mobile application in contrast to a server application, different teams will be involved in developing a distributed system. A requirement can be distributed, i.e. it requires the interaction between different subsystems to be satisfied.

In the present step, we mark distributed requirements to assign them to the responsible development team. In addition, we document dependencies of subsystems for satisfying requirements. For each requirement, we decide about its type and assign a set of responsible subsystems. A requirement that concerns at least two subsystems has to be considered as distributed, and in a distributed system there is at least one requirement concerning several subsystems.

Validation Conditions. We define two validation conditions for the third step of our method.

VC7. Only requirements concerning at least two subsystems have been classified as distributed.
VC8. At least one requirement has been defined as distributed.

Tool Support. To specify the type of requirement, our tool presents the list of requirements to the user where he/she can select the type. For distributed requirements, we provide a dialog to select the related subsystems. Using references to the corresponding machine domains, our tool documents the results in the model and updates the list of requirements.

Both stated validation conditions can be validated automatically using our tool.

5.4   Step 4: Decompose Context

In the first step of our method, we described the global context of the distributed system. As mentioned earlier, different teams will be involved in developing a distributed system. In the present step, we break down the global context in smaller units, one for each subsystem. Again, we make use of context diagrams which we call *Sub-Context Diagram* to document the results, one for each subsystem.

Such a sub-context diagram consists of the machine domain for the subsystem and the relevant problem domains. To express the relation between the subsystems, we introduce new elements to the context diagram, namely remote machines (represented by the symbol ⊡) and remote interfaces (dotted line). For each related subsystem with which communication exists, we add a remote machine domain and the corresponding remote interface.

The interfaces between machine and problem domains are taken from the global context definition, but the remote interfaces describing the communication between subsystems do not exist there and hence, need to be added.

The set of sub-context diagrams helps developers in focusing on the context of a concrete subsystem. However, we still document the relation to other subsystems.

Validation Conditions. To validate the application of the fourth step, we define the following five conditions:

VC9. There is one context diagram for each subsystem.

VC10. Each domain of the initial context diagram is contained in at least one context diagram of a subsystem.

VC11. Interfaces between machine and remote machine have been marked as *remote*.

VC12. Each context diagram contains all related subsystems represented by means of remote machine domains.

VC13. Only problem domains directly connected to the subsystem or via a connection domain are part of the context diagram.

Tool Support. Our tool automatically creates a sub-context diagram for each subsystem. It automatically adds related machines based on the requirement classifications taken from step three and the remote interfaces in-between. We also provide a wizard to select relevant problem domains, phenomena, and interfaces from the initial context. A graphical editor allows adjusting the generated diagrams. To ensure consistency between all steps, we make use of model references to the results of the previous steps.

Except for the last one, our tool allows to automatically evaluate the validation conditions. For the last step, it asks the user to confirm the manual validation.

5.5   Step 5: Select Frames

In the fifth step, we select suitable frames to describe the functional requirements. There are two types of frames: (i) problem frames (cf. Sect. 2.2 and [4]) and (ii) distributed frames (see Sect. 4). For non-distributed requirements, we consider problem frames and for distributed requirements, we consider distributed frames. Since the requirements have been documented in natural language, the selection requires manual effort. The specifications we provide for distributed frames help engineers in selecting appropriate frames, e.g. by considering the described context. A functional requirement is not necessarily restricted to a single frame. In some cases, it could be necessary to combine frames.

In case no suitable frame or combination exists, a new frame has potentially been identified. That frame has to be documented in the frame catalog using our template. This way, knowledge can be captured for further development projects.

Validation Conditions. There are three validation conditions for the fifth step:

VC14. For each distributed requirement, at least one distributed frame has been selected.
VC15. For each non-distributed requirement, at least one problem frame has been selected.
VC16. New frames have been added to the catalogue.

Tool Support. Currently, our tool does not support any frame specification (see Sect. 8). Therefore, the frame selection requires manual interaction based on the catalogue of frames and identified requirements.

5.6   Step 6: Create Problem Diagrams

The final step of our method is the creation of problem diagrams for the functional requirements we identified in the second step. For requirements not being classified as distributed, we create problem diagrams as proposed by Michal Jackson [10] based on the sub-context diagram for the responsible subsystem. To specify an interface in more detail, it is possible to add connection domains, e.g. a user interface.

To create problem diagrams, we instantiate the frame diagrams of the frames we selected in the previous step. To specify the interfaces between domains in more detail, we annotate its type according to the access vector as introduced in Sect. 3.

For requirements being classified as distributed, we create one problem diagram per involved subsystem. Those diagrams contain the relevant problem domains taken from the sub-context diagram and remote machines for subsystems related to the functional requirement. To connect machine and remote machines, we again make use of remote interfaces. The textual requirement description can be created by instantiating the corresponding textual pattern.

A distributed requirement is characterized by the communication between machine and remote machine for its satisfaction. Therefore, the requirement *refers to* or *constrains* at least one phenomenon of a remote machine. *Refers to* means that the remote machine triggers an event of the machine to be considered, and *constrains* means that the machine to be considered triggers an event of the remote machine. The annotated phenomenon describes that event.

Validation Conditions. For the final step of our method, we define four validation conditions.

VC17. Each functional requirement is contained in at least one problem diagram.
VC18. For each distributed requirement, there is a problem diagram for each involved subsystem.
VC19. A distributed requirement *refers to* or *constrains* at least one phenomenon of a remote machine.
VC20. The problem diagram is an instance of the corresponding frame diagram.

Tool Support. Using our tool, users can generate problem diagrams for each requirement and each subsystem, respectively. The initial structure of the diagrams can be generated automatically, i.e. requirement and machine. In addition, we provide a wizard that assists users of the tool in selecting relevant problem domains and interfaces from the model, and in adding connection domains. Again, we use references to existing model elements to ensure consistency between all diagrams.

Our tool can evaluate all validation conditions automatically, except the last one since the frame specifications are currently not part of the model.

5.7 Final Output

The final output of our method is a set of diagrams for each subsystem. The set consists of a context diagram for the subsystem and problem diagrams which describe the functional requirements to be satisfied by the subsystem. The set allows independent development of each system while still preserving dependencies to other subsystems. Since we document the results in one model, changes will be propagated throughout all method steps and diagrams.

6   Example

In the following, we apply our method to a part of a smart grid case study. The diagrams and tables we show in the following have been created with our tool.

6.1   Informal Scenario Description

For the present paper, we focus on a small part of the overall scenario that concerns the customer's home. The initial scenario description is as follows: The communication hub is the central gateway, for which software shall be developed. Smart meters measure the customer's power consumption. They transmit the data in given intervals to the communication hub where the data is stored. In addition, a customer can connect to the communication hub using a mobile application on a smartphone or tablet. Customers can configure the mobile application to connect to their communication hub and can then request a list of stored meter data.

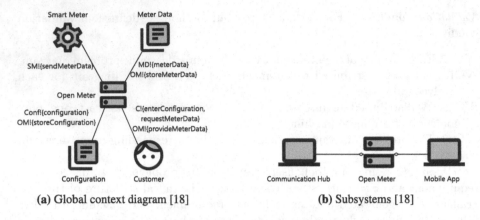

(a) Global context diagram [18]   (b) Subsystems [18]

Fig. 7. Case study - global context diagram & subsystems.

6.2   Step 1: Define Global Context and Subsystems

Our distributed system is called *Open Meter* 🖥, for which we present the global context diagram in Fig. 7a. We identified the stakeholder *Customer* ☺, who is able to enter a *Configuration* 🖼 for the mobile application and who can request previously stored meter data. We consider a *Smart Meter* ⚙ as existing technical equipment. Measured data will be stored persistently in the database which we call *Meter Data* 🖼.

In Fig. 7b on the right hand-side, we also provide an overview of the different subsystems that shall be developed. Our distributed system consists of two subsystems: The *Communication Hub* 🖵 will be realized as an embedded system for the gateway at customers' home. The *Mobile App* 🖵 will be realized as software for smartphones and tablets.

6.3   Step 2: Elicit Functional Requirements for DS

For our scenario, we consider three functional requirements:

Enter Configuration. Customers can configure the mobile application to connect to the communication hub.
Request Meter Data. Customers can request a list of their meter data via the mobile application.
Store Meter Data. In given intervals, smart meters send the measured data to the communication hub, where it is stored persistently.

6.4   Step 3: Identify Distributed Functional Requirements

Next, we identify those requirements that concern more than one subsystem.

Enter Configuration. Customers enter the configuration locally in the mobile application. There is no communication with other systems and therefore, the requirement is not considered as distributed.

Request Meter Data. To request the meter data, customers use their mobile application to access the communication hub. The communication hub then returns the stored data. Both subsystems are involved in that process, and therefore we consider the requirement as distributed.

Store Meter Data. Smart meters connect to a communication hub. There is no interaction with other subsystems.

6.5 Step 4: Decompose Context

Our scenario contains two subsystems, *Communication Hub* and *Mobile Application*. Hence, it is necessary to define one sub-context diagram for each.

Communication Hub. Figure 8a shows the context diagram for the *Communication Hub* 💻. The domain *Meter Data* 📱 represents the database where the communication hub stores the measured data persistently, and a *Smart Meter* ⚙ sends the measured data. Since the *Mobile App* 💻 is also part of the distributed system, it is represented as a remote machine. The interface between both subsystems is unreliable and therefore marked as a remote interface.

Mobile Application. For the *Mobile App* 💻, we develop the context diagram in Fig. 8b. It consists of the *Customer* ☺ who uses the application, a *Configuration* 📱, and the *Communication Hub* 💻, which is again connected to the machine with a remote connection. There are phenomena to enter the configuration and to request meter data.

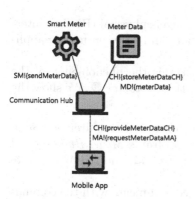

(a) Sub-context diagram for *Communication Hub* [18]

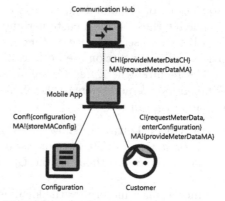

(b) Sub-context diagram for *Mobile Application* [18]

Fig. 8. Case study - sub-context diagrams.

6.6   Step 5: Select Frames

For the three requirements of our scenario, we select the following frames:

Enter Configuration. The requirement is non-distributed one. Since the customer (biddable domain) can enter the configuration (lexical domain), we select the problem frame *Simple Workpieces* [10].

Request Meter Data. The requirement is also not distributed. A smart meter (causal domain) stores the meter data (lexical domain). We choose the problem frame *Model Building* [10].

Store Meter Data. Store meter data is a distributed requirement. Therefore, we select a distributed frame. The requirement fits to the frame *Query (PF)*, since a customer (biddable domain) can request data from a remote resource (lexical domain).

In the next step, we create the diagrams according to the corresponding frame diagram.

6.7   Step 6: Create Problem Diagrams

There are three functional requirements in our scenario for which we present the corresponding problem diagrams in the following.

Enter Configuration. Since the requirement *Enter Configuration* is not a distributed requirement, there is only one problem diagram. It is an instance of the problem frame *Simple Workpiece* and consists of the *Customer* ☉, the *Mobile App* ▱, and the *Configuration* ▣. In addition, we decided to make the *User Interface* ⊡ of the mobile application explicit.

The interface between customer and user interface is physical (P). The interfaces between user interface and mobile application, and between mobile application and configuration are both local (L).

The requirement *Enter Configuration* ▱ constrains the phenomenon of the *Configuration* ▣ and refers to the phenomenon of the *Customer* ☉. We show the problem diagram in Fig. 9.

Store Meter Data. We show the problem diagram for the requirement *Store Meter Data* ▱ in Fig. 10. It is an instance of problem frame *Model Building* and consists of the *SmartMeter* ✿, the *Communication Hub* ▱, and the *Meter Data* ▣.

Since a smart meter uses the local network to communicate with the communication hub, the interface is classified as adjacent (A). Between communication hub and meter data, there is a local interface.

The requirement constrains the phenomenon of the *Meter Data* ▣ and refers to the phenomenon of the *Smart Meter* ✿.

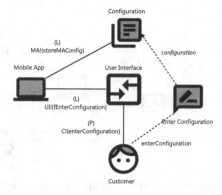

Fig. 9. Case study - problem diagram for *Enter Configuration* [18].

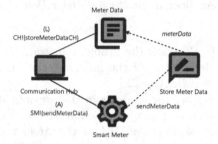

Fig. 10. Case study - problem diagram for *Store Meter Data* [18].

Request Meter Data. We identified the requirement *Request Meter Data* 🖾 as distributed, because it concerns both subsystems. Therefore, we create problem diagrams for the *Communication Hub* 🖳 and for the *Mobile App* 🖳. They are an instance of the problem frame *Query (DF)*.

Mobile Application. In Fig. 11a, we show the problem diagram for the requirement *Request Meter Data* 🖾 with regard to the *Mobile App* 🖳. It contains the machine, the *Customer* ☺ who initiates the request, the *User Interface* 🖼, and the remotely connected *Communication Hub* 🖾.

Between customer and user interface, we again consider a physical interface (P), and between user interface and mobile app, there is a local interface (L). Since mobile application and communication hub can communicate via the internet, the interface is annotated with network (N).

The requirement refers to the phenomenon *enterConfiguration* of the *Customer* ☺ and to the phenomenon *provideMeterDataCH* of the remote machine. It constrains the phenomenon *getMeterData* representing the event to retrieve the data from the database, and the phenomenon *fProvideMeterDataCH* of the *User Interface* 🖼 representing the feedback for the customer.

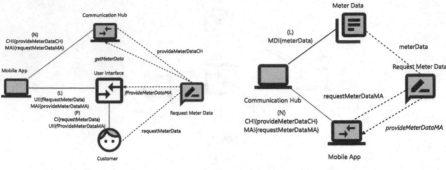

(a) Problem diagram for *Mobile App* [18]

(b) Problem diagram for *Communication Hub* [18]

Fig. 11. Problem diagram for *Request Meter Data* - Query (DF).

Communication Hub. We show the problem diagram for the *Communication Hub* 🖥 in Fig. 11b. It consists of the machine, the *Meter Data* 🖻, and the remotely connected *Mobile App* 🖥.

The types of interfaces are the same as in the previous diagrams.

The requirement refers to the phenomenon of the *Meter Data* 🖻 and to the phenomenon *requestMeterDataMA* of the *Mobile App* 🖥. In addition, the requirement constrains the phenomenon *provideMeterDataMA*, since the *Communication Hub* 🖥 initiates the event to provide the meter data to the customer.

The created diagrams which have been documented in the model can now be used for further analysis, e.g. with regard to security (cf. Sect. 8).

7 Related Work

In the following, we present related work that follows similar approaches or that may complement our work.

Haley argues that the problem frames notation does not allow to specify a *limited to many relation* between interfaces [7]. Therefore, the author suggests using cardinalities on interfaces. Cardinalities would extend our notation to be more precise in specifying the relations between the different subsystems, e.g. to state the number of concurrent instances.

The same author introduces so-called projection domains to document relations between different units of distributed architectures [8]. The approach neither provides detailed documentation of the context for each subsystem nor a method to systematically identify overlapping requirements.

Gol Mohammadi et al. propose a framework to combine goal-oriented requirements engineering with problem frames [11]. The proposed framework allows extending problem and context modeling approaches with soft-goals, e.g. for security. Using the framework in our method is a promising way to improve the context definition.

To decompose the requirements of a distributed system, Penzenstadler defines a catalog of criteria [12]. There are criteria for context, functionalities, and design of software. The presented catalog may help to further describe the subsystems we identified with our method. Therefore, it may complement our work.

Beckers and Faßbender describe a pattern-based approach for capturing quality requirements like performance [1] in distributed systems. Since we focus on functional requirements, the proposed pattern and our method can complement each other.

There are many design patterns that have been identified in the context of distributed systems (e.g., [2,5,9]). Some of those patterns capture aspects like security, as well. Currently, our method only addresses requirements engineering. By mapping distributed frames to appropriate design patterns, we can assist the design phase during software development.

Finally, Ramachandran and Mahmood discuss the state of the art in requirements engineering for distributed computing [13]. The authors put a special focus on cloud computing which became very popular in the last years. Currently, we do not focus on any specific type of distributed system. Their work may solve as an input to further analyze distributed frames in the context of cloud computing.

8   Conclusion

Summary. In this paper, we presented a pattern-based approach to characterize functional requirements for distributed systems. Following Jackson's problem frames approach, we introduced the so-called *Distributed Frames*. We first introduced a common template format to specify them. Next, we presented several examples of such frames using our template.

In addition, we provided an extension of our *RE4DIST* method that takes our distributed frames into account. The extension allows a pattern-based documentation of functional requirements, and functional requirements can systematically be described by instantiating a suitable frame. Our proposed Ecore model ensures consistency and traceability between the different steps of the method.

Finally, we exemplified the extended method and the application of our patterns based on a small case study.

Future Work. We plan to extend our tool which we developed in previous work [18]. We will embed the pattern catalog into the tool to support the selection and instantiation of appropriate frames. A frame instance can then be stored in the Ecore model which we presented in Sect. 3.

Currently, our distributed frames are only a small set of relevant patterns for requirements. We will go on with identifying additional frames, and we plan to make the catalog publicly available so that others can contribute, as well. Furthermore, we plan to develop a pattern system. In this system, each distributed frame can be further refined, for example, to capture specific aspects for Peer-to-Peer systems.

Due to unreliable connections between the different subsystems and continuous exchange of information, security and privacy are of special importance for distributed systems. With our method, we allow making those connections explicit. In previous work, we mapped security incidents to functional requirements [17]. We will extend the mapping with regard to distributed frames, and we will investigate in more detail how relevant threats can be identified automatically.

References

1. Beckers, K., Faßbender, S.: Peer-to-peer driven software engineering considering security, reliability, and performance. In: 7th International Conference on Availability, Reliability and Security, pp. 485–494, August 2012. https://doi.org/10. 1109/ARES.2012.26
2. Buschmann, F., Henney, K., Schmidt, D.C.: Pattern-Oriented Software Architecture, 4th edn. Wiley SEries in Software Design Patterns, Wiley (2007). http://www.worldcat.org/oclc/314792015
3. Choppy, C., Heisel, M.: Une approache à base de patrons pour la spécification et le développement de systèmes d'information. Approches Formelles dans l'Assistance au Développement de Logiciels - AFADL (2004)
4. Côté, I., Hatebur, D., Heisel, M., Schmidt, H., Wentzlaff, I.: A systematic account of problem frames. In: Hvatum, L.B., Schümmer, T. (eds.) Proceedings of the 12th EuroPLoP, Irsee, Germany, 4–8 July 2007, pp. 749–768. UVK - Universitaetsverlag Konstanz (2007). http://hillside.net/europlop/europlop2007/workshops/D3.pdf
5. Fernandez-Buglioni, E.: Security Patterns in Practice: Designing Secure Architectures Using Software Patterns, 1st edn. Wiley Publishing, New York (2013)
6. FIRST.org: Common Vulnerability Scoring System v3.1: Specification Document (2019)
7. Haley, C.B.: Using problem frames with distributed architectures: a case for cardinality on interfaces. In: Proceedings of the 2nd International Software Requirements to Architectures Workshop (STRAW 2003), May 2003. http://oro.open.ac.uk/3394/
8. Haley, C.B., Laney, R.C., Nuseibeh, B.: Using problem frames and projections to analyze requirements for distributed systems. In: Proceedings of the 10th International Workshop on Requirements Engineering: Foundation for Software Quality (REFSQ 2004), June 2004. http://oro.open.ac.uk/3393/
9. Hendrikx, K., Olivié, H.J., Duval, E.: Design patterns for distributed information systems. In: Dyson, P., Devos, M. (eds.) Proceedings of the 4th EuroPLoP, Germany, 7–11 July 1999, pp. 47–56. UVK - Universitaetsverlag Konstanz (1999). http://web.archive.org/web/20031011072203/. http://www.argo.be/europlop/Papers/Final/Hendrickx.ps
10. Jackson, M.A.: Problem Frames - Analysing and Structuring Software Development Problems. Pearson Education (2000). http://www.pearsoned.co.uk/Bookshop/detail.asp?item=100000000004768
11. Mohammadi, N.G., Alebrahim, A., Weyer, T., Heisel, M., Pohl, K.: A framework for combining problem frames and goal models to support context analysis during requirements engineering. In: Cuzzocrea, A., Kittl, C., Simos, D.E., Weippl, E., Xu, L. (eds.) CD-ARES 2013. LNCS, vol. 8127, pp. 272–288. Springer, Heidelberg (2013). https://doi.org/10.1007/978-3-642-40511-2_19

12. Penzenstadler, B.: DeSyRe: decomposition of systems and their requirements: transition from system to subsystem using a criteria catalogue and systematic requirements refinement. Ph.D. thesis, Technical University Munich (2010). http://mediatum.ub.tum.de/node?id=999357

13. Ramachandran, M., Mahmood, Z. (eds.): Requirements Engineering for Service and Cloud Computing. Springer, Cham (2017). https://doi.org/10.1007/978-3-319-51310-2

14. Steinberg, D., Budinsky, F., Paternostro, M., Merks, E.: EMF: Eclipse Modeling Framework 2.0, 2nd edn. Addison-Wesley Professional, Boston (2009)

15. Tanenbaum, A.S., Steen, M.V.: Distributed Systems: Principles and Paradigms, 2nd edn. Prentice-Hall Inc., Upper Saddle River (2006)

16. Wentzlaff, I., Specker, M.: Pattern-based development of user-friendly web applications. In: Proceedings of the 2nd International Workshop on Model-Driven Web Engineering (MDWE 2006), Palo Alto, USA. ACM (2006)

17. Wirtz, R., Heisel, M.: A systematic method to describe and identify security threats based on functional requirements. In: Zemmari, A., Mosbah, M., Cuppens-Boulahia, N., Cuppens, F. (eds.) CRiSIS 2018. LNCS, vol. 11391, pp. 205–221. Springer, Cham (2019). https://doi.org/10.1007/978-3-030-12143-3_17

18. Wirtz, R., Heisel, M.: RE4DIST: model-based elicitation of functional requirements for distributed systems. In: van Sinderen, M., Maciaszek, L.A. (eds.) Proceedings of the 14th International Conference on Software Technologies, ICSOFT 2019, Prague, Czech Republic, 26–28 July 2019, pp. 71–81. SciTePress (2019). https://doi.org/10.5220/0007919200710081

Efficient Diagnosis of Reconfigurable Systems with Incorrect Behavior and Faulty Components: A Case Study on SGrids

Yousra Hafidi[1,2,3,4](✉) [ID], Laid Kahloul[2], and Mohamed Khalgui[3,4] [ID]

[1] University of Tunis El Manar, Tunis, Tunisia
yousra_hafidi@hotmail.com
[2] LINFI Laboratory, Computer Science Department, Biskra University,
Biskra, Algeria
laid.k.b@gmail.com
[3] LISI Laboratory, National Institute of Applied Sciences and Technology,
University of Carthage, 1080 Tunis, Tunisia
khalgui.mohamed@gmail.com
[4] School of Electrical and Information Engineering, Jinan University,
Guangzhou, China

Abstract. This paper deals with the formal verification of reconfigurable discrete event systems. We use the formalism called reconfigurable timed net condition/event systems (R-TNCESs) which is a Petri net pattern that deals with reconfiguration properties. Systems can experience malfunctioning due to hardware failures or software errors. Model-based diagnosis algorithms are widely used in academia and industry to detect faulty components and ensure systems safety. The application of these methods on reconfigurable systems is impossible due to their special behavior. In this paper, we propose accomplishing techniques of backward reachability to make reconfigurable systems model-based diagnosis possible using R-TNCESs. The flexibility among reconfigurable systems allows them to challenge recent requirements of markets. However, such properties and complicated behavior make their verification task being complex and sometimes impossible. We deal with the previous problem by proposing a new methodology based on backward reachability of RDECSs using (R-TNCESs) formalism including improvement methods. The proposed methodology serves to reduce as much as possible redundant computations and gives a package to be used in model-based diagnosis algorithms. A real case study on smart electrical grids is adopted in order to demonstrate the paper's contributions. Finally, a performance evaluation is achieved using different factors and sizes to study benefits and limits of the proposed methodology among large-scale systems.

Keywords: Reconfigurable systems · Modeling and verification · Petri net · Backward reachability · Model-based diagnosis · Smart grids

© Springer Nature Switzerland AG 2020
M. van Sinderen and L. A. Maciaszek (Eds.): ICSOFT 2019, CCIS 1250, pp. 108–129, 2020.
https://doi.org/10.1007/978-3-030-52991-8_6

1   Introduction

Nowadays flexibility in manufacturing systems is challenging markets. For example, a system with fault tolerance should be dynamic and respond without any malfunction while hardware failures occur. Reconfigurable systems [1,2,15,28] have flexible configurations that allow them to switch from a configuration to another in order to respond for user requirements or to prevent from system malfunction [20,27]. However, their special behavior and properties of reconfiguration make of them complex discrete event systems. In fact, any failure or dysfunction of a critical system can result serious consequences. Reconfigurable systems like reconfigurable discrete event control systems (RDECS) [18] are often subjected to malfunctions that are due to hardware components breakdowns or software dismisses. A safe system should never reach an undesirable state during its working process [10].

Many research works ensure safety of systems using methods such as Model-based Diagnosis [5,8,22]. Model-based diagnosis (MBD) is a verification method that explains an observed system's malfunction [9]. When an abnormal system's behavior is observed, MBD method backtracks system execution in the model, and combines with predefined data to detect faulty components that cause this behavior. Backward reachability is frequently used to construct the backward state space that serves with model checking responding to system diagnosis problems. Model-checking [4] is a verification technique that explores possible system states in order to check if a system meets its specifications. If a required property is proved false, model checking provides the counterexample that falsified it. One of the main problems is how to check the largest possible state spaces and treat them as quick as possible with current means of processors and memories. Existing research works [4] have proven results for larger systems state spaces by including some clever algorithms. Consequently, more problems are covered.

Despite the advantage of system diagnosis method, there still a lack of research works on diagnosis of reconfigurable systems. Their special behavior as well as their reconfiguration properties [11,12,29] should be taken into consideration. In addition, the diagnosis of these complex systems like RDECSs needs optimization methods that improve the process and prevent unnecessary redundant computations.

In order to deal with previous problems, we propose in this paper the following contributions:

1. A backward reachability method for R-TNCESs formalism to facilitate reconfigurable systems diagnosis: backward reachability is used rather than forward reachability (for ordinary Petri nets, colored Petri nets ...etc. [7,25]) to solve systems diagnosis. R-TNCESs reverse rules and accomplishing techniques are proposed to run backward reachability of reconfigurable systems. Our motivation about using R-TNCESs formalism resides in the way that unlike most other formalisms, R-TNCESs are modular and support modeling of system reconfigurations. In addition, the composition of interconnected modules communicating with signals, deals with interactions that actually happen between

sensors and actuators in reconfigurable discrete event control systems [14], i.e., sensors send signals to activate actuators. By setting this method, the application of classical algorithms of model-based diagnosis on reconfigurable systems becomes possible using R-TNCESs.

2. A new methodology to cover a wider state space and resolve more problems. Diagnosis is a time and space consuming problem, and the proposed methodology in this paper includes improvement methods that serve to prevent redundancies during backward reachability analysis.

The purpose of this paper is to propose accomplishing methods to allow the application of classical model based diagnosis algorithms on reconfigurable systems using R-TNCES formalism. Note that the problem of applying the classical algorithms of model-based diagnosis is left outside the scope of this paper.

To the best of our knowledge, (1) no existing previous works have proposed methods for reconfigurable systems backward reachability, (2) no existing rules showing how to reverse a system modeled by R-TNCES formalism, and (3) no research works deal with optimization of R-TNCESs backward state space to improve model-based diagnosis abilities.

The paper's contribution is applied to a real case study of smart grids [24,33]: SGrid, which is an electrical distribution platform (from generators to consumers). Obtained results show that after applying proposed methods, classical algorithms of model based diagnosis becomes possible on R-TNCESs. In addition, the covered state space using new methodology is improved. A performance evaluation is achieved for different sizes of problems.

The present paper is an extended version of our previous paper [13]. The methodology is improved by new experiments and results on a well explained case study about smart grids.

The remainder of the paper is organized as follows. Section 2 recalls the most recent basic elements of R-TNCESs formalism, introduces backward reachability method concepts, presents the proposed R-TNCES reverse method that will be used as a basic element in backward reachability of R-TNCESs, and finally reminds Mu method that will be used to improve computations. Section 3 explains the main motivations of this paper, proposes the new methodology of backward reachability including Mu improvement method, presents the algorithm and computes its complexity. Section 4 is the experimentation part which contains some applications and results. Finally, Sect. 5 concludes this paper and describes the future work.

2   Preliminaries

In this section we first introduce an extension from Petri nets formalism [26] called reconfigurable discrete event/condition systems (R-TNCESs) [30]. R-TNCESs are used for formal modeling and verification of reconfigurable discrete event control systems. However, their verification is often expensive and needs some improvement methods. In this section, we present backward reachability analysis for R-TNCES and some basic elements proposed to improve the verification task.

2.1   R-TNCESs Formalism

According to the definition reported in [14,31], reconfigurable timed net condition/event systems (R-TNCESs) are formally defined by a couple $RTN = (B, R)$ where B (respectively, R) is the behavior (respectively, the control) module of a reconfigurable discrete event control system (RDECS). B is a union of multi-TNCESs represented by

$$B = (P, T, F, W, CN, EN, DC, V, Z_0)$$

where,

- P (respectively, T) is a superset of places (respectively, transitions),
- $F \subseteq (P \times T) \cup (T \times P)^1$ is a superset of flow arcs,
- $W : (P \times T) \cup (T \times P) \longrightarrow \{0, 1\}$ maps a weight to a flow arc, $W(x, y) > 0$ if $(x, y) \in F$, and $W(x, y) = 0$ otherwise, where $x, y \in P \cup T$,
- $CN \subseteq (P \times T)$ (respectively, $EN \subseteq (T \times T)$) is a superset of condition signals (respectively, event signals), (v) $DC : F \cap (P \times T) \rightarrow \{[l_1, h_1], \ldots, [l_{|F \cap (P \times T)|}, h_{|F \cap (P \times T)|}]\}$ is a superset of time constraints on input arcs of transitions, where
  $\forall i \in [1, \mid F \cap (P \times T) \mid]$, $l_i, h_i \in \mathbb{N}$ and $l_i < h_i$,
- $V : T \longrightarrow \{\vee, \wedge\}$ maps an event-processing mode (AND or OR) for every transition,
- $Z_0 = (M_0, D_0)$, where $M_0 : P \longrightarrow \{0, 1\}$ is the initial marking, and $D_0 : P \longrightarrow \{0\}$ is the initial clock position.

The graphical model of a TNCES is depicted in Fig. 1.

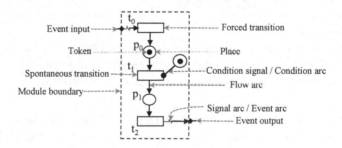

Fig. 1. Modules graphical model [13].

R is a set of reconfiguration rules such that rule r is a structure represented by

$$r = (Cond, s, x)$$

---

[1] Cartesian product of two sets: $P \times T = \{(p, t) \mid p \in P, t \in T\}$.

where,

- $Cond \rightarrow \{True, False\}$ is the pre-condition of r, i.e., r is executable only if $Cond = True$,
- $s : TN(^\bullet r) \rightarrow TN(r^\bullet)$ is the structure-modification instruction such that $TN(^\bullet r)$ (respectively, $TN(r^\bullet)$) represents the structure before (respectively, after) applying the reconfiguration r,
- $x : last_{state}(^\bullet r) \rightarrow initial_{state}(r^\bullet)$ is the state processing function. In this paper, we denote by r_{ij} the reconfiguration rule that transforms $TNCES_i$ to $TNCES_j$.

As reported in [14,31], structure-modification instructions are presented in Table 1. A place is denoted by x, a transition by y, a control component module by $\mathbb{CC}$, and the AND instruction to represent complex modification instructions is presented by ",".

Table 1. Structure-modification instructions of R-TNCESs [13].

N°	Instruction	Symbol
1	Add condition signals	$Cr(cn(x, y))$
2	Add event signals	$Cr(ev(y, y))$
3	Add control component	$Cr(\mathbb{CC})$
4	Delete condition signals	$De(cn(x, y))$
5	Delete event signals	$De(ev(y, y))$
6	Delete control component	$De(\mathbb{CC})$
7	Add place x with its marking $m(x)$	$Cr(x, m(x))$
8	Add transition y	$Cr(y)$
9	Add flow arc $fa(x, y)$ or flow arc $fa(y, x)$	$Cr(fa(x, y))$ or $Cr(fa(y, x))$
10	Delete place x	$De(x)$
11	Delete transition y	$De(y)$
12	Delete flow arc $fa(x, y)$ or flow arc $fa(y, x)$	$De(fa(x, y))$ or $De(fa(y, x))$
13	Modify transition's y event-processing mode to "AND"	$Mo(AND(y))$
14	Modify transition's y event-processing mode to "OR"	$Mo(OR(y))$

R-TNCESs semantic is defined by both the reconfiguration between TNCESs in behavior module B, and the firing of transitions in each TNCES. The former has the priority to be applied first when its pre-conditions are fulfilled. The latter depends on the rules of firing transitions in TNCESs and the chosen firing mode. Two kinds of transitions are distinguished, i.e., spontaneous and forced transitions. A transition t is called spontaneous if it is not forced by any other transition (i.e., there are no event signals incoming to t), otherwise it is called forced transition. Each type of transitions has its firing rules. The firing rules are described in detail in [31]. However for the firing mode, we adopt the mode in which only "*one spontaneous transition is fired by step*".

We use the concept of control components (CCs) which was firstly introduced in [17] in order to model RDECSs. This means that each configuration is a set of CCs interconnected with each other to compose a TNCES. The concept of CCs serves the modularity which enabels the readability and the re-usability of models.

Note that in this paper, we use non marked TNCESs which are TNCESs structures with no given initial marking and non marked R-TNCESs which are R-TNCESs with configurations represented by non marked TNCESs. We use non marked R-TNCESs to describe many possible systems in one model, i.e., each R-TNCES with a possible initial marking represents a system. In addition, by non marked R-TNCESs we are able to describe systems with missed information on their behavior.

2.2 Backward Reachability Analysis (BRA)

Backward reachability analysis (BRA) theory has been already used for ordinary Petri nets [3] and colored Petri nets [7]. BRA on ordinary Petri nets uses methods such as the reverse of the net, where arcs directions are just reversed (i.e., source becomes target and target becomes source). However, this method is disadvantageous for other high level Petri nets like R-TNCESs. We propose a method that helps to apply BRA on R-TNCESs and study its benefits comparing with other existed theories.

Backward reachability analysis (BRA) can be started from an undesirable state which leads the system to a critical behavior, and it highlights all possible scenarios that cause it. Backward reachability analysis are widely used in model-based diagnosis problems. Let (1) S be a system that works incorrectly, (2) M_S be an abstracted model of S, and (3) $OBS = \{o_1, o_2, ..., o_n\}$ be a set of states specifying the observed misbehavior. The model-based diagnosis method back-tracks the system states according to its behavior extracted from M_s, and gives sequences of initial states that are supposed to be reasons for this unpredictable misbehavior starting from OBS (Fig. 2).

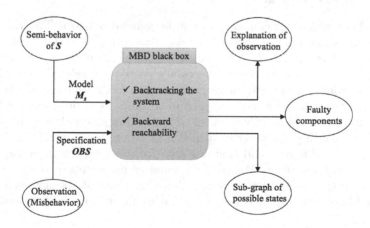

Fig. 2. Model based diagnosis and backward reachability [13].

This reasoning is beneficial when we have a non completed model of system S, i.e., sometimes system's behavior cannot be completely modeled 100%, thus, some parts are missed such as the initial state from which a system starts its process. In this case, model M_S is built from hardware components data and their interactions. Using Petri nets formalism, the missed behavior can be presented as lack of information about initial marking (i.e., initial state) in the model. Therefore, M_S is given as a Petri net model without initial marking (i.e., non marked Petri net). Suppose that we aim to explain a misbehavior of such system using the forward method, then all sequences with each possible combination of initial marking is generated. The problem is that in some cases, this reasoning costs a lot of extra time due to a huge number of initial marking possibilities that can even be infinite and not beneficial for the diagnosis process. Some diagnosis works take as an input a system that is modeled using Petri nets like M_s. Then, backward reachability analysis (BRA) is adopted to generate the system's state space starting from the undesirable state in OBS. The obtained state space serves to understand possible causes of resulted observations. The main strength point of this method is that it is able to have a model M_S that represents all possible systems with all combinations of inputs and parameters. Therefore, each real system of these possible ones in M_S is supposed to be diagnosed at the end of the process. One of BRA advantages is that it focuses on critical scenarios rather than all possible ones. Unfortunately, it is possible that the graph resulted from BRA be larger or infinite comparing with the original one obtained using the forward reachability analysis (FRA) [21] for a marked input system. For this case, BRA approach is practical only if the subsequent graph is smaller than the original one obtained by FRA approach. Therefore, generating backward reachability graphs is infeasible in some cases like the above one. In the next subsection, we define what is R-TNCES reverse that will be used to generate R-TNCES backward reachability graphs.

2.3   R-TNCES Reverse

Ordinary Petri nets reversion method can be generalized to R-TNCESs by (1) inverting arcs directions in the nets, and (2) adapting R-TNCESs semantics. The result is a reversed R-TNCES which is possible to be backward analyzed. Adapting R-TNCESs allows to add necessary procedures related to R-TNCESs semantic in order to complete the reversion and to facilitate the analysis among resulted structures. The reversion applied in ordinary Petri nets does not require adaptations, i.e., a simple reversion of arcs directions is sufficient to perform backward reachability. However in R-TNCESs, where the dynamic of this high level Petri net is different and contains more constraints, the inversion of arcs directions is not sufficient. We propose some complementary methods to R-TNCESs reversion method to consider the adaptation of token's evolution in this special Petri net, e.g., cases of, condition/event arcs, reconfigurations,.. etc.

We consider that the reverse of a non marked R-TNCES $RTN(B_{RTN}, R_{RTN})$ is an imaginary non marked R-TNCES given by

$$RTN^{-1}(B_{RTN}^{-1}, R_{RTN}^{-1})$$

where,

- B_{RTN}^{-1} is a set of reversed non marked TNCESs generated from original non marked TNCESs in B_{RTN} by using arcs inversion generic algorithm and reversed firing rules as in Table 2,
- R_{RTN}^{-1} is a set of reversed reconfiguration rules that are generated from original ones in R_{RTN} using Tables 3 and 4.

2.4   *Mu* Improvement Method

As reported in [14], Mu function improves the generation of accessibility graphs by reducing redundancies and unnecessary computations. Let $RS(B_{RS}, R_{RS})$ be an R-TNCES, where (1) $B_{RS} = \{C_1, ..., C_n\}$ is the behavior module containing $n > 1$ configurations $C_1, .., C_n$, and (2) R_{RTN} is the control module containing $k > 1$ reconfiguration rules: $r_{ij}, 1 \leq i, j \leq n$ that transforms the system from configuration C_i to configuration C_j. $\mu(AG(C_i), r_{ij})$ is the function that takes the accessibility graph of a configuration $AG(C_i)$ and transforms it into another accessibility graph of another configuration $AG(C_j)$ according to the structure-modifications in the applied reconfiguration rule r_{ij}, i.e., $r_{ij}.s$ is a list containing one or more structure-modification instructions defined in Table 1. Function Mu, generates new accessibility graphs of new configurations from already generated ones. Rather than computing each graph from zero, Mu helps to avoid repetitive computation and keep similar already computed parts of the state space. Mu function uses a set of rewriting rules on an already computed graph to transform it to a new graph. Table 5 presents some rewriting rules of Mu function. Other rewriting rules of all possible reconfiguration scenarios are presented and explained in [14]. A set of rewriting rules for each possible structure-modification instruction $SMI_m \in r_{ij}.s$, i.e., SMI_m denotes the structure-modification instruction symbol number m. We denote by (1) a and a': accessibility graph edges, (2) y, y_1, and y_2: R-TNCESs transitions, (3) $y_1 \frown y_2$ an event signal from y_1 to y_2, (4) $enb(s, y)$ a boolean function that returns 1 if the transition t is enabled in the state s or 0 otherwise, (5) src: $A \to S$ the function that returns the state representing the source node of the edge e and tg: $A \to S$ the function that returns the state representing the target node of the edge e, and (6) $SimulateFrom(s)$ the function that continues the simulation from a non-complete graph (i.e., a set of states and a set of edges), eventual enabled transitions are fired to compute the additional reachable states on the new structure, starting from the state s.

Table 2. R-TNCESs reversed firing rules [13].

Arcs	RTN	RTN^{-1}
Flow		
Event		
Condition		

Table 3. Reconfiguration rules inversion [13].

r	RTN	RTN^{-1}
$cond$	c	c^{-1}
S	S	S^{-1}
X	$TN(^{\bullet}r) \rightarrow TN(r^{\bullet})$	$TN(r^{\bullet}) \rightarrow TN(^{\bullet}r)$

3   Methodology

This section presents: our motivation in this paper, new proposed backward reachability methodology, algorithm and complexity.

3.1   Motivation

Model-based diagnosis (MBD) of systems [16] has attracted many interest since it ensures systems safety [5–7,22]. Some of diagnosis abilities is explaining the appearance of an observed system's misbehavior, determining the faulty components of the system, and defining what additional information need to be gathered to identify faulty components [9]. Backward reachability analysis is very important in model based diagnosis, i.e., it represents the principal function that backtracks the system process. Unfortunately, BRA is a complex function that is expensive in terms of computing time and memory. One of BRA high complexity reasons is that it generates branches of all possible systems. BRA function is important in complex systems diagnosis and it deserves to be improved.

Table 4. S^{-1}: Reversed structure modification instructions [13].

N°	RTN: S	RTN^{-1}: S^{-1}
1	$Cr(cn(x,\ y))$	$De(cn(x,\ y))$
2	$Cr(ev(y,\ y))$	$De(ev(y,\ y))$
3	$Cr(\mathbb{CC})$	$De(\mathbb{CC})$
4	$De(cn(x,\ y))$	$Cr(cn(x,\ y))$
5	$De(ev(y,\ y))$	$Cr(ev(y,\ y))$
6	$De(\mathbb{CC})$	$Cr(\mathbb{CC})$
7	$Cr(x,\ m(x))$	$De(x)$
8	$Cr(y)$	$De(y)$
9	$Cr(fa(x,\ y))/$ $Cr(fa(y,\ x))$	$De(fa(x,\ y))/$ $De(fa(y,\ x))$
10	$De(x)$	$Cr(x,\ 1)$ or $Cr(x,\ 0)$
11	$De(y)$	$Cr(y)$
12	$De(fa(x,\ y))/$ $De(fa(y,\ x))$	$Cr(fa(x,\ y))/$ $Cr(fa(y,\ x))$
13	$Mo(AND(y))$	$Mo(Or(y))$
14	$Mo(OR(y))$	$Mo(And(y))$

Despite its long success in systems diagnosis, BRA has a number of problems in use such as

1. Consideration of reconfigurable systems: the proposed algorithms in literature lacks from the consideration of some complex systems like reconfigurable ones. Contrarily to non-reconfigurable systems, reconfigurable ones have their own special dynamic behavior that needs to be particularly considered when they are backtracked.
2. Improvement of required time/memory: less research interests focus on optimizing the backward reachability function. Such an expensive function needs to include some optimization technique to improve required time and memory. This is beneficial because it makes backward reachability analysis easy and possible for complex systems such as reconfigurable ones (Table 5).

Petri nets [23] and their extensions are ones of the most widely used formalisms [19] that have been extensively exploited for modeling and analyzing concurrent, parallel and dynamic system. In this paper, we address the problem of reconfigurable systems backward reachability using Petri nets extension called R-TNCESs formalism [14,31,32].

Table 5. Mu rules [13].

m	SMI_m	Rewriting rules on accessibility graphs	Comments
(1)	$Cr(cn(x,y))$	a) $\forall a \in A, Label(a) = y \wedge \neg enb(src(a), y) ::=$ $A \leftarrow A \setminus \{a\}$.	a) For each edge labeled by y: if y is not enabled, then delete it.
(2)	$Cr(ev(y_1, y_2))$	a) $\forall a \in A, Label(a) = y_2 ::= A \leftarrow A \setminus \{a\}$. b) $\forall a \in A, Label(a) = y_1 \wedge enb(src(a), y_1 \curvearrowright y_2) ::=$ $A \leftarrow A \setminus \{a\} \cup \{a'\} \wedge Label(a') = y_1 \curvearrowright y_2 \wedge$ $src(a') = src(a) \wedge tg(a') = src(a) \overset{y_1 \curvearrowright y_2}{\longrightarrow}$.	a) Delete all edges labeled by y_2. b) For each edge labeled by y_1, check from its source state if $y_1 \curvearrowright y_2$ is enabled, then delete the edge labeled by y_1 and add a new edge labeled by $y_1 \curvearrowright y_2$.
(3)	$De(cn(x,y))$	a) $\forall s \in S, enb(s, y) ::= SimulateFrom(s)$.	a) In each state: if y is enabled, then continue simulation from this state.
(4)	$De(ev(y_1, y_2))$	a) $\forall a \in A, Label(a) = (y_1 \curvearrowright y_2) ::= A \leftarrow A \setminus \{a\}$ b) $\forall s \in S, enb(s, y_1) ::= SimulateFrom(s)$. c) $\forall s \in S, enb(s, y_2) ::= SimulateFrom(s)$.	a) Delete all edges labeled by $y_1 \curvearrowright y_2$. b) In each state if y_1 is enabled, then continue the simulation from this state. c) In each state if y_2 is enabled, then continue the simulation from this state.

3.2   Backward Reachability with Mu Method

In this subsection, we propose a new methodology for an efficient verification of reconfigurable systems. Foremost, we use a non marked R-TNCESs formalism for modeling reconfigurable systems. Then, specify as R-TNCESs states the set of system's situation(s) to be checked. Systems situations may represent undesirable states such as failures, or desirable ones such as required results. Therefore, situations are defined according to the problem and the type of the studied system (i.e., a detailed example that explains that in Subsect. 4.1). The suggested method in this paper uses the proposed backward reachability analysis method to generate the backward accessibility graph of the initial configuration. Then, it uses Mu method [14] to improve the computation of other backward accessibility graphs.

The proposed methodology represents a combination between Mu method and the suggested backward reachability analysis of R-TNCESs to generate backward reachability graphs. Let us have a reconfigurable system with n configurations such that $n \in \mathbb{N}$ and $n > 1$. The proposed method, as depicted in Fig. 3, uses the proposed BRA for R-TNCESs to compute backward accessibility graph $graph_1$ of initial configuration $conf_1$. After that, it employs Mu method to

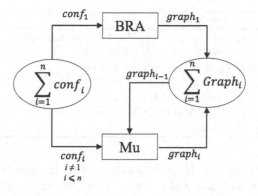

Fig. 3. BRA with Mu (the proposed methodology) [13].

generate other graphs of the other configurations. Old methods as explained in Fig. 4 should generate all graphs using BRA algorithm. Therefore, the difference between the proposed and the old methods is that the suggested one generates only one graph. Other graphs are generated from the initial one, and then, graph from another until the end of all system's configurations. However, in old methods, each graph is generated independently from others. In addition, Mu method is used previously in [14] with forward reachability analysis methods to generate forward reachability graphs. However, in this paper, Mu method is used with the proposed backward reachability analysis method to generate backward reachability graphs. This combination between both methods allows in one hand to backward analyze systems under reconfigurability constraints, and in another hand, to improve time and memory while generating all the graphs of such complex systems.

Fig. 4. BRA without Mu (old methods) [13].

3.3 Algorithm and Complexity

Algorithm 1 describes the proposed method of R-TNCES backward reachability analysis. The algorithm takes as inputs (1) RT a non marked R-TNCES structure, (2) $Configurations$ a set of TNCESs structures describing system's configurations, (3) $Reconfigurations$ a set of $Rules$ describing system's transformations, (4) $Conf_0$ a non marked TNCES structure describing the initial configuration of the system, and gives as output $Graphs$ the set of accessibility graphs of all the system.

Algorithm 1. GenerateGraphs.

> **Input**: $RT(Configurations$: Set of $TNCESs$; $Reconfigurations$: Set of
> $Rules) : R - TNCES$; $Conf_0 : TNCES$;
> **Output**: $Graphs$: Set of $Accessibility\ Graphs$;
> 1 $Graph_0 = BRA(Conf_0)$;
> 2 $AdaptingModel(RT, Conf_0, Graph_0)$;
> 3 $Graphs = GetGraphsWithMu(RT, Conf_0, Graph_0)$;
> 4 $Graphs \leftarrow Graph_0 \cup Graphs$;

Algorithm 1 uses some additional functions (1) BRA function that takes the initial configuration as input and returns its graph using the backward reachability analysis method described in Subsect. 2.2. (2) $AdaptingModel$ function that adapts RT so that Mu function, which was proposed for forward analysis, can be applied within the current backward analysis. (3) $GetGraphsWithMu$ function that computes other graphs using Mu. $GetGraphsWithMu$ function as described in Algorithm 2, takes the same inputs as in Algorithm 1, besides the initial accessibility graph $Graph_0$ that was already computed using BRA method. The algorithm uses $connections$ function to get the set of next reachable configurations from the graph of the current one. After that it recursively computes each new graph from the previous one and stops when (1) no next configurations are reachable, i.e., $SetC = Nil$, or (2) the graph is already computed, i.e, $Graph_i \in Graphs$.

Algorithm 2. GetGraphsWithMu.

> **Input**: $RT(Configurations$: Set of $TNCESs$; $reconfigurations$: Set of
> $Rules) : R - TNCES$; $Conf_0 : TNCES$; $Graph_0$: Accessibility Graph;
> **Output**: $Graphs$: Set of $Accessibility\ Graphs$;
> **Variables** : $SetC$: Set of $TNCESs$;
> 1 $SetC \leftarrow connections(Graph_0)$;
> 2 **if** $SetC \neq Nil$ **then**
> 3   **foreach** $Conf_i \in SetC$ **do**
> 4 $Graph_i = Mu(conf_i , conf_0, Graph_0)$;
> 5   **if** $graph_i \notin Graphs$ **then**
> 6 $Graphs \leftarrow graph_i \cup Graphs$;
> 7 $GetGraphsWithMu(RT, Conf_i, Graph_i)$;
> 8   **end**
> 9   **end**
> 10 **end**

The time complexity of the entire algorithm: Algorithm 1 in systems with at least 2 configurations is computed as follows

$$\mathcal{O}(1 * e^m + (\mid Configurations \mid -1) * n)$$

where, (1) $\mathcal{O}(e^m)$ is complexity of the BRA function used only once for computing the graph of the initial configuration, and (2) $\mathcal{O}(n)$ is complexity of Mu

function [14] used to compute other accessibility graphs, i.e., $(\mid Configurations \mid -1)$ times in the worst case when all configurations are reachable.

4   Experimentation

This section is composed of two subsections (1) a case study where paper's contributions are applied, and (2) performance evaluation where proposed and related methodologies are compared using different factors.

4.1   Case Study: SGrid Smart Grid

SGrid is an electricity platform and a modern electricity delivery system from generators to consumers, with self-healing and add-in-demand features. The studied SGrid is composed of four main levels of interconnected components: L1, L2, L3, and L4. Each level is composed of a set of electrical devices such as consumers, generators, transformers and/or actuators. Level L1 is the high voltage network that contains power generators such as nuclear power plants, coal plants and hydro-electric plants. The power generated is transmitted to level L2. Level L2 comprises a set of 8 transmission and sub-transmission elements that transfers electricity to different components of level L3. Level L3 is the distribution level that includes a set of 11 distributors, such that each distributor supplies one or more consumers by electricity according to their need. Finally, L4 is the consummation level which involves a set of 5 consumers like citizens' houses and small offices. In SGrid network, each element can have a local generator of power from renewable energy such as solar farms, wind farms, coat plants, nuclear plants, etc. Therefore, each component of the 4 levels can be both consumer and small generator of electricity in the same time. SGrid is: (1) a self-healing system that has the capacity to automatically recognize issues, correct the electricity interruption, and prevent from blackouts, (2) a flexible system with add-in-demand feature that allows it to augment the number of generators to increase electricity supply or new consumers to cover a larger area. SGrid deals with this by reforming its structure, i.e., adding/removing new connections, new elements. This usually happens in L3 (i.e., distribution level) which is the level the most concerned by transformations. The working process is simple: the electricity goes from generators to consumers passing by devices of transmitters and distributors. In the normal case, all consumers in L4 receive the necessary electricity that they need without blackouts thanks to SGrid self-adaptation. But in some unexpected cases, they meet insufficiency and interruptions. The issue is that in this case the abnormally is observed just in L4 devices. However, the reason can be in the input generators. The challenge is how to find in less as possible time the breakdown.

SGrid main working process is explained in Fig. 6

SGrid Modeling. In order to apply formal analysis techniques, it is necessary to mathematically model the studied system SGrid. We model SGrid using R-TNCES formalism already presented in Subsect. 2.1. SGrid is an R-TNCES (Fig. 5)

$$S(B_{FT}, R_{FT})$$

where,

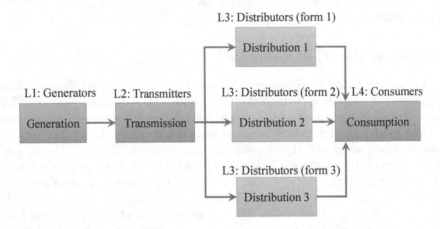

Fig. 5. SGrid main process.

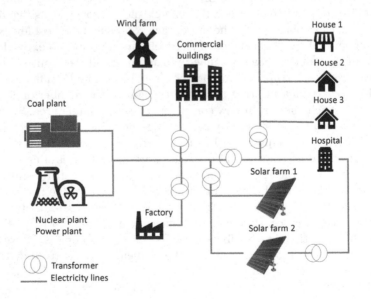

Fig. 6. SGrid Infrastructure.

- $B_S = \{c_1, c_2, c_3\}$: is the behavior module that contains all possible configurations, i.e., SGrid distribution forms are represented by R-TNCESs configurations, where C_1, C_2, and C_3 configurations respectively represent $Distribution_1$, $Distribution_2$, and $Distribution_3$ distribution modes. Each configuration is presented by a set of interconnected modules (Mdl_i) which are control components communicating with signals.
- $R_{FT} = \{r_{c_1-c_2}, r_{c_1-c_3}, r_{c_2-c_1}, r_{c_3-c_1}\}$ is the control module that involves all reconfiguration rules that transforms the system from a configuration to another.

The initial configuration c_1 of the studied system is represented by the TNCES that is graphically shown in Fig. 7. Other configurations c_2 and c_3 can be obtained by applying possible reconfiguration rules from R_S.

Considered reconfiguration rules are described as follows,

- $r_{c_1-c_2} = (Distributor_1$ breaks down; $De(Mdl_{10})$, $Cr(ev(t_{27}/Mdl_{13}, t_{42}/Mdl_{21}))$,
  $Cr(ev(t_{11}/Mdl_5, t_{27}/Mdl_{13})); (p_1, C_1) \rightarrow (p_1, C_2))$;
- $r_{c_1-c_3} = (Distributor_2$ breaks down; $De(Mdl_{11})$, $Cr(ev(t_{27}/Mdl_{13}, t_{42}/Mdl_{21}))$;
  $(p_1, C_1) \rightarrow (p_1, C_2))$.

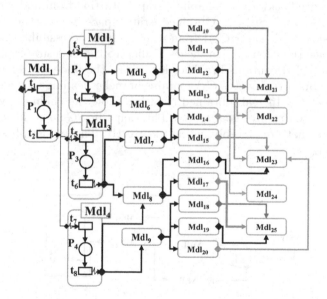

Fig. 7. Initial configuration of SGrid C_1.

SGrid Verification. We define a set of goal states St_i that represent undesirable behavior specified from observation. The observation in SGrid is simple, we notice that there is an abnormal behavior when for example the electricity cuts or when energy is insufficient for one or more consumers. We represent this case formally by an R-TNCES state, and we start backward reachability to obtain possible origins of this issue. In our case, the set of goal states is $\{(St_{goal_1}, C_1),$ $(St_{goal_2}, C_2), (St_{goal_3}, C_3)\}$ such that (1) (St_{goal_1}, C_1) represents a goal in configuration C_1, (2) (St_{goal_2}, C_2) represents a goal in configuration C_2, and (3) (St_{goal_3}, C_3) represents a goal in configuration C_3.

We use R-TNCESs reverse method, and obtain,

$$S^{-1}(B_S^{-1}, R_S^{-1})$$

where,

- $B_{FT}^{-1} = \{C_1^{-1}, C_2^{-1}, C_3^{-1}\}$, i.e., obtained using R-TNCESs reversed firing rules (Table 2) in each configuration,
- $R_S^{-1} = \{r_{c_1-c_2}^{-1}, r_{c_1-c_3}^{-1}\}$, i.e., obtained using Table 3

The set of considered S^{-1} reconfiguration rules are described as follows,

- $r_{c_1-c_2}^{-1} = (Distributor_1 \text{ works; } Cr(Mdl_{10}), De(ev(t_{27}/Mdl_{13}, t_{42}/Mdl_{21})),$
  $De(ev(t_{11}/Mdl_5, t_{27}/Mdl_{13})); (p_1, C_2) \rightarrow (p_1, C_1));$
- $r_{c_1-c_3}^{-1} = (Distributor_1 \text{ works; } Cr(Mdl_{11}), De(ev(t_{27}/Mdl_{13}, t_{42}/Mdl_{21}));$
  $(p_1, C_3) \rightarrow (p_1, C_1)).$

Now, we compute backward reachability graphs starting from undesirable states St_{goal_1}, St_{goal_2}, and St_{goal_3}. Obtained state space is a set of sub-graphs $\{subG(C_1), subG(C_2), subG(C_3)\}$ from whole system accessibility graphs. Sub-graphs: (1) $subG(C_1)$ contains branches leading to the undesirable state St_{goal_1} in C_1, (2) $subG(C_2)$ contains branches leading to the undesirable state St_{goal_2} in C_2, and (3) Sub-graph $subG(C_3)$ contains branches leading to the undesirable state St_{goal_3} in C_3. In real, obtained branches show the chain of system components that acted to give goal states. This helps in $SGrid$ to identify the set of components that are possibly acting incorrectly. The sub-graph $subG(C_1)$ is depicted in Fig. 8.

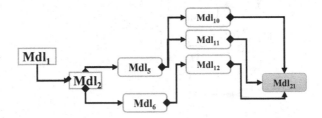

Fig. 8. Backward reachability graph of St_{goal_1}: $subG(C_1)$.

After computing sub-graph $subG(C_1)$, we use Mu method (Subsect. 2.4) to compute other subgraphs from the already computed one $subG(C_1)$. Sub-graphs $subG(C_2)$ and $subG(C_3)$ are depicted in Figs. 9, 10.

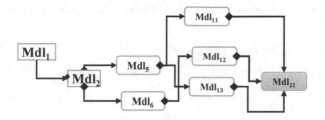

Fig. 9. Backward reachability graph of St_{goal_2}: $subG(C_2)$.

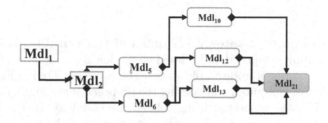

Fig. 10. Backward reachability graph of St_{goal_3}: $subG(C_3)$.

The advantage of using backward reachability, is that it focuses on explaining the appearance of an undesirable behavior i.e., other behavior of system is not included in the verification. By using the proposed methodology, we were able to successfully apply backward reachability analysis for the studied reconfigurable system $SGrid$ using R-TNCESs formalism.

4.2   Performance Evaluation

In this section, we first study results obtained for the same case study using different methodologies. Then, we study the evaluation in large scale systems using different factors. Finally, we summarize in a comparison table limits and benefits of the proposed method and previous related ones.

Comparison with Related Works Methods. For the same system $SGrid$, we apply our proposed methodology, and methodologies proposed in related works, then, we compare obtained results.

We notice that the total number of computed states is almost the half in current methodology compared to previous ones. Backward reachability helped to identify only critical scenarios and their related states rather than all possible system's behavior. And Mu method helps to improve the generation of the system's states space without computations redundancies. This can serve the verification of reconfigurable systems such as $SGrid$ with complex behavior using less time and memory.

Table 6. Number of states with the proposed methodology VS related methodologies.

Configuration	Number of states		
	Related work 1 [31]	Related work 2 [14]	Current work
C_1	25	25	8
C_2	24	1	8
C_3	24	5	8
Total	73	31	24

Number of Computed States VS Number of Undesirable States. In this subsection, we apply proposed and related methodologies in a large scale system using different number of undesirable states. The curve depicted in Fig. 11 shows that the number of computed states using the proposed methodology is less than the number of states generated using related methodology. In the best cases, backward reachability generates less states starting from the undesirable states to the source (possible initial marking), however, forward methods generate all possible branches with all possible initial markings.

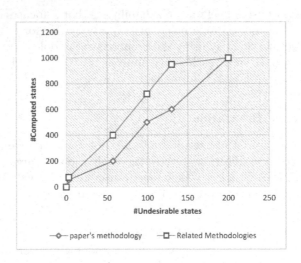

Fig. 11. Computed states VS undesirable states [13].

5   Conclusion

The paper's work deals with the backward reachability of reconfigurable systems and its application on smart electrical grids verification. The proposed method allows the applicability of backward reachability methods on reconfigurable systems modeled by R-TNCESs. The suggested methodology allows to compute backward reachability graphs using improvement methods that reduce repetitive computations.

The application of the proposed methodology in a real case study which is a smart grid network has displayed how backward reachability analysis becomes possible using R-TNCESs. The performance evaluation has shown that the proposed methodology for RDECSs improved verification for large scale systems.

Perspectives of this research work includes: (1) considering the application of model-based diagnosis (2) comparison with other different formalisms, (3) consideration of probabilistic constraints in computing branches, and (4) including the proposed improvement method in a tool in order to automatize it and profit from its gain.

References

1. Aissa, Y.B., Bachir, A., Khalgui, M., Koubaa, A., Li, Z., Qu, T.: On feasibility of multichannel reconfigurable wireless sensor networks under real-time and energy constraints. IEEE Trans. Syst. Man Cybern. Syst. (2019)
2. Aissa, Y.B., Mosbahi, O., Khalgui, M., Bachir, A.: New scheduling mechanism in multi-channel reconfigurable WSN under QoS and energy constraints. In: 32nd Annual European Simulation and Modelling Conference 2018, pp. 187–191 (2018)
3. Anglano, C., Portinale, L.: B-W analysis: a backward reachability analysis for diagnostic problem solving suitable to parallel implementation. In: Valette, R. (ed.) ICATPN 1994. LNCS, vol. 815, pp. 39–58. Springer, Heidelberg (1994). https://doi.org/10.1007/3-540-58152-9_4
4. Baier, C., Katoen, J., Larsen, K.: Principles of Model Checking. MIT Press, Cambridge (2008)
5. Bennoui, H., Chaoui, A., Barkaoui, K.: Distributed causal model-based diagnosis based on interacting behavioral Petri nets, pp. 99–106 (2009)
6. Berghout, Y.M., Bennoui, H.: Distributed diagnosis based on distributed probability propagation nets. Int. J. Comput. Sci. Eng. $18(1)$, 72–79 (2019)
7. Bhandari, G.P., Gupta, R., Upadhyay, S.K.: Colored Petri nets based fault diagnosis in service oriented architecture. Int. J. Web Serv. Res. (IJWSR) $15(4)$, 1–28 (2018)
8. Cong, X., Fanti, M.P., Mangini, A.M., Li, Z.: Decentralized diagnosis by Petri nets and integer linear programming. IEEE Trans. Syst. Man Cybern. Syst. (2017). https://doi.org/10.1109/TSMC.2017.2726108
9. De Kleer, J., Kurien, J.: Fundamentals of model-based diagnosis. IFAC Proc. Vol. $36(5)$, 25–36 (2003)
10. Dubinin, V., Vyatkin, V., Hanisch, H.M.: Synthesis of safety controllers for distributed automation systems on the basis of reverse safe net condition/event systems. In: Proceedings of the Trustcom/BigDataSE/ISPA, vol. 3, pp. 287–292. IEEE (2015)
11. Gharsellaoui, H., Gharbi, A., Khalgui, M., Ahmed, S.B.: Feasible automatic reconfigurations of real-time OS tasks. In: Handbook of Research on Industrial Informatics and Manufacturing Intelligence: Innovations and Solutions, pp. 390–414. IGI Global (2012)
12. Ghribi, I., Abdallah, R.B., Khalgui, M., Li, Z., Alnowibet, K., Platzner, M.: R-codesign: codesign methodology for real-time reconfigurable embedded systems under energy constraints. IEEE Access 6, 14078–14092 (2018)

13. Hafidi, Y., Kahloul., L., Khalgui., M.: New methodology for backward analysis of reconfigurable event control systems using R-TNCESs. In: Proceedings of the 14th International Conference on Software Technologies - Volume 1: ICSOFT, pp. 129–140. INSTICC, SciTePress (2019). https://doi.org/10.5220/0007979901290140

14. Hafidi, Y., Kahloul, L., Khalgui, M., Li, Z., Alnowibet, K., Qu, T.: On methodology for the verification of reconfigurable timed net condition/event systems. IEEE Trans. Syst. Man Cybern. Syst. (99), 1–15 (2018)

15. Hafidi., Y., Kahloul., L., Khalgui., M., Ramdani., M.: On improved verification of reconfigurable real-time systems. In: Proceedings of the 14th International Conference on Evaluation of Novel Approaches to Software Engineering - Volume 1: ENASE, pp. 394–401. INSTICC, SciTePress (2019). https://doi.org/10.5220/0007736603940401

16. Hamscher, W., Console, L., de Kleer, J. (eds.): Readings in Model-based Diagnosis. Morgan Kaufmann Publishers Inc., San Francisco (1992)

17. Khalgui, M., Mosbahi, O., Li, Z., Hanisch, H.M.: Reconfigurable multiagent embedded control systems: from modeling to implementation. IEEE Trans. Comput. **60**(4), 538–551 (2011)

18. Khalgui, M., Rebeuf, X., Simonot-Lion, F.: A behavior model for IEC 61499 function blocks. In: Proceedings of the 3rd Workshop on Modelling of Objects, Components, and Agents, pp. 71–88 (2004)

19. Khawla, B., Molnár, B.: An FSM approach for hypergraph extraction based on business process modeling. In: Demigha, O., Djamaa, B., Amamra, A. (eds.) CSA 2018. LNNS, vol. 50, pp. 158–168. Springer, Cham (2019). https://doi.org/10.1007/978-3-319-98352-3_17

20. Lakhdhar, W., Mzid, R., Khalgui, M., Li, Z., Frey, G., Al-Ahmari, A.: Multiobjective optimization approach for a portable development of reconfigurable real-time systems: from specification to implementation. IEEE Trans. Syst. Man Cybern. Syst. (2018)

21. Leveson, N.G., Stolzy, J.L.: Analyzing safety and fault tolerance using Time Petri nets. In: Ehrig, H., Floyd, C., Nivat, M., Thatcher, J. (eds.) TAPSOFT 1985. LNCS, vol. 186, pp. 339–355. Springer, Heidelberg (1985). https://doi.org/10.1007/3-540-15199-0_22

22. Liu, B., Ghazel, M., Toguyéni, A.: Model-based diagnosis of multi-track level crossing plants. IEEE Trans. Intell. Transp. Syst. **17**(2), 546–556 (2016)

23. Murata, T.: Petri nets: properties, analysis and applications. Proc. IEEE **77**(4), 541–580 (1989)

24. Naidji, I., Smida, M.B., Khalgui, M., Bachir, A.: Non cooperative game theoretic approach for residential energy management in smart grid. In: The 32nd Annual European Simulation and Modelling Conference, Ghent, Belgium, pp. 164–170 (2018)

25. Pózna, A.I., Gerzson, M., Leitold, A., Hangos, K.: Colored Petri net based diagnosis of process systems (2016)

26. Qin, M., Li, Z., Zhou, M., Khalgui, M., Mosbahi, O.: Deadlock prevention for a class of Petri nets with uncontrollable and unobservable transitions. IEEE Trans. Syst. Man Cybern. Part Syst. Hum. **42**(3), 727–738 (2012)

27. Ramdani, M., Kahloul, L., Khalgui, M.: Automatic properties classification approach for guiding the verification of complex reconfigurable systems. In: Proceedings of the 13th International Conference on Software Technologies - Volume 1: ICSOFT, pp. 591–598. INSTICC, SciTePress (2018). https://doi.org/10.5220/0006863005910598

28. Ramdani., M., Kahloul., L., Khalgui., M., Hafidi., Y.: R-TNCES rebuilding: A new method of CTL model update for reconfigurable systems. In: Proceedings of the 14th International Conference on Evaluation of Novel Approaches to Software Engineering - Volume 1: ENASE, pp. 159–168. INSTICC, SciTePress (2019). https://doi.org/10.5220/0007736801590168

29. Wang, X., Khalgui, M., Li, Z.: Dynamic low power reconfigurations of real-time embedded systems. In: PECCS, pp. 415–420 (2011)

30. Zhang, J., Frey, G., Al-Ahmari, A., Qu, T., Wu, N., Li, Z.: Analysis and control of dynamic reconfiguration processes of manufacturing systems. IEEE Access **6**, 28028–28040 (2017)

31. Zhang, J., Khalgui, M., Li, Z., Mosbahi, O., Al-Ahmari, A.: R-TNCES: a novel formalism for reconfigurable discrete event control systems. IEEE Trans. Syst. Man Cybern. Syst. **43**(4), 757–772 (2013)

32. Zhang, S., Wu, N., Li, Z., Qu, T., Li, C.: Petri net-based approach to short-term scheduling of crude oil operations with less tank requirement. Inf. Sci. **417**, 247–261 (2017)

33. Ziouche, L., Meskina, S.B., Khalgui, M., Kahloul, L., Li, Z.: Smart grid rebuilding based on cloud computing architecture. In: 2019 IEEE International Conference on Systems, Man and Cybernetics (SMC), pp. 2259–2266. IEEE (2019)

Software Systems and Applications

GA-PPI-Net: A Genetic Algorithm for Community Detection in Protein-Protein Interaction Networks

Marwa Ben M'barek[1,2($\boxtimes$)] (iD), Amel Borgi[1,3], Sana Ben Hmida[2] (iD), and Marta Rukoz[2]

[1] LIPAH, Faculté des Sciences de Tunis, Université de Tunis El Manar, 2092 Tunis, Tunisia
marwa.benmbarek@fst.utm.tn
[2] LAMSADE CNRS UMR 7243, Paris Dauphine University, PSL Research University, Place du Maréchal de Lattre de Tassigny, Paris, France
marwa.ben-mbarek@dauphine.eu, sana.mrabet@dauphine.psl.eu, marta.rukoz@lamsade.dauphine.fr
[3] Institut Supérieur d'Informatique, Université de Tunis El Manar, 1002 Tunis, Tunisia
Amel.Borgi@insat.rnu.tn

Abstract. Community detection has become an important research direction for data mining in complex networks. It aims to identify topological structures and discover patterns in complex networks, which presents an important problem of great significance. In this paper, we are interested in the detection of communities in the Protein-Protein or Gene-gene Interaction (PPI) networks. These networks represent a set of proteins or genes that collaborate at the same cellular function. The goal is to identify such semantic and topological communities from gene annotation sources such as Gene Ontology. We propose a Genetic Algorithm (GA) based approach to detect communities having different sizes from PPI networks. For this purpose, we introduce three specific components to the GA: a fitness function based on a similarity measure and the interaction value between proteins or genes, a solution for representing a community with dynamic size and a specific mutation operator. In the computational tests carried out in this work, the introduced algorithm achieved excellent results to detect existing or even new communities from PPI networks.

Keywords: Community detection · Genetic algorithm Protein-Protein or gene-gene interaction networks · Semantic Similarity · Gene Ontology

1 Introduction

Diverse kinds of networks such as the computer network, the biological network, the power system network and the social media network have emerged and are changing our daily life with the development of science and technology [7]. Network becomes the engine of scientific research activities in the 21st century, and the active topic across disciplines. Many real-world networks are rather complex, characterised by big data volume, dynamics, interactivity and heterogeneity [7]. In recent years, one of the outstanding property of networks, i.e., the community [12], has become a hot research topic of modern network science. Community detection is one of the theoretical underpinnings of network science, social science, physical science, biological science, etc. It

© Springer Nature Switzerland AG 2020
M. van Sinderen and L. A. Maciaszek (Eds.): ICSOFT 2019, CCIS 1250, pp. 133–155, 2020.
https://doi.org/10.1007/978-3-030-52991-8_7

can yield useful insights into the structural organization of a network and can serve as a basis for understanding the correspondence between structure and function (specific to the domain of the network). Identifying the community allows us to obtain some important information about the relationship and interaction among nodes.

In this paper, we are interested in detecting communities in biological networks. Biological networks have been observed to be highly modular where a tightly connected group of genes (nodes) are involved in similar biological functions. These groups are referred to as communities, modules, or clusters. Communities detected from biological networks are usually responsible for a common phenotype and are useful in providing insights pertaining to biological functionality. Community detection methods play a crucial role in obtaining these functional modules [52]. Biological networks, such as Protein–Protein interaction networks, gene regulatory networks, gene co-expression networks, metabolic networks and signaling networks provide a mathematical representation of biological systems. In this work, we mainly focus on Protein-Protein or Gene-Gene interaction networks known as PPI networks. Their nodes correspond to proteins or genes and the edges correspond to pairwise interactions between genes or proteins. These communities give us an idea about the perception of the network's structure. The ultimate goal in biology is to determine how genes or proteins encode function in the cell.

This work is multidisciplinary as it brings the field of biology and computer science in the broad sense. Thus, the goal is to find communities having a biological sense (that participate in the same biological processes or that perform together specific biological functions) from gene annotation sources. To achieve this task, we have combined three levels of information:

1. Semantic level: information contained in biological ontologies such as Gene Ontology GO [2] and information obtained by the use of a similarity measure such as GS2 [40], it assesses the semantic similarity between proteins or genes;
2. Functional level: information contained in public databases describing the interactions of proteins or genes such as Search Tool for Recurring Instances of Neighbouring Gene (STRING) database [24];
3. Networks level: information contained in pathway databases that present community of proteins or genes such as KEGG database [19].

The performed tests in [16], revealed that genes or proteins in the same community of the biological pathway database KEGG are semantically similar and are interacting. From this affirmation, we have proposed to take into account the similarity between proteins or genes that are annotated by terms of Gene Ontology (GO). In a previous work, we have tested different similarity measures to determine the most suitable one for this problem that is GS2 [5].

Community detection sheds light on the functionalities of complex networks. Thus far, a large number of community detection methods have been proposed in the literature [7]. Meanwhile, various methods based on the evolutionary algorithms (EAs) have been proposed. EAs are a class of artificial intelligent optimisation metaheuristics inspired by biological evolution, such as reproduction, mutation, recombination, and selection. These metaheuristics are notable for their good local learning and global searching abilities and have been developed for successfully solving a wide range of optimisation problems. The EAs based mining methods can automatically determine the clusters of the complex networks which makes it very convenient for practical applications. The essence of the EAs based community detection methods is to first model the network community detection task as different optimisation problems and then design suitable metaheuristics to deal with them. EA based algorithms are found to solve diverse kind of complex optimisation problems and are used to overcome some drawbacks such as scaling up of network size. Indeed some of the community detection algorithms are unsuitable for very large networks and require a priori knowledge about the community structure, as the number and the size of communities which is not easy or impossible to obtain in real-world networks [48]. The vast majority of optimization methods proposed to detect communities in PPI networks use only graph topology and do not use similarity measures between proteins or genes [36].

This paper presents a new community detection algorithm in PPI networks based on Genetic Algorithm (GA). This work is an extension of a previous method [6]. Therefore, we propose a GA based approach that allows to find communities of proteins or genes. Alike the previous algorithm, the proposed method uses the similarity measures between proteins or genes and tries to find the best community by maximizing the concept of community measure. This measure is based on semantic similarity and interaction between proteins or genes. Moreover, we propose a new specific mutation operator adapted to our problem. The algorithm outputs the final proteins/genes community by selectively exploring the search space. Experiments on real datasets show the ability of the proposed approach to correctly detect communities having different sizes.

This paper is organized as follows. The next section provides the background of literature survey to community's detection methods. Section 3 defines the problem of community detection in PPI networks. Section 4 describes the biological field and the data used to formalize the problem. Section 5 depicts our proposed algorithm for community detection. In Sect. 6, experimental results on real data sets are presented and analyzed. Finally, Sect. 7 draws the conclusion and the future works.

2 Network Community Detection Related Works

Network community detection has an important role in the networked data mining field. Community detection helps to discover latent patterns in networked data and it affects the ultimate knowledge presentation [7]. The task for network community detection is to divide the whole network into small parts or groups which are also called communities. There is no uniform definition for community in the literature, but in academic domain, a community (also called a cluster or a module) is a group of nodes that are connected densely inside the group but connected sparely with the rest of the network. Radicchi et al. [38] propose two definitions of community. These definitions are based on the degree of a node (or valency)[1]. In the first definition, a community is a subgraph in a strong sense: each node has more connections within the community than the rest of the graph. In the second definition, a community is a subgraph in a weak sense: the sum of all incident edges in a node is greater than the sum of the out edges.

The problem of community detection has been receiving a lot of attention, in recent years, and many different approaches have been proposed. The literature survey is

---

[1] The degree of a node is the number of edges incident to the node.

divided into two categories: community detection based on analytical approaches and those based on evolutionary approaches [32].

Analytical methods firstly split networks into subgroups according to their topological characteristics, then the modularity assessment is carried out. The modularity is defined as the fraction of edges inside communities minus the expected value of the fraction of edges, if edges fall at random without regard to the community structure. Values of modularity approaching 1 indicate strong community structure. A well known algorithm in this category is the one presented by Girvan and Newman [12, 27]. It is a divisive hierarchical clustering method based on an iterative removal of edges from the network. The edge removal splits the network in communities. The removed edges are chosen by using betweenness measures (that represents the number of shortest paths between all vertex pairs that run along the edge). The idea underlying the edge betweenness comes from the observation that if two communities are joined by a few inter-community edges, then all the paths from vertices in one community to vertices in the must pass through these edges. Paths determine the betweenness score to compute for the edges. By counting all the paths passing through each edge, and removing the edge scoring the maximum value, the connections inside the network are broken. This process is repeated, thus dividing the network into smaller components until a stop criterion is reached. The criterion adopted to stop the division is the modularity. Newman in [26] presents an agglomerative hierarchical algorithm that optimizes the concept of modularity. Thus the algorithm computes the modularity of all the clusters obtained by applying the hierarchical approach, and returns as result the clusters having the highest value of modularity [26].

Analytical algorithms do not reach the expected successful results in community detection from complex networks. Therefore, various evolutionary based algorithms have been proposed to provide different approaches to solve the community detection problem [3]. Many community evaluation criteria have been proposed and quantities of methods that combine either single objective or multiobjective EAs with community detection have emerged. Most if not all of these methods share the common feature that they model the community detection problem as an optimization problem to solve them [7]. The single objective methods optimize a single property, while the multiobjective approaches simultaneously optimize competing objectives. The most popular single evaluation criterion is the modularity proposed by Newman and Girvan [27]. Since 2002, several methods that divide networks into clusters according to the modularity criterion have been developed [3]. The authors presented in [47] and [23] an approach based on a GA to optimize the network modularity introduced by Newman and Girvan [12]. However, some studies have indicated that the optimization of modularity has several drawbacks [7]. First, it has the resolution limitation, i.e., maximising the modularity can fail in finding communities smaller than a fixed scale, even if these communities are well defined. The scale depends on the total size of the network and the interconnection degree of the communities [11]. Second, maximizing the modularity is proved to be NP-hard [7]. These drawbacks can constitute a weakness for all those methods whose objective is to optimize the modularity. To avoid the resolution limitation of modularity, many multi-resolution models have been developped [7]. Pizzuti [33] has proposed an algorithm named GA-Net and has used a special assessment function called community score. This community score takes one parameter r which is hard to tune because higher values of r help to detect communities and low values of this paramter return no communities. A modification of the modularity has been proposed in [21] with the concept of modularity density. The authors prove that modularity density has a number of advantages with respect to modularity, such as detecting communities of different sizes.

Single objective optimization identifies a single best solution that gives insights on the graph organization. However, this solution could be biased toward a particular structure inherent inside the criterion to optimize [7]. These methods have obtained very good results on both artificial and real-world networks [32]. The intuitive notion of community that the number of edges inside a community should be much higher than the number of edges connecting to the remaining nodes of the graph, has two different objectives: 1) maximizing the internal connection links and 2) minimizing the external connection links [32]. Thus, on the basis of these objectives, many multi-objective community models are established. The first proposal framework to uncover community structure has been presented by Pizzuti [34,35]. In particular, the method introduce two objectives: maximizes the community score proposed by [33] and minimizes the community fitness put forward by [20]. Then, the fast elitist non-dominated sorting genetic algorithm (NSGA-II) proposed in [10] has been applied. A variation of this method has been proposed by Agrawal [1]. The objectives to minimize are the modularity proposed by Newman and Girvan [26] and the community score proposed by Pizzuti [33]. Surveys on the selection of objective functions in multiobjective community detection can be found in Shi et al. [43,44].

Multi-objective evolutionary approaches, like the single objective ones, are able to discover community structures of quality comparable with, or even better than, those obtained by analytical methods. Optimizing multiple objectives allows a simultaneous evaluation of community structure from different perspectives, then it is the user's responsibility to choose a solution [7]. The choice of the objectives to optimize should take into account the suggestions given by Shi et al. [45], where a comparison of several objective functions in a multi-objective framework has been performed [32].

The use of evolutionary methods for community detection presents a number of advantages [32]:

- During the search process, the communities' number is generated automatically.
- Domain-specific knowledge can be incorporated inside the method, such as biased initialization, or specific variation operators instead of random, allowing a more effective exploration of the state space of possible solutions.
- The efficient implementations of population-based models can be realized to deal with large size networks.

Most evolutionary approaches to detect communities have been applied in social networks and use only graphical topology and no semantic similarity between nodes. [36]. In this paper we propose a new approach based on GA to detect semantic and topological communities in biological networks. This new algorithm tries to find the best community of proteins or genes by maximizing the concept of community measure. This measure is based on the graph topology (interaction) and the semantic similarity between nodes.

3 Problem Definition

A PPI network is modelled as a graph $G = (V, E)$ where V is a set of objects, called nodes or vertices, and E is a set of links, called edges, that connect two elements of V. Communities are groups of nodes (i.e. proteins or genes) that are more connected to each other than to any node else in a network. Often these groups of nodes correspond to a common process, purpose, or function. Therefore, it is reasonable to hypothesize that determining communities on biological networks may shed new light on groupings of genes with common biological function or features [50]. In this work, we explain a community C as a group of genes or proteins that are semantically similar and interact with each other. A set of genes $C = G_1, G_2, ..., G_n$ is a community if it checks the following propriety:

$$\forall\, G_i, G_j \in C, i \neq j,\ Sim(G_i, G_j) \geq \nabla_S\ or/and\ Interaction(G_i, G_j) \geq \nabla_I \quad (1)$$

where:

- Each gene G can be annotated with a set of GO (Gene Ontology) terms [8]. We use TP to denote the set of GO terms that annotate a gene G. More formally, the set of annotations of a gene G is:

$$A(G) = \{TP/TP \in GO\ and\ TP\ annotates\ the\ Gene\ G\} \quad (2)$$

- $Sim(G_i, G_j)$: the similarity value between two genes G_i and G_j. To calculate the similarity between two genes, we need to use a measure allowing to compare sets of terms that annotate these genes thus we can quantify the similarity between these sets. In this work, we use the semantic similarity measure GS2 (GO-based similarity of gene sets) [40]. This measure averages the similarity contributed by each gene in C. Each gene is compared with the remaining set of genes by calculating how closely that gene follows the functionality distribution of the remaining genes. The functionality distribution is represented by the distribution of ancestor GO terms for each gene [40].
- Interaction (G_i, G_j): the score of interaction between two genes extracted from STRING Database [24]. This score explains the protein-protein or the gene-gene associations known and predicted according to different criteria in a bibliographic reference.
- ∇_S and ∇_I are two thresholds. They are defined for both the semantic and the interaction criteria respectively. Their values are fixed according to the recommendations of our biological expert.

4 Used Data

To understand this work, we define some terms that are important for our discussion:

- A biological network is a multiple biological pathways interacting with each other, example of biological networks: PPI networks [25].

- Protein-Protein interaction (PPI) networks are commonly modeled via graphs, whose nodes represent proteins and whose edges, that are undirected and possibly weighted, connect pairs of interacting proteins. They are essential to almost every process in a cell, so understanding PPIs is crucial for understanding cell physiology in normal and disease states. It is also essential in drug development, since drugs can affect PPIs. PPI networks are mathematical representations of the physical contacts between proteins in the cell [28].
- A biological pathway is a series of actions among molecules in a cell that leads to a certain product or a change in the cell [25]. There are many types of biological pathways such as metabolic pathways or Gene-regulation pathways.

For more details of PPI network's structure, we have combined three information's levels: semantic level, functional level and network level. We describe below the used data recovered from different sources for these three levels.

4.1 Semantic Level: Gene Information

GO Vocabulary Structure

An ontology is a formal representation of a body of knowledge within a given domain. Ontologies usually consist of a set of classes (or terms or concepts) with relations that operate between them. The GO describes the knowledge of the biological and biomedical domain with respect to three aspects [53]:

- Cellular Component (CC): the parts of a cell or its extracellular environment;
- Molecular Function (MF): the elemental activities of a gene product at the molecular level, such as binding or catalysis;
- Biological Process (BP): operations or sets of molecular events with a defined beginning and end, pertinent to the functioning of integrated living units: cells, tissues, organs, and organisms.

The GO ontology is structured as a directed acyclic graph, where each GO term is a node, and the relationships between the terms are edges between the nodes. GO is loosely hierarchical, with 'child' terms being more specialized than their 'parent' terms, but unlike a strict hierarchy, a term may have more than one parent term. Each GO term within the ontology has a term name (which may be a word or string of words), a unique alphanumeric identifier (which start by GO:), a definition with cited sources, and a namespace indicating the domain to which it belongs. Terms may also have synonyms (which are classed as being exactly equivalent to the term name, broader, narrower, or related), references to equivalent concepts in other databases, and comments on term meaning or usage. The three GO aspects (cellular component, biological process, and molecular function) are disjoint, meaning that is not relations operate between terms from the different ontologies. Hence GO is three ontologies. In this work, we focus on the BP aspects. To obtain data of this aspect, we precisely focus on the relationship "is-a" and "part of" in order to identify the inheritance relationship between GO terms. From this source, we have extracted the unique identifier and the name of all the terms related to the BP aspect.

Gene Ontology Annotation GOA

A GO annotation represents a link between a gene product type and a molecular function, biological process, or cellular component type (a link, in other words, between the gene product and what that product is capable of doing, what biological processes it contributes to, and where in the cell it is capable of functioning in the natural life of an organism) [17]. From this database, we get a set of GO annotation for each gene of BP aspect. For example, the MEIKIN gene is annotated by the following GO terms' sets: "GO: 0007060", "GO: 0010789", "GO: 0016321", "GO: 0045143", "GO: 0051754".

Semantic Similarity

The authors state, in [16], that genes of the same community are semantically similar and interact with each other. From this assertion, we supposed that genes belonging to the same community are similar and tried to find the best similarity measure between genes. A gene can be annotated with various GO terms. To determine the similarity between two genes, we need to use an approach allowing to compare sets of terms that annotate these genes. Thus, we can quantify the similarity between these sets. Several methods of determining semantic measures have been proposed in the last few decade. There are three main approaches for measuring semantic similarity between the objects of an ontology [39,49]. The first family' approaches is node-based approaches: the main data sources are the nodes and their properties. One concept commonly used in these approaches is information content, which measures how specific and informative a term is. The most popular node-based approaches are Resnik's [39], Lin's [22], Rel's [41] and Jiang and Conrath's [18] methods. They were originally developed for the WorldNet, and then applied to GO [30]. The second family of approaches is edge-based approaches: they are based mainly on counting the number of edges in the graph path between any two terms. The most common technique selects either the shortest path or the average of all paths when more than one path exists (Wu and Palmer, 1994). Among this family of approaches, there is the method of Rada [37] and the one of Wu and Palmer [51]. The third family of approaches are hybrid ones:

1. Wang and al. [49] developed an hybrid measure in which each edge is given a weight according to the type of relationship. For a given term c_1 and its ancestor c_a , the authors define the semantic contribution of c_a to c_1, as the product of all edge weights in the "best" path from c_a to c_1, where the "best" path is the one that maximizes the product. Semantic similarity between two terms is then calculated by summing the semantic contributions of all common ancestors to each of the terms and dividing by the total semantic contribution of each term's ancestors to that term.
2. Ruths and al. [40] proposed GS2 (GO-based similarity of gene sets), a novel GO-based measure of genes set similarity. The measure quantifies the similarity of the GO annotations among a set of genes by averaging the contribution of each all gene's GO terms and their ancestor terms with respect to the GO vocabulary graph.

In order to choose the adequate measure of similarity, we have performed several tests [5]. The best results were obtained with the GS2 measure. In the remainder of our work, we use the measure GS2 to characterize the similarity between genes.

4.2 Functional Level: Interaction Between Genes

We use the STRING (Search Tool for the Retrieval of Interacting Genes/Proteins) database in order to study the interaction between genes. This database is a biological database and web resource of known and predicted protein-protein or gene-gene interactions. It contains information from several sources, including experimental data, computational prediction methods and public text collections. It is freely accessible and it is regularly updated [24,46]. From this database, we extract the couples of genes or proteins that are interacting, the mode of interaction between these couple of genes and the interaction value which defines the number of citations of this interaction in the literature. This value is scaled between zero and one. It indicates the estimated likelihood that a given interaction is biologically meaningful, specific and reproducible, given the supporting evidence [24].

4.3 Network Level: Biological Pathways Databases

Among the various biological pathways databases, we cite those that we have used.

Reactome: is a free online database of human biological pathways and processes. The basic unit used to describe the data is the reaction [9].

Biocarta: catalogues community of several species. It makes it possible to visualize, construct or identify the networks mapping the known genomic and proteomic relationships. It offers a synthesis of these paths and represents them by graphs [29].

Ec number (Enzyme Commission Number): is a numerical classification scheme for enzymes (proteins that act as biological catalysts), based on the chemical reactions they catalyze. The chemical reaction catalyzed is the specific property that distinguishes one enzyme from another. It specify enzyme-catalysed reactions [15].

BBID (Biological Biochemical Image Database): is a WWW accessible relational database of archived image from different article that describe regulatory pathways. Pathway information is annoted and can be queried [4].

KEGG (Kyoto Encyclopedia of Genes and Genomes): is a knowledge base for systematic analysis of gene functions, linking genomic information with higher order functional information. The genomic information is stored in the GENES database, which is a collection of gene catalogs for all the completely sequenced genomes and some partial genomes with up-to-date annotation of gene functions [19].

The biological pathway database used to test the proposed approach is KEGG as it was the one proposed by our biology expert. In this database, we focused on the biological pathway which represent the communities name and the genes related to a community. The other biological pathway databases are used to validate the experimental results as explained in Sect. 6.

4.4   The Used Data' Summary

Based on what has been illustrated from Sect. 4.1 to Sect. 4.3, the used data is summarized as:

– A gene or protein is described by an ID, a name and a set of terms that annotate it. For example, the UBC gene is presented as follows: ID: 728637, NAME: UBC, Annoted terms: [GO:0000082, GO:0000086, GO:0000122, GO: 0000165, GO:0000186, GO:0000187, GO:0000209, GO:0000278, GO:0000423, GO:0000715, GO:0000724, GO:0002223, GO:0002224, GO:0002474, GO:0002479, GO:0002755, GO:0002756, GO:0005975, GO:0005978, GO:0006006, GO:0006281, GO:0006283, GO:0006289, GO:0006297, GO:0006302, GO:0006351, GO:0006367, GO:0006915, GO:0006977, GO:0007166, GO:0007173, GO:0007 179, GO:0019985].
– Data related to the interaction between two genes. For example, the interaction between the UBC gene and the PIK3R1 gene is: NameGene1: "UBC", NameGene2: "PIK3R1", Interaction: "Binding", Interaction Score: 0.57.
– The biological pathway is described by a community name and a set of genes. These data are extracted from different pathway databases presented in subsection 4.3.
– The semantic similarity value computed by the GS2 method.

Figure 1 summarizes the sources of these extracted data. The first goal is to obtain information about a gene. Therefore, we get a set of GO terms of BP aspect that identify such gene from GO and GOA. Then, we acquire the interaction between couple of genes from STRING database.

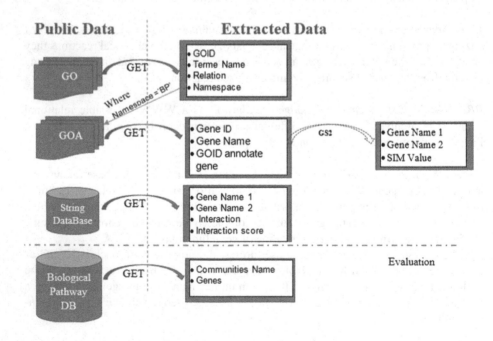

Fig. 1. A summary of used data [5].

5 Proposed Approach

GAs have proved to be competitive alternative methods to traditional optimization and search techniques and they have been applied to solve different classes of problems in diverse research and application areas such as planning and scheduling, machine learning, neural nets evolution and pattern recognition [13] and [31]. Thus, they are also suitable for solving the community detection problem. In this section, we describe the genetic algorithm used in this work as well as the genetic representation and operators. GA evolves a population of individuals that are candidate solutions to the problem. At each generation, fittest solutions are selected for the reproduction step. In our approach, an individual is a set of proteins or genes that form a community. In our approach, an individual is a set of proteins or genes that form a community. To evaluate a solution, we propose a fitness function based on a community measure. The performed tests in [16] revealed that genes or proteins in the same community of the biological pathway database KEGG are semantically similar and are interacting. Thus, the community measure uses the similarity value and the interaction score of every pair of genes making up the solution. Moreover, we modify the steps of GA to satisfy the needs of our algorithm. Thus, we propose a new specific mutation operator and insert some additional steps during the population initialization. The detected communities have different sizes. The algorithm works as follows:

Algorithm 1. GA-PPINet: General Algorithm.

Require: algorithm parameters, problem instance
Ensure: best solution to the optimisation problem
    Begin
 1: Initialize population
 2: Evaluate the initial population
 3: **for** $i = 1$ to max_iteration **do**
 4:    Select parents for mating
 5:    **for** each pair of candidates in the set of parents **do**
 6:        generate an offspring through genetic operator - crossover and mutation - with respectively a probability pc and pm
 7:        evaluate the fitness of the offspring
 8:        Replace the worst existing individual in the population by the obtained offspring
 9:    **end for**
10: **end for**
    End

The steps of the proposed GA are presented in the following subsections.

5.1 Genetic Representation

A solution to our problem, corresponding to an individual in GA terms, is a community of proteins or genes. It is represented by a vector T. In this representation, each individual S stores: the size n of the individual (the community) that is the number of proteins or genes in the community, the average value of similarity denoted *AVGSim* (Eq. 3), the average interaction value denoted *AVGInteraction* (Eq. 4) of each two genes or proteins and the list of the n components. Each component (gene or protein) is designed by its name. Figure 2 illustrates the representation of an individual adopted in our algorithm.

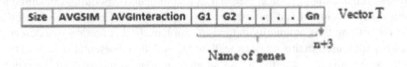

Fig. 2. Example of individual representation designing a community [6].

The similarity average *AVGSim* and the interaction average *AVGInteraction* of a community solution S are computed using respectively the Eqs. 3 and 4.

$$AVGSim(S) = \sum_{i,j \in [1,n],\ i \neq j} SIM_{GS2}(G_i, G_j)/n \tag{3}$$

$$AVGInteraction(S) = \sum_{i,j \in [1,n],\ i \neq j} InteractionValue(G_i, G_j)/n \tag{4}$$

Where:

- G_i and G_j are two different genes in the community S;
- n: the size of the community S;
- $SIM_{GS2}(G_i, G_j)$: the similarity value between two genes in S, it is calculated using the semantic similarity measure GS2 [40];
- $InteractionValue(G_i, G_j)$: the value of an interaction between two genes in S extracted from STRING Database [24].

5.2 Population Initialization

The initialization of the first population in GA (step 1 in the Algorithm 1) is an important step which can affect the quality of the final solution as well as the running time of the algorithm. In this work, we define the population as a two-dimensional array of individuals initialized respecting the following steps. To initialize this population:

- Get randomly a set of communities from the KEGG pathway database and create randomly the population with the recovered genes. The population is composed by individuals having different sizes.
- Compute the similarity value using the GS2 measure and get the interaction score of each two genes of this group from the created "interaction" table.
- Calculate the average similarity value and the average interaction score of each group forming this population.

Figure 3 presents an example of an initial population with five individuals having different sizes.

5	0.553	0.398	PDHA2	MTHFD2L	RAC2	GRHPR	ANAPC1			
8	0.793	0.543	ANAPC5	SOS1	CDC16	AURKA	IL4	ANAPC2	ccNB2	BUB1B
5	0.340	0.410	RFK	HYI	GPI	UBC	IGF1R			
7	0.578	0.687	HSD3878	PFKP	LDHAL6B	FBXW7	ACSM3	MAX		
6	0.632	0.591	ALPP	BPGM	PLK1	HK3	HK1	KEAP1		

Fig. 3. Example of an initial population with five individuals [6].

5.3 Fitness Function

The fitness function (also known as the evaluation function) evaluates the performance of a given solution. It takes as input a candidate solution S to the problem and produces as output how better "fit" the solution is fit with respect to the considered problem. The choice of the fitness function is a critical step for obtaining good solutions. In the context of community detection, the most popular function is modularity, originally introduced by Girvan and Newman [12]. In this work, we don't directly take into account the modularity, nevertheless the topological propriety of a community is taken into account through the interaction score between proteins or genes. Moreover, the fitness function is enriched with semantic information. So, the used fitness function is based on topological and semantic similarity measures. Indeed, we used a defined fitness function based on the computation of the average similarity value and the average interaction score of each two genes existing in the community S. We start from the assertion [16] that genes in the same community S are semantically similar and interact with each other. The fitness function is defined as follows [5]:

$$F(S) = W_1\, AVGSim(S) + W_2\, AVGInteraction(S) \tag{5}$$

With:

- AVGSim and AVGInteraction defined in 3 and 4 respectively.
- W_1 and W_2 : weights$\in [0, 1]$.

5.4 Selection and Replacement

Selection is the stage of a GA in which individual are chosen from a population (step 4 in Algorithm 1) to be parents which mate and recombine to create offspring for the next generation. It is very crucial to the convergence rate of the GA as good parents drives individuals to fitter solutions. The problem is how to select these individuals. In literature, there are many methods to select the best individuals such as roulette wheel selection, tournament selection, rank selection, elitism, etc. [14]. The tournament selection method is used for this work. In K-Way tournament selection, we select K individuals from the population at random and select the best out of these to become a parent. The same process is repeated for selecting the next parent. It is an extremely popular selection method in GA due to its efficiency and simple implementation [14]. Once an offspring is generated, it is inserted into the population respecting the Steady State GA replacement where the new offspring replace the worst solution in the current population.

5.5   Genetic Operators

After the generation of an initial population, a GA carries out the genetic operators to generate offspring based on the initial population. Once a new generation is created, the genetic process is performed iteratively until an optimal result is found or a maximum number of generations is met. Crossover and mutation are two basic operators of GA. The performance of GA depends essentially on them. These operators guide the algorithm towards a solution to a given problem. Their goal is to both exploit the best solutions and explore the search space. For this work, we used the multi-point crossover: it is equivalent to performing two single-point crossovers with different crossover points. Here, two crossover points are picked randomly from the parent where the crossover points do not exceed the longest parent size. Then, the content in between the two points is swapped between the two parents to get two new offsprings. This operator is usually applied with a high probability (pc) [32]. Figure 4 presents a graphical illustration to better understand this kind of crossover. In this example, two crossover points are chosen at random in position 1 and 4. Then two offsprings (ch1, ch2) are generated by exchanging the values of the selected parents (P1, P2).

P1	PDHA2	MTHFD2L	RAC2	GRHPR	ANAPC1			
P2	ANAPC5	SOS1	CDC16	AURKA	IL4	ANAPC2	CCNB2	BUB1B

Ch1	PDHA2	SOS1	CDC16	AURKA	ANAPC1			
Ch2	ANAPC5	MTHFD2L	RAC2	GRHPR	IL4	ANAPC2	CCNB2	BUB1B

Fig. 4. Example of application of the two points crossover operator on two communities [6].

The mutation is an operator used to maintain and introduce genetic diversity insight the population along the evolution. It alters some genes in the individual, promoting the diversification of the population. However, the mutation must not be too destructive and nullify the process of finding an optimal solution [32]. Thus, it is usually applied with a low probability (pm). If the probability is very high, the GA gets reduced to a random search [32].

For GA-PPINet, we propose a specific mutation operator called 'Optimized Community Mutation (OCM)' with two variants: OCM1 (Algorithm 2) and OCM2 (Algorithm 3). These operators can better meet the objectives of our problem. They should allow a better exploration of the search space than the random mutation. Their goal is to maximize the chance of creating a better solution than the original one. These operators can integrate a new gene in order to replace a gene having a poor quality or to enlarge the size of the community.

To mutate a solution S, the two mutation operators alter only one gene at a time and uses a score function, denoted GS, applied to each gene in S. This score (GS) is equal to the sum of the average similarity and the average interaction score of a gene in a community. It helps us to detect the gene having the best score in a community as well as the gene having the worst score. It is defined as follows:

$$AVGSim(G) = \sum_{i=1}^{n-1} Sim_{GS2}(G, G_i)/n - 1 \tag{6}$$

$$AVGInteraction(G) = \sum_{i=1}^{n-1} InteractionValue(G, G_i)/n - 1 \tag{7}$$

$$GS(G) = AVGSim(G) + AVGInteraction(G) \tag{8}$$

Where:

- $G \neq G_i$;
- $Sim_{GS2}(G, G_i)$: The similarity value of a gene G compared to the other genes in the community;
- $InteractionValue(G, G_i)$: The interaction score of a gene G compared to the others in the community;
- n: size of an individual (community).

The first mutation operator *OCM1* is applied according to the following steps [6]:

Algorithm 2. OCM1 algorithm.

1: Select in a solution S a gene having the highest score GS that will be called "bestGene";
2: Randomly search a gene G' from the "interaction" table with which the "bestGene" interacts and $G' \notin S$;
3: Get the gene having the lowest score GS in S, it will be called "worstGene";
4: **if** $GS("worstGene") \leq \theta$ (ie $\theta = 0.5$) **then**
5:     replace the "worstGene" by the gene G' selected in the second step;
6: **else**
7:     insert into the end position of the solution the gene G' selected in the second step and update the size.
8: **end if**

The second operator *OCM2* is applied according to the Algorithm 3. The main goal of OCM1 is to improve the solution quality by replacing the worst gene if it has low interaction/similarity score, or enlarge the community otherwise. OCM2 differs from OCM1 in steps 5 to 8 where the GS score of the new gene is considered for the final decision of the mutation action to apply on S. To better understand the optimized mutation procedure, a graphical illustration is given in Fig. 5.

6 Experimental Results

In this section, we study the effectiveness of our approach on real datasets (Pathways selected from KEGG Pathway database). The GA-PPI-Net algorithm has been written in python, using the inspyred[2] Genetic Algorithms framework. We first carried out tests

---

[2] https://pythonhosted.org/inspyred/.

Algorithm 3. OCM2 algorithm.

1: Select in a solution S a gene having the highest score GS that will be called "bestGene";
2: Randomly search a gene G' from the "interaction" table with which the "bestGene" interacts and $G' \notin S$;
3: Get the gene having the lowest score GS in S, it will be called "worstGene";
4: **if** $GS("worstGene") \leq GS(G')$ and $GS("bestGene") \geq GS(G')$" **then**
5:     replace the "worstGene" by the new gene G';
6: **else if** the score of the $GS("bestGene") < GS(G')$ **then**
7:     insert at the end position of the solution S the gene G' and update the size.
8: **end if**

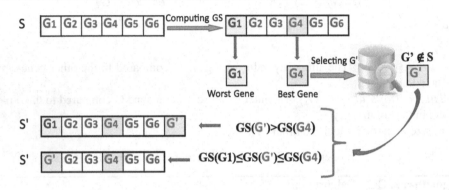

Fig. 5. OCM2 illustration.

to tune the GA parameters. Different parameters values were tested: generation number set at 100, 300 and 500, size of the population set at 10, 20, 30, 70 and 100, crossover rate set at 0.5, 0.6, ...1 and mutation rate set at 0,01, 0.1, 0.2, ..., 0.5. Based on these tests, we choose the combination of the parameters values giving the best results (highest values of fitness function), namely: population size 30, generation number 100, crossover rate 0.8, and mutation rate 0.01. Moreover, a weak value of mutation probability allows to prevent the algorithm to be blocked in a local minimum. Concerning the size of individual in the initial population, we fix it in the range of 5 to 40 [6]. The different values of the fitness function's weights are $W_1 = W_2 = 0.5$ [5].

For the evolutionary methods optimizing the network modularity (Sect. 2), a solution is a community structure of the PPI network. With GA-PPINet, a solution is a potential community in the PPI network with optimized interaction/similarity score. Two optimal solutions might have similar fitness but they are composed with different sets of genes/proteins and have different sizes. In order to check the ability of GA-PPINet to successfully detect communities in a PPI network, we use randomly selected proteins or genes that are present in known communities from the reference pathway database KEGG. More precisely, our approach has been tested with five datasets proposed by our biological expert. In total, we have 595 genes by removing the redundant genes, as described in Table 1. These datasets correspond to real and existing communities and are collected from the KEGG pathway database.

Table 1. The used datasets.

Datasets	Number of genes
Apoptosis[3]	88
B cell receptor signalling pathway[4]	75
Purine metabolism[5]	159
Rna degradation[6]	159
Oocyte meiosis[7]	114
Total	595

[3]https://www.genome.jp/dbget-bin/www_bget?pathway:hsa04210
[4]https://www.genome.jp/dbget-bin/www_bget?pathway:hsa04662
[5]https://www.genome.jp/dbget-bin/www_bget?pathway:hsa00230
[6]https://www.genome.jp/dbget-bin/www_bget?pathway:hsa03018
[7]https://www.genome.jp/dbget-bin/www_bget?pathway:hsa04114

The evaluation consists in verifying how GA-PPINet is likely to find gene or proteins communities existing in the KEGG pathway database. Actually, the tests showed that our approach allowed to detect communities of genes or proteins existing in KEGG database or even new communities having high interaction and high similarity between its genes or proteins and that do not appear in KEGG.

We performed tests to find communities. We run our approach 20 times with proteins or genes chosen randomly from the five proposed datasets showed in Table 1. And, we retained each time the best community. Thus, we have 20 best communities with sizes varying from 5 to 40. Details about the twenty obtained communities are summarized in Table 2. The fitness value varies from 0.43 and 0.84, the AVGInteraction value varies from 0.4 and 0.79 and the AVGSim value varies from 0.5 and 0.89. These results are considered as satisfactory according to the two measures of interaction and similarity. However, for all obtained solutions, the question that arises is how they will be evaluated.

Table 2. Details about sizes and different measures for the best obtained communities over 20 runs.

N°	Size community	AVGSim	AVG interaction	Fitness value	N°	Size community	AVGSim	AVG interaction	Fitness value
1	13	0.64	0.49	0.56	11	8	0.74	0,69	0.72
2	8	0.81	0.77	0.79	12	7	0.56	0.48	0.52
3	15	0.62	0.67	0.65	13	11	0.50	0.40	0.45
4	23	0.52	0.44	0.48	14	6	0.70	0.50	0.60
5	13	0.59	0.53	0.56	15	12	0.51	0.38	0.45
6	10	0.61	0.43	0.51	16	25	0.58	0.48	0.53
7	7	0.86	0.73	0.80	17	23	0,53	0.42	0.47
8	6	0.89	0.79	0.84	18	7	0.65	0.52	0.59
9	28	0.65	0.64	0.65	19	6	0.77	0.65	0.71
10	9	0.66	0.54	0.60	20	24	0.74	0.56	0.65

To evaluate these communities, the biology expert proposed to check if they exist in KEGG or other biological pathway databases. Each new community *Rnew* founded by our algorithm is presented to the DAVID tools (Database for Annotation Visualization and Integrated Discovery), which compares this community with others in different databases and gives the percentage of *Rnew*'s genes that belong to the existing communities in those databases. DAVID bioinformatics resources consist of an integrated biological knowledge-base and analytic tools that aim at systematically extracting biological meaning from large gene/protein lists. It is the most popular functional annotation programs used by biologists [42]. It takes as input a list of genes and exploits the functional annotations available on these genes in a public database such as, KEGG Pathways, Biocarta, Reactome, BBID and EC Number in order to find common functions that are sufficiently specific to these genes. Comparing a community *Rnew* founded by our approach to the datasets used to create the initial population, allows to evaluate the ability of our method to rebuilt communities with the initial proteins or genes.

Table 3. Communities' detection: experimental results compared to the datasets.

Pathway databases	Percentage min	Percentage max
Apoptosis	15%	88%
B cell receptor signalling pathway	20%	75%
Purine metabolism	23%	100%
Rna degradation	–	34%
Oocyte meiosis	19%	78%

Table 3 demonstrates that the obtained communities correspond to some "parts" of the real communities and in some cases to a complete network (percentage 100%). Therefore, GA-PPINet is able to efficiently rebuilt communities with the initial used proteins or genes. Figure 6 presents a community with 23 genes which 9 are from the Purine dataset (i.e the percentage is 40%), 8 genes from Oocyte dataset (i.e the percentage 35%) and the others are from different KEGG pathways. Additional tests in a further work, should be conducted to confirm these results.

We evaluate also the obtained communities by checking if they exist in other biological pathway databases. The biological databases used to evaluate our results are Biocarta, Reactome, BBID and EC Number and KEGG pathway database. These databases are used to compare the found communities by our approach with other communities. The results of this evaluation are shown in Table 4.

The results presented in Table 4 show that the new communities obtained by our approach correspond to some "parts" of real communities existing in other biological pathway databases, and in some cases to a complete network (percentage 100%). These results are considered very satisfactory by the biology expert. They constitute an initial validation of our algorithm and show the relevance of the used fitness function and the genetic operator. These tests should be supplemented on a larger scale with other datasets and different communities.

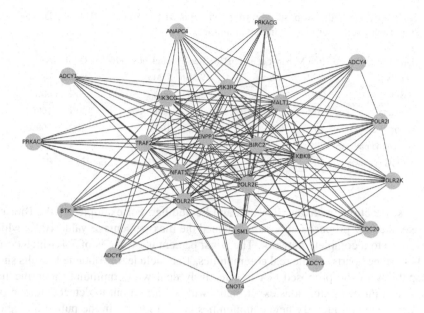

Fig. 6. An example of an obtained community with 23 genes.

Table 4. Evaluation of new communities.

Pathway databases	Percentage min	Percentage max
BBid	20%	60%
Biocarta	30%	100%
Ec number	30%	100%
Reactome pathway	25%	100%
KEGG pathway	33%	95%

Moreover, we compare the results obtained by our new algorithm *GA-PPI-Net* with the proposed genetic in [6] and in [5] where the communities have a fixed predetermined size. We name these approaches Ben M'barek et al. 2018 and Ben M'barek et al. 2019 respectively. A thorough comparison is not easy because the obtained communities for both propositions haven't the same sizes and the same constitution. Hence, the same datasets proposed by the biological expert (Table 1) and the same GA parameters were used for both approaches. The three algorithms were executed 20 times. Table 5 illustrates the comparison' results. We also used the DAVID tools to estimate the recovery rate of the found communities with existing communities in different biological databases.

From Table 5, we find that the new proposed approach the good performance to detect communities having different sizes with respect to Ben M'barek et al. (2019) approach and Ben M'barek et al. (2018) approach to detect communities having the same sizes. Our new method achieves the highest percentage 100% in three pathway

Table 5. Comparison of the proposed algorithm with Ben M'barek et al. (2018) and Ben M'barek et al. (2019) approaches for identifying communities.

Pathway Database	Ben M'barek et al. (2018)		Ben M'barek et al. (2019)		GA-PPINet	
	%Min	%Max	%Min	%Max	%Min	%Max
BBid	20%	30%	25%	50%	20%	60%
Biocarta	20%	60%	20%	66%	30%	100%
Ec number	20%	70%	10%	100%	30%	100%
Reactome pathway	20%	70%	14%	100%	25%	100%
KEGG pathway	20%	90%	15%	100%	33%	95%

databases: Reactome pathway, Biocarta and Ec number. For example, on the Biocarta database, the new proposed approach obtained the max percentage value 100% which corresponds to a complete network. The worst percentage value is of 7% which corresponds to some "parts" of the real communities. To conclude, the obtained results show the capability of the proposed GA to effectively deal with community identification in networks. Further extensions experiments will be carried out to detect communities with larger size and identify new communities not yet known in the public biological databases.

7   Conclusion

In this paper, we have proposed an approach based on GA to detect communities from the PPI network. This approach is a generalization of a previous work. It introduces the concept of community measure and searches for an optimal partitioning of the network by maximizing these measures. Our contribution in this paper is twofold. First, we apply GA to community detection in PPI networks. Second, we modify the previous proposed specific mutation operator adapted to the considered biological problem. Dense communities existing in the network are obtained at the end of the evolution by selectively exploring the search space, without the need to know in advance the community size. The experimental results showed the ability of our approach to correctly detect communities having different sizes and containing proteins/genes semantically similar and interacting. Future research will aim at extending the proposed fitness function by adding the modularity value and applying a multi-objective optimization to improve the quality of the results.

Acknowledgements. We would like to show our gratitude to Dr. Walid BEDHIAFI (Laboratoire de Génétique Immunologie et Pathologies Humaines, Université de Tunis El Manar) for assistance to comprehend the biological fields and for the interpretation of the results.

References

1. Agrawal, R.: Bi-objective community detection (BOCD) in networks using genetic algorithm. In: Aluru, S., et al. (eds.) IC3 2011. CCIS, vol. 168, pp. 5–15. Springer, Heidelberg (2011). https://doi.org/10.1007/978-3-642-22606-9_5

2. Ashburner, M., et al.: Gene ontology: tool for the unification of biology. Gene Ontol. Consortium. Nat. Genet. **25**(1), 25–29 (2000). https://doi.org/10.1038/75556
3. Atay, Y., Koc, I., Babaoglu, I., Kodaz, H.: Community detection from biological and social networks: a comparative analysis of metaheuristic algorithms. Appl. Soft Comput. **50**, 194–211 (2017). https://doi.org/10.1016/j.asoc.2016.11.025
4. Becker, K.G., White, S.L., Muller, J., Engel, J.: BBID: the biological biochemical image database. Bioinformatics **16**(8), 745–746 (2000). https://doi.org/10.1093/bioinformatics/16.8.745
5. Ben M'barek, M., Borgi, A., Bedhiafi, W., Hmida, S.B.: Genetic algorithm for community detection in biological networks. Procedia Computer Science **126**, 195–204 (2018)
6. Ben M'barek, M., Borgi, A., Hmida, S.B., Rukoz, M.: Genetic algorithm to detect different sizes' communities from protein-protein interaction networks. In: Proceedings of the 14th International Conference on Software Technologies - Volume 1: ICSOFT, pp. 359–370. INSTICC, SciTePress (2019). https://doi.org/10.5220/0007836703590370
7. Cai, Q., Ma, L., Gong, M., Tian, D.: A survey on network community detection based on evolutionary computation. Int. J. Bio-Inspired Comput. **8**(2), 84–98 (2016). https://doi.org/10.1504/IJBIC.2016.076329
8. Camon, E., et al.: The Gene Ontology Annotation (GOA) Project: Implementation of GO in SWISS-PROT, TrEMBL, and InterPro. Genome Res. **13**(4), 662–672 (2003). https://doi.org/10.1101/gr.461403
9. Croft, D., et al.: Reactome: a database of reactions, pathways and biological processes. Nucleic Acids Res. 39(Database issue), D691–697 (2011). https://doi.org/10.1093/nar/gkq1018
10. Deb, K., Pratap, A., Agarwal, S., Meyarivan, T.: A fast and elitist multiobjective genetic algorithm: Nsga-ii. IEEE Trans. Evol. Comput. **6**(2), 182–197 (2002)
11. Fortunato, S., Barthélemy, M.: Resolution limit in community detection. PNAS **104**(1), 36–41 (2007). https://doi.org/10.1073/pnas.0605965104
12. Girvan, M., Newman, M.E.J.: Community structure in social and biological networks. Proc. Natl. Acad. Sci. U.S.A. **99**(12), 7821–7826 (2002). https://doi.org/10.1073/pnas.122653799
13. Goldberg, D.E.: Genetic Algorithms in Search, Optimization and Machine Learning, 1st edn. Addison-Wesley Longman Publishing Co. Inc., Boston (1989)
14. Goldberg, D.E., Deb, K.: A comparative analysis of selection schemes used in genetic algorithms. In: Foundations of Genetic Algorithms, pp. 69–93. Morgan Kaufmann (1991)
15. Green, M.L., Karp, P.D.: Genome annotation errors in pathway databases due to semantic ambiguity in partial EC numbers. Nucleic Acids Res. **33**(13), 4035–4039 (2005). https://doi.org/10.1093/nar/gki711. https://academic.oup.com/nar/article/33/13/4035/1094428d
16. Guo, X., Liu, R., Shriver, C.D., Hu, H., Liebman, M.N.: Assessing semantic similarity measures for the characterization of human regulatory pathways. Bioinformatics **22**(8), 967–973 (2006). https://doi.org/10.1093/bioinformatics/btl042
17. Hill, D.P., Smith, B., McAndrews-Hill, M.S., Blake, J.A.: Gene Ontology annotations: what they mean and where they come from. BMC Bioinformatics **9**(5), S2 (2008). https://doi.org/10.1186/1471-2105-9-S5-S2
18. Jiang, J.J., Conrath, D.W.: Semantic similarity based on corpus statistics and lexical taxonomy. arXiv:cmp-lg/9709008, September 1997. arXiv: cmp-lg/9709008
19. Kanehisa, M., Goto, S.: KEGG: kyoto encyclopedia of genes and genomes. Nucleic Acids Res. **28**(1), 27–30 (2000)
20. Lancichinetti, A., Fortunato, S., Kertesz, J.: Detecting the overlapping and hierarchical community structure in complex networks. New J. Phys. **11**(3), 033015 (2009)
21. Li, Z., Zhang, S., Wang, R.S., Zhang, X.S., Chen, L.: Quantitative function for community detection. Phys. Rev. E **77**(3), 036109 (2008)

22. Lin, D.: An information-theoretic definition of similarity. In: Proceedings of the 15th International Conference on Machine Learning, pp. 296–304. Morgan Kaufmann (1998)

23. Liu, X., Li, D., Wang, S., Tao, Z.: Effective algorithm for detecting community structure in complex networks based on GA and clustering. In: Shi, Y., van Albada, G.D., Dongarra, J., Sloot, P.M.A. (eds.) ICCS 2007. LNCS, vol. 4488, pp. 657–664. Springer, Heidelberg (2007). https://doi.org/10.1007/978-3-540-72586-2_95

24. Mering, C.V., Huynen, M., Jaeggi, D., Schmidt, S., Bork, P., Snel, B.: STRING: a database of predicted functional associations between proteins. Nucl. Acids Res. **31**(1), 258–261 (2003). https://doi.org/10.1093/nar/gkg034

25. National Human Genome Research Institute (NHGRI): Biological Pathways Fact Sheet (2015). https://www.genome.gov/27530687/Biological-Pathways-Fact-Sheet

26. Newman, M.E.J.: Fast algorithm for detecting community structure in networks. Phys. Rev. E **69**(6) (2004). https://doi.org/10.1103/PhysRevE.69.066133, arXiv: cond-mat/0309508

27. Newman, M.E.J., Girvan, M.: Finding and evaluating community structure in networks. Phys. Rev. E **69**(2) (2004). https://doi.org/10.1103/PhysRevE.69.026113, arXiv: cond-mat/0308217

28. Nibbe, R.K., Chowdhury, S.A., Koyutürk, M., Ewing, R., Chance, M.R.: Protein-protein interaction networks and subnetworks in the biology of disease. Wiley Interdiscip. Rev. Syst. Biol. Med. **3**(3), 357–367 (2011)

29. Nishimura, D.: BioCarta. Biotech Softw. Internet Rep. **2**(3), 117–120 (2001). https://doi.org/10.1089/152791601750294344

30. Pesquita, C., Faria, D., Falcão, A.O., Lord, P., Couto, F.M.: Semantic Similarity in Biomedical Ontologies. PLoS Comput. Biol. **5**(7) (2009). https://doi.org/10.1371/journal.pcbi.1000443

31. Petrowski, A., Ben-Hamida, S.: Evolutionary Algorithms. Wiley, Hoboken, April 2017. google-Books-ID: fvRRCgAAQBAJ

32. Pizzuti, C.: Evolutionary computation for community detection in networks: a review. IEEE Trans. Evol. Comput. **22**(3), 464–483 (2018). https://doi.org/10.1109/TEVC.2017.2737600

33. Pizzuti, C.: GA-Net: a genetic algorithm for community detection in social networks. In: Rudolph, G., Jansen, T., Beume, N., Lucas, S., Poloni, C. (eds.) PPSN 2008. LNCS, vol. 5199, pp. 1081–1090. Springer, Heidelberg (2008). https://doi.org/10.1007/978-3-540-87700-4_107

34. Pizzuti, C.: A multi-objective genetic algorithm for community detection in networks. In: 2009 21st IEEE International Conference on Tools with Artificial Intelligence, pp. 379–386. IEEE (2009)

35. Pizzuti, C.: A multiobjective genetic algorithm to find communities in complex networks. IEEE Trans. Evol. Comput. **16**(3), 418–430 (2011)

36. Pizzuti, C., Rombo, S.E.: Algorithms and tools for protein-protein interaction networks clustering, with a special focus on population-based stochastic methods. Bioinformatics **30**(10), 1343–1352 (2014). https://doi.org/10.1093/bioinformatics/btu034

37. Rada, R., Mili, H., Bicknell, E., Blettner, M.: Development and application of a metric on semantic nets. IEEE Trans. Syst. Man Cybern. **19**(1), 17–30 (1989). https://doi.org/10.1109/21.24528

38. Radicchi, F., Castellano, C., Cecconi, F., Loreto, V., Parisi, D.: Defining and identifying communities in networks. PNAS **101**(9), 2658–2663 (2004). https://doi.org/10.1073/pnas.0400054101

39. Resnik, P.: Semantic similarity in a taxonomy: an information-based measure and its application to problems of ambiguity in natural language. arXiv:1105.5444 [cs], May 2011. https://doi.org/10.1613/jair.514, arXiv: 1105.5444

40. Ruths, T., Ruths, D., Nakhleh, L.: GS2: an efficiently computable measure of GO-based similarity of gene sets. Bioinformatics **25**(9), 1178–1184 (2009). https://doi.org/10.1093/bioinformatics/btp128

41. Schlicker, A., Domingues, F.S., Rahnenführer, J., Lengauer, T.: A new measure for functional similarity of gene products based on Gene Ontology. BMC Bioinformatics **7**, 302 (2006). https://doi.org/10.1186/1471-2105-7-302

42. Sherman, B.T., Huang, D.W., Tan, Q., Guo, Y., Bour, S., Liu, D., Stephens, R., Baseler, M.W., Lane, H.C., Lempicki, R.A.: DAVID Knowledgebase: a gene-centered database integrating heterogeneous gene annotation resources to facilitate high-throughput gene functional analysis. BMC Bioinformatics **8**, 426 (2007). https://doi.org/10.1186/1471-2105-8-426

43. Shi, C., Yu, P.S., Cai, Y., Yan, Z., Wu, B.: On selection of objective functions in multi-objective community detection. In: Proceedings of the 20th ACM International Conference on Information and Knowledge Management, pp. 2301–2304. ACM (2011)

44. Shi, C., Yu, P.S., Yan, Z., Huang, Y., Wang, B.: Comparison and selection of objective functions in multiobjective community detection. Comput. Intell. **30**(3), 562–582 (2014)

45. Shi, C., Zhong, C., Yan, Z., Cai, Y., Wu, B.: A multi-objective approach for community detection in complex network. In: IEEE Congress on Evolutionary Computation, pp. 1–8. IEEE (2010)

46. Snel, B., Lehmann, G., Bork, P., Huynen, M.A.: STRING: a web-server to retrieve and display the repeatedly occurring neighbourhood of a gene. Nucl. Acids Res. **28**(18), 3442–3444 (2000). https://doi.org/10.1093/nar/28.18.3442

47. Tasgin, M., Bingol, H.: Community Detection in Complex Networks using Genetic Algorithm. arXiv:cond-mat/0604419, April 2006. arXiv: cond-mat/0604419

48. Tasgin, M., Herdagdelen, A., Bingol, H.: Community Detection in Complex Networks Using Genetic Algorithms. arXiv:0711.0491 [physics], November 2007. arXiv: 0711.0491

49. Wang, J.Z., Du, Z., Payattakool, R., Yu, P.S., Chen, C.F.: A new method to measure the semantic similarity of GO terms. Bioinformatics **23**(10), 1274–1281 (2007). https://doi.org/10.1093/bioinformatics/btm087

50. Wilson, S.J., Wilkins, A.D., Lin, C.H., Lua, R.C., Lichtarge, O.: Discovery of functional and disease pathways by community detection in protein-protein interaction networks. In: Pacific Symposium on Biocomputing 2017, pp. 336–347. World Scientific (2017)

51. Wu, Z., Palmer, M.: Verbs semantics and lexical selection. In: Proceedings of the 32Nd Annual Meeting on Association for Computational Linguistics, pp. 133–138. ACL 1994, Association for Computational Linguistics, Stroudsburg, PA, USA (1994). https://doi.org/10.3115/981732.981751

52. Xu, B., Lin, H., Yang, Z.: Ontology integration to identify protein complex in protein interaction networks. Proteome Sci. **9**(1), S7 (2011). https://doi.org/10.1186/1477-5956-9-S1-S7

53. Zhao, Y., Dong, J., Peng, T.: Ontology classification for semantic-web-based software engineering. IEEE Trans. Serv. Comput. **2**(4), 303–317 (2009). https://doi.org/10.1109/TSC.2009.20

From Formal Test Objectives to TTCN-3 for Verifying ETCS Complex Software Control Systems

Rabea Ameur-Boulifa[1] , Ana Cavalli[2] , and Stephane Maag[2](✉)

[1] LTCI, Télécom ParisTech, Institut Polytechnique de Paris, Palaiseau, France
rabea.ameur-boulifa@telecom-paristech.fr
[2] Samovar, CNRS, Télécom SudParis, Institut Polytechnique de Paris,
Palaiseau, France
{ana.cavalli,stephane.maag}@telecom-sudparis.eu

Abstract. The design of a practical but accurate software methodology to guarantee systems correctness and safety is still a big challenge. Where test coverage is dissatisfying, formal analysis grants much higher potential to discover errors or safety vulnerabilities during the design phase of a system. However, formal verification methods often require a strong technical background that limits their usage. In this paper, we present a framework based on testing and verification to ensure the correctness and safety of complex distributed software systems. As a result of the application of our methodology we obtain a more reliable system, in terms of functionality, safety and robustness and a reduction of the time necessary for verification. In order to show the applicability of our solution we applied it on a real industrial case study, that is the European Train Control System (ETCS) [14]. We specify the system using the SDL language [24], and we use a test generation tool to generate abstract test cases in TTCN-3. Based on these standardized tests, we verify using model-checking, some critical properties of the system, in particular these regarding safety requirements. We analyse a real train accident and we demonstrate how the accident could have been avoided if the ETCS system was used.

Keywords: Formal verification · Safety · Model checking · Software control systems

1 Introduction

The difficulty of the implementation and the time required for testing and verifying complex software systems (e.g., embedded systems, control systems, etc.) involve high challenges. In most cases, the deadline is not met, products being launched several months late and without achieving the required performance targets. Within that context, many efforts have been done in the processes of software validation and in particular in the testing of these systems from the

M. van Sinderen and L. A. Maciaszek (Eds.): ICSOFT 2019, CCIS 1250, pp. 156–178, 2020.
https://doi.org/10.1007/978-3-030-52991-8_8

verification of formal specifications. However, very few works have been devoted to the verification of models from the testing phases although languages and formal transformation have been proposed.

In our paper, a framework based on formal methods that performs the methods and techniques necessary to automate the development and verification processes, is proposed. The expected result consists in a more reliable system, in terms of functionality, safety and robustness and a reduction of the time necessary for verification. We aim at verifying software systems from the standardized definition of their test objectives formally modeled.

We demonstrate the usefulness and efficiency of our framework in applying it on a real industrial case study, the European Train Control System (ETCS) [14]. European railways have evolved over the past 150 years within national boundaries, resulting in a variety of train control systems. To increase interoperability, the European Union has decided to standardize the European system of trains control, producing the European Train Control System (ETCS). This standard is mandatory within the European Union since 2015. Several research initiatives are trying to develop frameworks to ensure interoperability between different European train systems [3, 8, 11, 31, 37]. The requirements specification of ETCS describes the behavior of the system as well as a number of functional requirements. The formal description of these requirements demands a formalism that takes into account different behavioral scenarios under different conditions, and functional requirements as these related to the position, speed and acceleration of the train.

This paper is built upon a previous work of the authors. The automatic generation of efficient test cases from the TestGen-IF tool has already been defined in [1]. This paper expands this work by proposing how to manage the limitations of TestGen-IF without impacting the verification capabilities. For that purpose, we herein formally specify the system using the SDL language [24], focusing on the description of two main components of the standard, the On-Board Unit (OBU) and the Radio Block Center (RBC). We use the PragmaStudio tool to generate abstract test cases in TTCN-3. The advantage to use this tool regarding our previous work, is the reduction of the number of test cases as well as a standardized way of defining test suites. Furthermore, these suites can be executed through well defined testing architecture. Based on these standardized test objectives, we verify using model-checking, some critical properties of the system, in particular these regarding safety requirements. Besides, one of the main motivations of the work presented in this paper is to avoid train accidents. For instance, the train accident that happened in Spain[1] could be avoided by verifying different scenarios that illustrate the weaknesses of the train system used in Spain at the moment of the accident and we demonstrate how the accident could have been avoided if the ETCS was used. In the test cases generation section, we consider the scenario of the accident and the test objectives we have developed for this scenario show how the accident could be avoided if the ETCS system was used.

---

[1] El Pais Journal, 24th of July 2013, https://elpais.com/ccaa/2013/07/24/galicia/1374693125_734192.html.

In summary, the main contributions of this paper are:

- the design of an integrated framework suitable for software developers. The proposed framework is composed by a tool-chain for automating test generation, together with mechanisms to transform tests in properties to be verified by formal verification;
- we provide a ETCS specification based on the SDL language and based on standardized test objectives we generate the corresponding tests in TTCN-3 format;
- a transformation that converts the generated tests to MCL-formulas in such a way that automatic and exhaustive verification of critical properties will be possible on application;
- an example illustrating the approach and its practical use by applying our framework on a complex real case study, showing how the ETCS system, can contribute to avoid train accidents.

The paper is organized as follows. Section 2 presents the related works on the verification and testing of complex systems and the relation between testing and verification techniques. In Sect. 3, the motivations and contributions of this work regarding the prevention of train accidents are presented. In Sect. 4, basic concepts and definitions for the modelling of the system, and the description of test objectives are described. Section 5 gives the language for the properties specification and the rules for the transformation of test objectives into formal properties to be verified on the formal model. In Sect. 6, the formal specification of the ETCS system is provided as well as the results of the experimentation performed on it. Finally, Sect. 7 gives the conclusion and perspectives of this work.

2   Related Works

Verification and testing of complex systems (e.g., train or avionic software and industrial control systems) have been studied for many years. Several models and techniques have been proposed to either test the systems [4,19,33] or verify their formal models [6,28]. In the following, we cite the works from which we get inspired.

Many works have defined languages or approaches to model complex systems. In [38], a UML profile named R-UML has been proposed to model and then verify flexible control systems. The model is enriched in order to consider the management of resource sharing. Besides, a transformation model to state machines is used for the verification process. Also, the authors of [5] proposed a Pi-calculus-based approach through transformation of sequence diagrams for the verification process. An interesting mapping is formally defined to analyse and verify well-defined properties. Models transformation is of high importance and has been well described in a very recent survey [26]. The transformation is also performed in our approach in order to apply model-checking. However, although these studies propose high semantics and transformation rules, the authors do not propose experiments on real case studies and the properties to be checked are not provided. Besides, in our approach, our transformation through models and languages are easily applied in a sense that the procedures are tooled (based on Fiacre [18] - see Sect. 6.4).

We also get inspired of the researches on testing and verification of complex software control systems. [27] presents an interesting survey for modeling, testing, and verifying embedded control systems. The authors note that model-based development approaches are crucial in industrial contexts. They also raise the challenging consolidation between testing and verification processes in software systems. In this area, papers like [36] experimented an incremental methodology of deductive verification assisted by test generation. Though the proposal is very promising, it tackles the software code with no formal state machines. Nevertheless, relevant combination between test and verification was introduced. Time constraints in the validation processes are also very important. In [35], the authors studied them and proposed an approach to represent and refine them among various abstraction levels. Besides, they verified timing constraints on a complex system. In our paper, such information has also been raised and we noted the importance of such constraints in the model as well as into the verification phase.

It was shown in the survey of Fraser et al. [17] that testing could be performed from verification processes. Many efficient techniques and tools have been developed in that purpose. Still in that way, the authors of [16] have recently presented the use of model-checking for automated test cases generation applied to a standardized complex aerospace system. However, all these works present the use of verification for testing without raising the issue of the test objectives. Although a recent interesting document about bridging the gap between testing and verification approaches has been published by Microsoft Research [21], the methods always propose to apply verification to testing. In our work, we present a way for verifying a formal specification from standardized test objectives in the context of the European Control Train Systems (ETCS). Such verification purposes are not new as depicted in the well-known report published by the CMU on TCS [37]. In [20], a dynamic model is proposed for model-checking of the European TCS specifications. UML, LTL and a model-based methodology is successfully applied and the author clearly focus that work as an entry point for generating test cases. In a more recent work [25], the authors proposed a novel testing platform based on virtual laboratory. Braking events have been tested using faults injection. However, as mentioned, although these works are very interesting, none of them started from standardized test objectives (eventually automatically generated) to the verification of the models. This is what we tackle in our work we herein propose.

Besides, considering safe properties, in [40], the authors provide a definition of a safety management and signaling system integration model according to the CENELEC standards. They present an interesting approach based not only on train safety properties but also these regarding passengers' safety. They take into account the safety requirements for the Communication-Based Train Control

(CBTC) system, to define a safety assurance and assessment method based on safety verification and validation. This approach had been applied in many urban rail transit lines of Beijing.

3   Motivation

As mentioned in the introduction, in the actual context, the train system across Europe suffers from some deficiencies, which caused several severe accidents in the recent period. Safety and security become crucial aspects that require special consideration.

In this paper, we analyse the scenario of the train accident from Spain, Santiago de Compostela on Wednesday the 24th of July, 2013 and tested it for the case in which the ETCS would have been used.

According to the reports, the train involved in the accident was using the "Automatic Braking and Announcement of Signals" (ASFA) legacy system, a widely deployed automatic warning system on the Spanish rail network. The train derailed at high speed on a curve, as it was running at about twice the speed limit of 80 km per hour on that portion. Even if the train driver mentioned going at too high a speed, this does not necessarily mean that his guilt is completely acknowledged. Security systems should have ensured that not one cause results in a crash. We will present, in the following, the main principles of ASFA and ERTMS systems, showing how the accident would not have been produced in case the ERTMS system was used.

In both train systems, the train route is divided into cantons, sections between signals, along the routes.

In the ERTMS System - The European Rail Traffic Management System, which is the standard that comprises also the ETCS system, the beacons are disposed in a such a way that every two beacons there is a minimum distance of two meters.

The signaling system takes the information of the route and sends it to the beacons. The train, going on the beacons, reads the information so that the onboard computer manages it. The speed is regulated throughout the trajectory and less control of the driver is required.

By comparison with the ERTMS System, the ASFA System, provides more control to the driver. The ASFA system functions on the following principle: there are 2 beacons for each signal at a distance of 300 m between each other. The signaling system takes the information of the route and sends it to the two beacons. The train, going on the beacons, reads the information and sends it to the driver. The driver must act according to the information received (to reduce speed, to stop . . .). The ASFA system provides no regulation of the speed during the journey and it requires more attention from the driver.

The ASFA beacons provide information about two issues. If the train goes faster than 200 km/h, the beacon stops the train. The other situation is if the tracks are occupied, in which case, a red or yellow signal is activated and may halt the train. But if the train goes under 200 km/h, the speed is left up to the driver. In the situation of the accident there were some signals available to the driver (a light signal telling that the train is going to run on the Santiago tracks, a sign indicating that a tunnel is coming up) that should indicate at a point that the speed should be reduced, but no automatic speed regulation was applied. In the case of the ETCS system, the on-board equipment always co-operates with the ETCS trackside equipment. The on-board computer calculates the maximum allowed speed, monitors the real speed and controls the driver's indicators.

Consequently, considering the circumstances of the accident, due to the on-board control unit a train under ETCS security system would have had automatically detected and reduced the high speed on that portion of track and the accident could have been avoided. We illustrate this scenario in the experimental section of the paper.

4 Basics

In this section, we introduce all formal languages, techniques and tools that are used in our paper. Several concepts have been utilized in parallel to focus on system verification purpose.

4.1 Formal Specification Language - EFSM

There exist several modelling languages, such as the symbolic state machines [34], logic languages [13], etc. to specify complex systems when the number of exchanged messages, data and parameters is important.

In our approach, we describe each process (the behaviour of each component of our system) in terms of a machine modeled by an Extended Finite State Machine (EFSM) [29].

Definition 1. *An EFSM M is defined as : $M = (I, O, S, x, T)$ with I, O, S, x and T respectively a set of input symbols, a set of output symbols, a set of states, a vector of variables and a set of transitions. Each transition $t \in T$ is a 6-tuple defined as : $t = (s_t, q_t, i_t, o_t, P_t, A_t)$ where*

- *s_t is the current state,*
- *q_t is the next state,*
- *i_t is an input symbol,*
- *o_t is an output symbol,*
- *$P_t(x)$ a predicate on the values of the variables,*
- *$A_t(x)$ an action on the variables.*

[12]

4.2   The SDL Language

The Specification and Description Language SDL standardized by ITU-T [24] is widely used to specify complex communicating systems. This language has evolved according to user needs. It provides new concepts needed by designers to specify systems more and more complex. We have chosen SDL since it is based on the semantic model of Extended Finite State Machine (EFSM) [30]. Its goal is to specify the behavior of a system from the representation of its functional aspects. The description of the functional aspects is provided at different abstraction levels. The most abstract is the one describing the system, while the lowest is the specification of abstract machines composed by signals, channels, tasks, etc. Two kinds of properties may describe these functional aspects: the architectural and behavioral properties. The first one denotes the architecture of the system, that is the connection and organisation of the elements (blocks, processes, etc.). The second one describes the behaviors of the entities after an interaction with the environment. These reactions are described by tasks, transitions between states, and are based on the EFSMs.

A verification on local variable values imposes a condition (predicate) on moving to the next state. The actions associated with a transition include: verification on local variable (that can impose conditions, predicates, to move to the next state), the execution of tasks (assignment or informal text), procedure calls, dynamic creation of processes in order to include new mobile nodes into a system for instance (SDL contains the concepts of "type" and "instance of type"), arming and disarming timers, etc. SDL supports objects that permit to define generic types that could be validated and used in different contexts.

SDL is a very interesting language for our purpose in terms of specification of course but also to target the Labelled Transition Systems (LTS for short) used in our previous work [1]. Indeed, many tools (such as PragmaStudio[2]) allow first, to unfold SDL specification to LTS (for example for verification goals), and secondly to translate SDL in the language IF [9] dedicated to model our test objectives. We describe in the following these two formalisms.

4.3   Labelled Transition Systems

Labelled Transition Systems are strongly based on the definition and semantics of Symbolic Transition Graph with Assignment [22]. The LTS extends the general notion of Labelled Transition Systems by adding parameters and value-passing features. Transitions are labelled by parameterised actions, to which are attached a set of parameters and variables.

Definition 2. *(LTS) A Labelled Transition System is a rooted directed graph where each state s is associated with a finite set of free variables and each edge is labelled by a triple $s \xrightarrow{([b], \alpha, \boldsymbol{x}:=e)} s'$. Where b is a boolean expression, e is a data expression (which may includes variables), x ranges over data variables, $\boldsymbol{x} := \boldsymbol{e}$ is a multiple assignment and α ranges over a set of abstract action algebras.*

---

[2] http://pragmadev.com/product/index.html.

The set of abstract actions is a set of action algebras that can encode naturally usual point-to-point message passing calculi using $?a(x_1, \ldots, x_n)$ for inputs, $!a(v_1, \ldots, v_n)$ for outputs. Figure 6 shows the graphical representation of the two LTSs depicting the behaviour of the OBU (On-Board Unit) and RBC components (Radio Block Center).

The parallel composition of processes and their communication is defined through parameterised Network (pNet) [2,23]. pNets are tree-like networks of processes. They provide means to represent in a structured and hierarchical way the behaviour of processes, represented as labelled transition systems (LTS with value-passing messages). Composition of pNets is realized by synchronisation vectors that relate the actions of (a subset of) the subnets, with a global action that will be exported at the next level.

Figure 5 gives a graphical representation of pNets. The pNet shown in this example is represented by a set of four boxes: OBU, RBC, GETSPEED and RELEAS-ESPEED boxes inside the ETCS_SYSTEM box (hierarchy). Each box representing parameterised process (which can be formed of other pNets or LTS and that have parameters and local variables), is surrounded by labelled ports encoding a particular sort of the corresponding pNet. The ports are interconnected through edges for communication and synchronisation. Edges are translated to synchronisation vectors.

4.4   The IF Language

IF is a language based on the semantic temporized state machines, allowing the description of existing concepts into specification formalisms [9]. A real-time system described using IF language is composed of processes running in parallel and interacting asynchronously through shared variables and message exchanges via communication channels. The description of a system in IF consists in the definition of data types, constants, shared variables, communication signals and processes. The signals set is divided into inputs and outputs provided by the environment of a current state machine or sent to its environment, respectively. One of the main advantages of the IF language is the ease of use to formally specify test objectives as described in the next section.

4.5   Test Objectives

In our work, we focus on the functional properties to be tested on a system or implementation (namely implementation or system under test (SUT)). In that context, a test objective describes a particular functionality of a SUT by specifying the property to be checked in the system implementation. It is an observable action of the system that once described in IF language [10] is used for guiding the space exploration of the system's states.

A test objective is described as a conjunction of conditions, including the following optional conditions: instance of a process with an identifier, a state of the system (a source state or a destination state), an action of the system (a message sent, a message received, an internal action), a variable of the process or a clock of the process, specifying a value and its state (active or inactive). Table 1 shows the general structure of a test objective in the IF description.

Table 1. General structure of test objective [1].

$$TO = TO_1 \wedge TO_2$$
$$TO_1 = P_1 \wedge P_2 \wedge \cdots \wedge P_5$$
$$P_1 = process : instance = \{proc\}id$$
$$P_2 = state : source = s_1$$
$$P_3 = state : destination = s_1'$$
$$P_4 = input\ action : \alpha_1(parameters)$$
$$P_5 = variable : (v_1 = value)*$$

$$TO_2 = Q_1 \wedge Q_2 \wedge \cdots \wedge Q_5$$
$$Q_1 = process : instance = \{proc\}id$$
$$Q_2 = state : source = s_2$$
$$Q_3 = state : destination = s_2'$$
$$Q_4 = output\ action : \alpha_2(parameters)$$
$$Q_5 = variable : (v_2 = value)*$$

From a test objective described in IF and the SDL specification of the system, we may generate a set of test cases within a commonly used notation, namely TTCN-3 [15]. Basically, a test case is a sequence of input and output actions with eventual pre-post conditions. It represents a trace of an LTS that satisfies the test objective. We briefly describe the TTCN-3 notation in the next section.

4.6 Testing and Test Control Notation Version 3

The ETSI standard for Testing and Test Control Notation version 3 (TTCN-3[3]) [15,39] is a test specification language for black-box testing of complex distributed systems. The syntax looks similar to programming languages (e.g., C, C++, JAVA) and therefore easy to understand and apply. It is a powerful language for all types of reactive system test specification. TTCN-3 is referred as an Abstract Test Suite (ATS) and is used for expressing the configuration and behavior of abstract test system and test cases.

5   Framework - From Test Objectives to Verified Properties

Our goal is to use formal methods both to increase the quality of such systems through enhancing the verification activity, and to prevent unnecessary

[3] http://www.ttcn-3.org.

tests. However, since we aim at a general approach for specifying properties, we advocate to use the test objectives to generate formal specifications or properties that may be used for proving or disproving the correctness of the systems. As described before (Sect. 4.5) test objectives express the desired or unexpected behaviour of a system in terms of input and output actions. Their distinctive features are typically the dealing with data parameters that are generally abstracted away in formal models because verification problems are undecidable for infinite systems. Furthermore, the crucial characteristic of our models is the parameterized action.

Precisely, MCL (Model Checking Language) is a language for expressing properties that addresses this crucial matter: representing and handling data, and reasoning about their value.

5.1 Property Language

Basic MCL logic extends action in modal μ-calculus with data variables [32], so it suits for describing the property of concurrent systems. Indeed, MCL language provides high-level operators facilitating the construction of formulas. It allows to handle in a natural way the data values present in the LTSs and to reason about systems described in value-passing process algebras such as LOTOS.

The MCL formulas are logical formulas built over regular expressions using boolean operators, modalities operators (the necessity operator denoted by [ ] and the possibility operator denoted by ⟨ ⟩), maximal fixed point operator (denoted by μ) and data-handling constructs inspired from functional programming languages. From LTS's point of view, a transition sequence starting at the initial state and satisfying a regular formula ϵ can be expressed in MCL either as an example for the ⟨ϵ⟩true formula, or as a counterexample for the [ϵ]false formula. For specifying transition sequences, MCL uses regular formulas.

A regular formula is a logical formula built from action formulas, traditional and extended regular expression operators, namely concatenation (.), choice (|), and transitive- reflexive closure (*).

An action formula is a logical formula built from action predicates which includes action patterns, and the "**tau**" constant operator. Action pattern can either action for matching values denoted by $\{\alpha\,!e_1\ldots!e_n\}$, or action for extracting and storing values denoted by $\{\alpha\,?x_1:T_1\ldots?x_n:T_n\}$ where α is an action name, e_i is an expression, variable name or function name, x_i is a variable name and T_i is a basic data type. It is important to note that the usage of ! and ? symbols in MCL specification has different meaning from the notation introduced in LTS models. They enable to match a given value against an expression or to extract and store it in a variable. MCL also uses other specific notations: the "**true**" constant is used to match a value of any action formula and the wildcard clause "**any**" matches a value of any type.

5.2   Encoding Test Objectives into MCL Formula

We define the transformation of IF test objectives into MCL specification by associating to each test objective a MCL formula expressing a liveness property. Consider TO a test objective:

$$TO = "process : instance=\{proc\}id"$$
$$\wedge"state : source=s" \wedge"input\ action : \alpha_1(x_1, .., x_n)"$$
$$\wedge"output\ action:\alpha_2(x'_1, .., x'_n) \wedge"state : destination=s'"$$

The encoding of test objective TO is the following MCL property pattern:

$$[\mathbf{true}*.\{\alpha_1?x_1:T_1 \ldots ?x_n:T_n\}]\ \mathrm{inev}(\{\alpha_2 \dagger x'_1 \ldots \dagger x'_n\})$$

where $\{\alpha_1?x_1 : T_1 \ldots ?x_n : T_n\}$ and $\{\alpha_2 \dagger x'_1 \ldots \dagger x'_n\}$ are the input action and the output action resp. Note that for dataless actions, brackets can be omitted. And such that $\dagger x$ can be either $!x$ or $?x : T$ depending on whether x'_i consists of matching values with data x_i (encoded $!x_i$) or extracting and storing them in typed variables (encoded $?x_i : T_i$). MCL uses the usual datatypes e.g., *bool, nat, string*.

The predicate inevitability of an action α denoted $\mathrm{inev}(\alpha)$ expresses that a transition labelled with α is eventually reached from the current state. It can be defined in MCL using fixed point operator by the following macro definition:

macro $\mathrm{inev}(\alpha)=$
  μ X.(<**true**> **true and** [**not** (α)] X)
macro_end

meaning that as long as there has been no α action, there is always an execution leading to α. It is important to note that our translation does not care about the conditions on the states which are involved in test objectives. For the formal verification, the pointing of the states of a system is useless information. Because the approach checks properties by means of an exhaustive search of all possible states that the system could reach.

Concerning the variables that we have not considered in the given general test objective. They are also translated but not in completely automatic manner. The translation requires sometimes the intervention of the user. As mentioned earlier, such as a programming language, MCL offers constructors to facilitate the handling of data values. Thus, for encoding the variable conditions that are not empty, we use such constructors, in particular the **where** constructor. The action pattern ending with the optional clause "**where b**" means that the pattern matches an action if and only if the guard (boolean expression) **b** is true. The guard can be the equality check, i.e, like **where** $v_i = val_i$.

6 Experiments

6.1 ETCS System

Our work has been experimented on a formal model of the European Train Control System (ETCS). The ETCS is a part of the European standard that defines the European Railway Traffic Management System[4].

The normative documents describe ETCS as a train control standard, based on in-cab equipment, an On-Board Unit (OBU) able to supervise train movements and to stop it according to the permitted speed at each line section, along with calculation and supervision of the maximum train speed at all times [14]. The information is received from the ETCS equipment beside the track. For that purpose, the OBU runs concurrently with a Radio Block Center (RBC). Basically, this standard is proposed in order to improve the safety in European railways. The trains running limits are stated by movement authorities.

The train control system ensures the reception of messages like safety distance, speed limitations and controls the driving according to these limitations. Secondly, the safety is increased by the supervision of train driving. As illustrated in the Fig. 1, data are used by the on-board ETCS equipment to supervise the train drivers[5]. Therefore, the on-board equipment has to know both information regarding the route as well as information regarding the train.

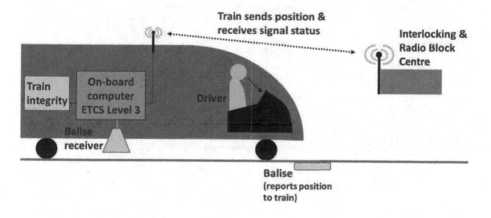

Fig. 1. The ETCS system [1].

This train data is introduced by the train driver before starting the journey. Based on the track data and on the data entered by the driver, the on-board subsystem calculates a dynamic speed profile, calculates a set of braking curves for train

---

[4] http://www.ertms.net/.

[5] https://medium.com/@POST_UK/moving-block-signalling-b9b0b9f498c2.

movement supervision and commands the brake application, if necessary[6]. A high performance is given by an increasing speed and capacity due to a track-train transmission system and the on-board equipment knowledge. The track-train transmission system uses precise information about running limits and consequently, supervises a train permanently to avoid that the speed limits exceed. The on-board equipment knowledge about train running limits is used to inform drivers through displays, allowing the railways to increase the running speeds without worrying about shortening the time period for track side signal observation.

6.2   ETCS Formal Specification in SDL

We designed our SDL specification using the PragmaStudio tool through two main blocks and processes. The architecture of our system is represented in the Fig. 2. It consists of the communication of the two components (OBU and RBC) through the channels carrying the different signals (packet messages).

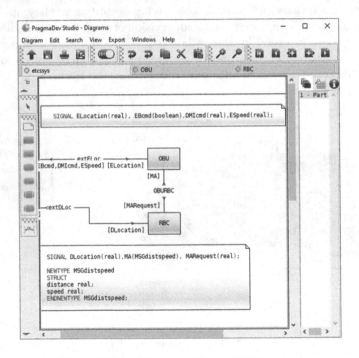

Fig. 2. SDL architecture of the ETCS system.

In each SDL block, one process modeling the behavior of the components is integrated, receiving and sending the signals using ports. These processes are illustrated by the Fig. 3 and Fig. 4. Input/output messages, variables, parameters, guards, clocks and decisions are represented. A procedure call has also

---

[6] https://ec.europa.eu/transport/modes/rail/ertms_en.

been specified to represent the behavior of the ReleaseSpeed as noted in Fig. 5. Besides, the procedure allowing to get the speed has been supposed belonging to the environment of the SDL process.

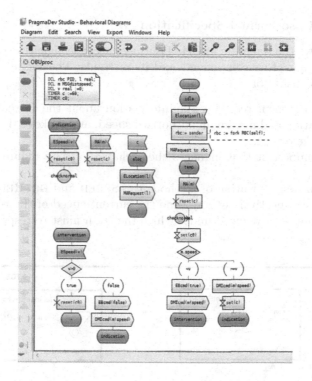

Fig. 3. SDL process of the OBU.

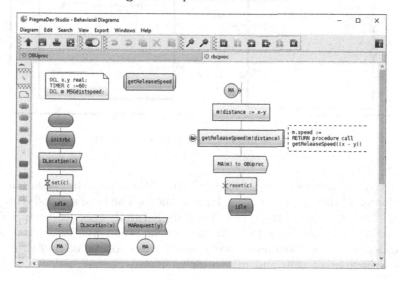

Fig. 4. SDL process of the RBC.

From this formal specification, we are now able to generate several sequence diagrams, to describe diverse use cases, flows and by simulation, to provide TTCN-3 sequences as we depict in the following.

6.3   A Use Case Formal Specification

The Fig. 5 shows the semantic model of our use case, the signature of interfaces, and the behaviour of its components and its methods. The overall architecture of the system consists of:

- The OBU component receiving the information about the current speed, the current location and maximum authorized speed, and makes a decision to the issue to brake or not,
- The RBC component that manages the exchange of data required for a safe train travel,
- A behavioural specification of methods GETSPEED and GETRELEASESPEED that returns respectively at any time the current speed of the train and the maximum authorized speed under which the train must to respect.

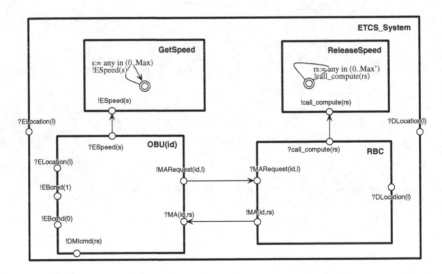

Fig. 5. pNet model for the ETCS system [1].

In this section we describe only the structure of the pNets, the communication among them and the behaviour of the local methods. The local methods compute regularly the new value of the speed. They are naturally encoded as an infinite loop of actions that returns a random value in the range $[0 \ldots max\_value]$ such that max_value is the maximum value of speed attainable by each of them. The internal behaviour of OBU and RBC components are represented by the LTSs given in Fig. 6.

The ETCS system as specified in the European standard uses a clock. Each component owns a clock which is synchronized with clocks of the other components. Particularly, the RBC component receives a location of a danger point for a certain period of time. In our models, we abstract away this kind of detail and represent the receiving of a location of danger point as an infinite loop.

The OBU *Component.* The OBU receives the current estimated location (?ELocation(l)) of the train from the environment. This location is encapsulated in a request sending to the RBC (!MARequest(id, l)). Thus, it receives in return a release speed consisting of a limited speed under which the train must to respect (?MA(id, rs)). The local method GETSPEED will fill the current speed with the calculated value (?ESpeed(s)). If the current speed s of the train is less than or equals to the limited speed, it can continue to operate. Otherwise, if the current speed s exceeds the maximum authorized speed, an emergency brake is applied (!EBcmd(1)). The brake is hold until the train totally stops. The OBU sends a Driver Machine Interface command to display speed information to the driver (!DMIspeed(rs)).

The RBC *Component.* The RBC receives the Danger locations that are sent from the environment (?DLocation(l)). Based on this information and the estimated location report received from the OBU, the RBC computes release speeds by calling the method RELEASESPEED (!call_computation(rs)). The release speed is then sent to OBU via the (!MA(id, rs)) message.

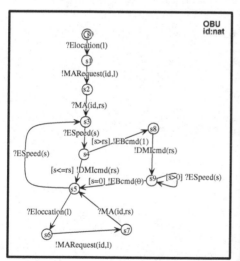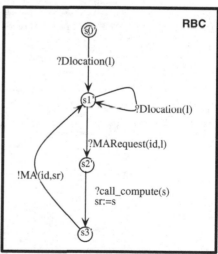

Fig. 6. Model for ETCS system [1]

Test Objectives for Automatic Verification. A critical property of the ETCS that is particularly crucial to be verified is the ability of the system of taking over control if the driver appears to be going too fast. Among scenarios describing this property we consider the following:

Example 1. Scenario in which the train is in the indication state (encoded s_5), running at 120 km/h while the release speed is 80 km/h, thus OBU has to generate a brake command and to pass to the intervention state (encoded s_8) – by traversing the normal state (encoded s_3)–. The associated test objective is formulated in the IF description (where {OBU}0 is used to identify the first instance of process OBU) as follows:

$$TO = "process : instance = \{OBU\}0" \wedge " variable\ rs = 80"$$
$$\wedge " state : source = s_5 " \wedge " variable\ s = 120"$$
$$\wedge " state : source = s_8 " \wedge " output\ action : \mathtt{EBCMD1}"$$

In our previous work [1], we used the TestGen-IF tool to generate efficient test cases. However, as it has been noted, the system dealt with data variables over a domain leading to a huge number of generated test cases. In this extended paper, we used the SDL specification of our ETCS system as well as the PragmaStudio tool to generate abstract test cases in TTCN-3. The technique covers the whole SDL model according to the test objectives but does not give numerical data to the variable. Instead, the variable are kept for future test cases concretization and execution. Therefore, the number of the test cases was drastically reduced. We illustrate in the Fig. 7 the TTCN-3 test cases obtained for our previous mentioned TO and generated from our SDL specification.

Fig. 7. Our generated TTCN-3 test file.

6.4   Experimental Results

The source specification was written in the intermediate format Fiacre language [7]. The Fiacre language provides syntax for data types and expressions, definition of LTSs, and a form of composition of processes by synchronization on channels. Then we run a combination of CADP tools [18], the most important ones are ceasar.open for generating transition systems from Fiacre programs, ocis the interactive simulator, and Evaluator4, the model-checker that deals with the MCL logic. All the tools provided by the CADP toolbox are command-line tools, but also integrated into graphical user interface (GUI). Through the Xeuca interface (see Fig. 8) CADP toolbox allows an easy access to the offered functionalities.

From a finite model pNet of ETCS we have computed the LTS of the global system. Choosing small values for the domain of parameters, i.e. [0..4] intervals for all data, we obtain an LTS with 662 states and 3615 transitions.

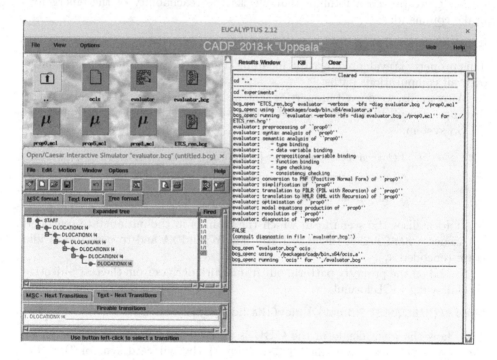

Fig. 8. Graphical user-interface of CADP [1].

To formally verify the correct execution of the different scenarios, we generated several properties in MCL in precise and generic way; they express various facets of the system. Some properties express global correctness of the application, seen from the (external) ETCS point of view, and that reveals the feasibility of several scenarios or the impossibility of some errors.

First, we started by verifying usual properties the system is deadlock-free. As well, we verified a property expressing that each scenario is acyclic, i.e. specifying the absence of unfair execution actions, which is characterized using the infinite looping operator (denoted by @ operator):

[true∗] <true> @

Not surprisingly, this property does not hold for all scenarios. By using ocis simulator (as depicted in Fig. 8), we visualize the cause, this is because the RBC processor can stay in its state after receiving a ?DLocation(l). Indeed, since we abstracted away the clock, the RBC process can be engaged in a circular receiving loop of danger locations that are sent from the environment. However, under the hypothesis that this action is performed over a time period, such a cycle is executed at most a finite number of times. Thus, cycles of this form should not be considered a problem, and the model is refined, for instance by allowing only a finite number of actions.

Next, we proved a formula that checks the reachability of the emergency brake command:

[true∗."EBCMD1"] true

This property is evaluated to TRUE meaning that the break command is reachable over all computations paths.

Afterwards, we proved properties that we generated from test objectives. For instance, consider the following test objective checking global correction of the ETCS system:

$$TO = "process : instance = \{RBC\}0"$$
$$\wedge "state : source = s_0'" \wedge "input\ action : \texttt{MAREQUEST}(id)"$$
$$\wedge "output\ action : \texttt{MA}(id, sr)" \wedge "state : destination = s_1'"$$

It formalises the scenario in which the train is in the initial state (encoded s_0') issues a MAREQUEST, thus the RBC has to send MA and to pass to the idle state (encoded s_1').

Based on the property pattern, our framework derives from the test objective the following MCL formula:

[true∗.({MAREQUEST ?id:nat})] inev({MA !id ?any})

Note how the identifier *id* of the OBU is extracted from a transition label by the first action predicate {MAREQUEST ?id:nat} (by wildcard symbol ?) and is used subsequently in the property. This property is evaluated to TRUE meaning that for each possible request of a train (*id* being the identifier of an OBU), the return of the corresponding movement authority permission is reachable with some returned value of speed (denoted **any**).

From the test objective given in the Example 1, our framework generates also a MCL formula although in a less systematic way:

[true∗.{MA ?any ?v_1:nat}.(not{ESPEED ?any})∗.{ESPEED ?v_2:nat where $v_2 > v_1$}] inev("EBCMD 1")

This formula expresses a general property for verifying that OBU issues a brake command at each state whenever speed is greater than releaseSpeed. Actually, the test objective does not specify the input action but the value of the variables s and rs ($s = 120$ and $rs = 80$), and the output action: EBCMD1. It is specified that the speed of the train is greater than the release speed. By analysis of the models of the train, we look for the actions that set the value of these variables, we use them to express the assignment instead of the variables assignment. As it can be noted, the variable s is set by the action ESPEED sets and the variable rs is set by the action MA. Thereby, for these actions that are used in the formula, it is explicitly expressed that the argument of the first is greater than the argument of the second. Note that the values 80 and 120 of the variables are not set in the formula to express this safety property in a general form. It is evaluated to TRUE: once an RBC delivers a release speed, upon the first speed exceeding this limit the train always issues the brake command.

Behavioural model generated is also used to verify other properties, and other scenarios. For instance, the scenario that caused the Spain train accident (see footnote 1) can be expressed by a combination of properties: – property specifying the capability of the ETCS system of taking over control if the driver appears to be going too fast; – and a property specifying the inability of the train to move without being controlled by the RBC.

The first property is the one that encodes the test objective given in Example 1. However, for the second the purpose is to ensure that the train (the OBU unit) can only evolve if it receives messages from RBC unit. This can be expressed by the following MCL formula:

[(not {MA ?any ?any})*.{DMICMD ?any}.(not {MA ?any ?any})*.{MA ?any ?any}]
false

This property is evaluated to TRUE, meaning that the displaying action of the OBU (DMICMD ?any) cannot be performed before receiving the message (MA ?any ?any) from RBC. Note that in the formula the train's progress is simulated by the displaying action. Indeed as mentioned before, we produced behavioural models where we abstract away some details, in particular the move action simulating the movement of the train. Because of this, we consider that any other action that does not loop on the initial state (encoded s_0) or on the stop state (encoded s_5) can simulate the movement.

7   Conclusion and Perspectives

In this paper we have presented a framework for the generation of logical properties from test objectives with the aim of verifying properties of complex distributed systems. A test objective provides a convenient description for generating test cases to be executed to achieve a particular software testing requirement. The system has been described using the SDL language and we used the Pragmadev test generation tool to generate the test cases, which are represented in the standard notation TTCN3 facilitating the execution of the tests. We also describe the translation of such test objectives to MCL properties. MCL properties enable the exhaustive verification of critical properties; the correctness of applications has been proved by using the model checking technique. We have analysed a real train accident and showed that could be avoided if the ETCS safety rules were applied.

As a future work, we are planning to refine the behavioural model by taking time into consideration. Preliminary modifications allow to encode implicitly the notion of time and go beyond the issues raised by its abstraction. However, from the test objectives point of view, it would be interesting to study what could be the property pattern corresponding to the test objective involving the clock. Moreover, we will consider the eventual changes of the model parameters due to the clock phases over the time.

Finally, our framework could be extended to take into account other aspects in order to offer the ability to analyse non-functional properties.

References

1. Ameur-Boulifa, R., Cavalli, A.R., Maag, S.: Verifying complex software control systems from test objectives: application to the ETCS system. In: Proceedings of the 14th International Conference on Software Technologies, ICSOFT 2019, Prague, Czech Republic, 26–28 July 2019, pp. 397–406 (2019). https://doi.org/10.5220/0007918203970406
2. Ameur-Boulifa, R., Henrio, L., Kulankhina, O., Madelaine, E., Savu, A.: Behavioural semantics for asynchronous components. J. Log. Algebraic Methods Program. **89**, 1–40 (2017)
3. Andres, C., Cavalli, A., Yetvushenko, N.: On modeling and testing the european train control system, technical report 09013 lor, telecom sudparis. Technical report, March 2013
4. Abbaspour Asadollah, S., Inam, R., Hansson, H.: A survey on testing for cyber physical system. In: El-Fakih, K., Barlas, G., Yevtushenko, N. (eds.) ICTSS 2015. LNCS, vol. 9447, pp. 194–207. Springer, Cham (2015). https://doi.org/10.1007/978-3-319-25945-1_12
5. Belghiat, A., Chaoui, A.: A Pi-calculus-based approach for the verification of UML2 sequence diagrams. In: 2015 10th International Joint Conference on Software Technologies (ICSOFT), vol. 2, pp. 1–8. IEEE (2015)
6. Bérard, B., et al.: Systems and Software Verification: Model-checking Techniques and Tools. Springer, Heidelberg (2013). https://doi.org/10.1007/978-3-662-04558-9
7. Berthomieu, B., et al.: The syntax and semantics of FIACRE. In: Deliverable number F.3.2.11 of project TOPCASED (2012)
8. Bougacha, R., Wakrime, A.A., Kallel, S., Ayed, R.B., Collart-Dutilleul, S.: A model-based approach for the modeling and the verification of railway signaling system. In: Proceedings of the 14th International Conference on Evaluation of Novel Approaches to Software Engineering, pp. 367–376. SCITEPRESS-Science and Technology Publications, Lda (2019)
9. Bozga, M., Graf, S., Mounier, L.: IF-2.0: a validation environment for component-based real-time systems. In: Brinksma, E., Larsen, K.G. (eds.) CAV 2002. LNCS, vol. 2404, pp. 343–348. Springer, Heidelberg (2002). https://doi.org/10.1007/3-540-45657-0_26

10. Bozga, M., Graf, S., Ober, I., Ober, I., Sifakis, J.: The IF toolset. In: Bernardo, M., Corradini, F. (eds.) SFM-RT 2004. LNCS, vol. 3185, pp. 237–267. Springer, Heidelberg (2004). https://doi.org/10.1007/978-3-540-30080-9_8

11. Bundell, G.A.: Aspects of the safety analysis of an on-board automatic train operation supervisor. In: 2009 IEEE International Conference on Systems, Man and Cybernetics, pp. 3223–3230. IEEE (2009)

12. Cavalli, A.R., Grepet, C., Maag, S., Tortajada, V.: A validation model for the DSR protocol. In: 24th International Conference on Distributed Computing Systems Workshops (ICDCS 2004 Workshops), 23–24 March 2004, Hachioji, Tokyo, Japan, pp. 768–773 (2004). https://doi.org/10.1109/ICDCSW.2004.1284120

13. Che, X., Lalanne, F., Maag, S.: A logic-based passive testing approach for the validation of communicating protocols. In: ENASE 2012 - Proceedings of the 7th International Conference on Evaluation of Novel Approaches to Software Engineering, Wroclaw, Poland, 29–30 June 2012, pp. 53–64 (2012)

14. ERTMS Commission Group - European Commission: delivering an effective and interoperable European Rail Traffic Management System (ERTMS) – the way ahead. Technical report, SWD(2017), p. 375, November 2017. https://ec.europa.eu/transport/sites/transport/files/swd20170375-ertms-the-way-ahead.pdf

15. ETSI-ES-201-873-1: Methods for testing and specification (MTS), the testing and test control notation version 3, part 1: Ttcn-3 core language, v4.11.1. Technical report, April 2019

16. Ferrante, O., Scholte, E., Rollini, S., North, R., Manica, L., Senni, V.: A methodology for formal requirements validation and automatic test generation and application to aerospace systems. Technical report, SAE Technical Paper (2018)

17. Fraser, G., Wotawa, F., Ammann, P.E.: Testing with model checkers: a survey. Softw. Test. Verification Reliab. 19(3), 215–261 (2009)

18. Garavel, H., Lang, F., Mateescu, R., Serwe, W.: CADP 2010: a toolbox for the construction and analysis of distributed processes. In: Abdulla, P.A., Leino, K.R.M. (eds.) TACAS 2011. LNCS, vol. 6605, pp. 372–387. Springer, Heidelberg (2011). https://doi.org/10.1007/978-3-642-19835-9_33

19. Garousi, V., Felderer, M., Karapıçak, Ç.M., Yılmaz, U.: Testing embedded software: a survey of the literature. Inf. Softw. Technol. 104, 14–45 (2018)

20. Ghazel, M.: Formalizing a subset of ERTMS/ETCS specifications for verification purposes. Transp. Res. Part C Emerg. Technol. 42, 60–75 (2014)

21. Godefroid, P.: Between testing and verification: Dynamic software model checking (2016)

22. Hennessy, M., Lin, H.: Symbolic bisimulations. Theor. Comput. Sci. 138(2), 353–389 (1995)

23. Henrio, L., Madelaine, E., Min, Z.: pNets: an expressive model for parameterised networks of processes. In: 2015 23rd Euromicro International Conference on Parallel, Distributed, and Network-Based Processing, pp. 492–496. IEEE (2015)

24. ITU-T: Recommandation Z.100: CCITT Specification and Description Language (SDL, 1999, updated 2019). Technical report, ITU-T, October 2019

25. Jesus Valdivia, L., Solas, G., Añorga, J., Arrizabalaga, S., Adin, I., Mendizabal, J.: ETCS on-board unit safety testing: saboteurs, testing strategy and results. Promet-Traffic Transp. 29(2), 213–223 (2017)

26. Kahani, N., Bagherzadeh, M., Cordy, J.R., Dingel, J., Varró, D.: Survey and classification of model transformation tools. Softw. Syst. Model. 18(4), 2361–2397 (2018). https://doi.org/10.1007/s10270-018-0665-6

27. Kapinski, J., Deshmukh, J.V., Jin, X., Ito, H., Butts, K.: Simulation-based approaches for verification of embedded control systems: an overview of traditional and advanced modeling, testing, and verification techniques. IEEE Control Syst. Mag. **36**(6), 45–64 (2016)

28. Karna, A.K., Chen, Y., Yu, H., Zhong, H., Zhao, J.: The role of model checking in software engineering. Front. Comput. Sci. **12**(4), 642–668 (2018). https://doi.org/ 10.1007/s11704-016-6192-0

29. Lee, D., Yannakakis, M.: Principles and methods of testing finite state machines - a survey. IEEE Trans. Comput. **84**, 1090–1123 (1996)

30. Lee, D., Yannakakis, M.: Principles and methods of testing finite state machines - a Survey. Proc. IEEE **84**, 1090–1123 (1996)

31. Liu, Y., Tang, T., Liu, J., Zhao, L., Xu, T.: Formal modeling and verification of RBC handover of ETCS using differential dynamic logic. In: 2011 Tenth International Symposium on Autonomous Decentralized Systems, pp. 67–72. IEEE (2011)

32. Mateescu, R., Thivolle, D.: A model checking language for concurrent value-passing systems. In: Cuellar, J., Maibaum, T., Sere, K. (eds.) FM 2008. LNCS, vol. 5014, pp. 148–164. Springer, Heidelberg (2008). https://doi.org/10.1007/978-3-540-68237-0_12

33. Merouane, K., Grepet, C., Maag, S.: A methodology for interoperability testing of a manet routing protocol. In: International Conference on Wireless and Mobile Communications, p. 5, March 2007. https://doi.org/10.1109/ICWMC.2007.2

34. Mouttappa, P., Maag, S., Cavalli, A.: Using passive testing based on symbolic execution and slicing techniques: application to the validation of communication protocols. Comput. Netw. **57**(15), 2992–3008 (2013)

35. Mubeen, S., Nolte, T., Sjödin, M., Lundbäck, J., Lundbäck, K.-L.: Supporting timing analysis of vehicular embedded systems through the refinement of timing constraints. Softw. Syst. Model. **18**(1), 39–69 (2017). https://doi.org/10.1007/ s10270-017-0579-8

36. Petiot, G., Kosmatov, N., Giorgetti, A., Julliand, J.: How test generation helps software specification and deductive verification in Frama-C. In: Seidl, M., Tillmann, N. (eds.) TAP 2014. LNCS, vol. 8570, pp. 204–211. Springer, Cham (2014). https://doi.org/10.1007/978-3-319-09099-3_16

37. Platzer, A., Quesel, J.-D.: European train control system: a case study in formal verification. In: Breitman, K., Cavalcanti, A. (eds.) ICFEM 2009. LNCS, vol. 5885, pp. 246–265. Springer, Heidelberg (2009). https://doi.org/10.1007/978-3-642-10373-5_13

38. Salem, M.O.B., Mosbahi, O., Khalgui, M., Frey, G.: R-UML: An UML profile for verification of flexible control systems. In: Lorenz, P., Cardoso, J., Maciaszek, L.A., van Sinderen, M. (eds.) ICSOFT 2015. CCIS, vol. 586, pp. 118–136. Springer, Cham (2016). https://doi.org/10.1007/978-3-319-30142-6_7

39. Willcock, C., Dei, T., Tobies, S., Keil, S., Engler, F., Schulz, S.: An Introduction to TTCN-3, 2nd edn. Wiley Publishing, Hoboken (2011)

40. Yan, F., Gao, C., Tang, T., Zhou, Y.: A safety management and signaling system integration method for communication-based train control system. Urban Rail Transit **3**(2), 90–99 (2017). https://doi.org/10.1007/s40864-017-0051-7

Service Robots: A Unified Framework for Detecting, Opening and Navigating Through Doors

Tatsuya Harada[1], Antonio Tejero-de-Pablos[1(✉)], Stefano Quer[2]ⓘ,
and Francesco Savarese[1,2]

[1] Machine Intelligence Lab., The University of Tokyo, Tokyo, Japan
`antonio-t@mi.t.u-tokyo.ac.jp`
[2] Department of Control and Computer Engineering,
Politecnico di Torino, Turin, Italy

Abstract. For an autonomous robotic system, detecting, opening, and navigating through doors remains a very challenging problem. It involves several hard-to-solve sub-tasks such as recognizing the door frame and the handle, discriminating between different type of doors and their status, and opening and moving through the doorway. Previous works often tackle single individual sub-problems, assuming that the robot is moving in a well-known static environments or it is already facing the door handle. However, ignoring navigation issues, using specialized robots, or restricting the analysis to specific types of doors or handles, reduce the applicability of the proposed approach. In this paper, we present a unified framework for the door opening problem, by taking a navigation scenario as a reference. We implement specific algorithms to solve each sub-task and we describe the hierarchical automata which integrates the control of the robot during the entire process. We build a publicly available data-set which consists in 780 images of doors and handles crawled from Google Images. Using this data-set, we train a deep learning neural network, exploiting the Single Shot MultiBox Detector, to recognize doors and handles. We implement error recovery mechanisms to add robustness and reliability to our robot, and to guarantee a high success rate in every task. We carry-out experiments on a realistic scenario, the "Help Me Carry" task of the RoboCup 2018, using a standard service robot, the Toyota Human Support Robot. Our experiments demonstrate that our framework can successfully detect, open, and navigate through doors in a reliable way, with low error rates, and without adapting the environment to the robot.

Keywords: Service robotics · Door opening · State machines · Object detection · Autonomous system

1 Introduction

Today the greatest challenge in robotics is to create robots which are able to perform increasingly complex tasks autonomously and with little previous

© Springer Nature Switzerland AG 2020
M. van Sinderen and L. A. Maciaszek (Eds.): ICSOFT 2019, CCIS 1250, pp. 179–204, 2020.
https://doi.org/10.1007/978-3-030-52991-8_9

knowledge about the environment around them. Former approaches concentrate on static (unchanging) environments, with little or no interaction between the robot and the environment. Latter frameworks have modeled non-static environments, and at a bare minimum, they must navigate in and interact with them autonomously.

The first attempts of human-robot cooperation focused on robots capable of guiding people in human coexisting environments [4,13,23]. Minerva [32] was installed in the Smithsonian's National Museum of American History during two weeks in 1998. The evolutionary Mobot Museum Robot Series [31] were permanently installed robots which have operated in public spaces for many years. However, influenced by the aging population problem, service robotics has focused on the design of robots to assist elderly people, or people with mobility impairments, in their daily life at home [12]. Current approaches emphasize the ability to autonomously navigate unknown environments (such as houses or offices), to perform common tasks (such as picking up objects or delivering articles), and to interact with humans [9]. For example, the Defense Advanced Research Projects Agency (DARPA) Robotics Challenge (DRC) program recently conducted a series of prize-based competition events to develop and demonstrate technology for disaster response [11,17,19]. The DRC Finals required robots to perform eight tasks: Drive, Egress, Door, Valve, Wall, Surprise, Rubble, and Stairs. Door opening has drawn attention not only because it is a very common task but also because of its complexity. In the "Door" task of the DRC, the robot was supposed to open a door and to travel through a 91.4 cm (36 in.) doorway, without the human assistance. Very detailed specifications were used to simplify the task. The doorway had no physical threshold, and the door could be opened inward (away from the robot). The handle was a standard American with Disabilities Act-compliant lever, which released the latch in either the up or the down direction. The task was considered complete when all points of robot ground contact were past the door threshold.

In general, a robust unified pipeline including navigation and door opening, which does not rely on prior knowledge of the environment or on the characteristics of the door, requires the following tasks: Detection of the door, estimation of the type and status of the door, understanding of the opening direction, recognition and grasping of the handle, and navigation through the door. Many existing approaches tackle this pipeline only partially and they concentrate on independent tasks, often neglecting navigation issues. Many other techniques suppose that the robot initially faces the door. Unfortunately, the position of the robot with respect to the door can greatly influence the success of the handle detection process, meaning that the robot needs to know the position of the door within the environment to proceed correctly. Thus, these strategies are not suitable for realistic scenarios in which the robot is moving and interacting with a dynamically changing environment. Moreover, while an off-the-shelf system is desirable, most of the existing approaches use custom-made robots which imply very high costs and completely hinder reproducibility.

In this work, we present a unified framework to open doors while navigating the environment. We assume the robot navigates an unmodified house, that is, a house furnished with common furniture pieces and with non-automatic doors. We consider robot navigation in a structured environment, admitting semantic navigation. This allows studying the door opening problem from the perspective of a realistic navigation problem. We suppose no prior knowledge of the properties of the doors such that these attributes (i.e., door width, handle position, and opening direction) are estimated at run-time. We also recognize whether the door is closed or partially open, whether it has to be pushed or pulled, and we perform appropriate actions to open it. We present a detailed hierarchical automata model of our framework. Using this model, we decompose the overall task into sub-tasks, and we perform proper error recovery during all main phases. We solve the implied sub-problems adopting a unified approach, providing detailed explanations of the resulting automata. To automatic detect doors and handles, we leverage a deep learning approach based on the Single Shot MultiBox Detector (SSD). In order to train such a detector, we build and make available the "MIL-door" data-set[1], including 780 different images of doors and handles. After the door and the handle have been detected, depth images are used to evaluate the location of the handle with a higher precision. This strategy allows our robot to recognize doors and handles even while navigating through unknown environments, that is, without previously knowing their existence.

While the majority of the proposed solutions use specific architectures, such as the Personal Robot 2 (PR2) robotic platform [21] or other custom-made robots [17], we implemented our framework into a standard general purpose robot, namely, the Toyota Human Support Robot (HSR) [33], To evaluate it, we chose a complex task among the RoboCup 2018 [26] challenges, namely the "Help Me Carry" task. In this task, the user instructs the robot to fetch an object in a specific location in a different room, and he awaits for the robot to return. We force the robot to follow different paths on the outward journey and on its way back (with different doors along the two paths) and we dynamically change the environment status during its trip. After that, we focus on the sub-task of grasping an handle, forcing our HSR platform to deal with a large variety of doors and handles. We present extensive experimentation showing low failure rate and a very efficient recovery procedure, able to rectify errors in the majority of the cases. Overall, our analysis show the high reproducibility and the broad applicability of our approach.

It has to be noticed that this work is an extended version of the conference paper [29]. While the conference paper focuses only on a few steps of the entire work-flow, the current one describes the entire process with more details, more accurate author's considerations and hints on the work done. Abstract, introduction, contributions, related works, and conclusions have been completely rewritten and are now organized in a completely different way. The core sections include new details and some extra descriptive pictures. An explicit section on

---

[1] The data set is publicly available at https://www.mi.t.u-tokyo.ac.jp/projects/mildoor.

future works has also been added to indicate our current effort in the area. References are now more complete and updated.

1.1   Contributions

The principle of the proposed framework is to provide a comprehensible solution to the problem of door opening in a unified fashion. That is, while most related works focus only in individual modules (e.g., door detection [7], door unlatching [25], we tackle the entire problem end to end: From the moment the robot starts navigating the environment to the moment the robot traverses the door and reaches its destination. The direct benefit of such a unified framework is its high applicability to solve a real-world door-opening problem. Moreover, to the best of our knowledge, current literature does not contain any method or evaluation for amalgamating all the required modules to solve the end-to-end door opening problem. Building such a framework is challenging, given the complexity of the system obtained when combining all modules. To successfully build the proposed framework, we identified the following design requirements:

- Comprehensibility: The end-to-end door opening problem involves multiple behaviors. A state-machine implementation should follow an understandable relationship among the modules, and consider all possible cases in the task pipeline.
- Robustness: The framework should be able to handle an error at any point of the state machine execution.
- Reproducibility: Other researchers should be able to re-implement our framework. For that, explicitly specifying the parameter values used and other implementation details is essential, but not enough. Deploying the framework on a standard platform is also preferable over a closed implementation.

In this research, in order to achieve comprehensibility, our implementation of the framework follows a hierarchical structure of state machines. In order to achieve robustness, we also define an error recovery module that can deal with errors at any point of the door opening. The error recovery module behaves in a hierarchical fashion, to adapt to the state machine structure of our network. In order to achieve reproducibility, we provide the necessary details as well as sharing the datasets built for the training. In addition, we employed the Toyota HSR standard robot platform to deploy our framework and conduct our experiments.

To sum up, our contributions are the following:

- We present a unified framework to open doors while our robot navigates through an unmodified house. We suppose no prior knowledge of the property of the doors or the handles, as these characteristics are estimated at run-time. Our robot autonomously recognizes doors and handles, it performs automatic door type detection, and it executes appropriate actions to open and to traverse it.
- We describe our framework using a hierarchical automata model. The model is adopted to decompose the overall task into sub-tasks and to perform proper

error recovery during all main phases. A deep learning neural network is used to detect doors and handles in the unknown environment.
- We implement our framework into a standard general purpose robot, the Toyota Human Support Robot. We analyze our robot's behavior during the "Help Me Carry" task in a realistic scenario, and we check it with several type of doors and handle. Overall, we prove the high reproducibility and the broad applicability of our approach.

1.2 Roadmap

The remainder of the paper is organized as follow. Section 2 reports details on related and recent works in the same area. Section 3 describes our hardware and software platforms, and our semantic navigation framework. Section 3.4 overviews our solution from the point of view of an automata model. It also presents the door opening problem, and it explains our solutions to solve all sub-tasks, It finally introduces a realistic scenario, i.e., the "Help Me Carry" task, which we take as a reference. before and after making contact with the door. Section 5 describes the experiments we run to evaluate our framework. Finally, Sect. 6 summarizes our conclusions, and it discusses future research lines.

2   Related Works

In the field of computer vision, many research groups have proposed solutions to the problem of navigating an environment and interacting with it. Other works have focused more on recognizing door frameworks and handles, and moving through the doorways. The challenging task of door opening while navigating the environment has also received a lot of attention.

Rhee et at. [25] develop an indoor service robot equipped with a manipulator, with 6 degree of freedom and a multi-fingered hand, specifically adapted to door opening. As appropriately managing sensors and motions is essential for a service robot system, the authors propose active sensing methodologies in order to overcome uncertainty problems in real environments.

Kim et al. [6] employ cheap three-axis force sensors to successfully open a door using a home service robot called Hombot, which is equipped with an anthropomorphous manipulator arm.

Petrovskaya et al. [24] present a unified, real-time, algorithm that simultaneously models the position of the robot within the environment, as well as the objects to be manipulated. The approach is motivated by the fact that the state of an object significantly impacts the navigation task, thus the authors' goal is to simultaneously model a dynamic environment and to localize the robot within it.

Aude et al. [2] propose a new algorithm to enable a robot to autonomously find and cross doors within an unknown environment based on two main features: The identification of long straight lines and the determination of the baseboard's angle and position. They also restrict the robot's knowledge about the environment to the door's width and they detect door frames through image manipulation based on Gaussian and Sobel Filters and Hough Transforms.

Ott et al. [22] focus on the task of opening a door with no previous knowledge of the door size or on the door opening trajectory. The whole application is divided into three sub-tasks: The localization of the door handle, the turning and opening of the door handle, the movement through the door hinge until the door is sufficiently wide open. The exact localization of the door handle with respect to the mobile platform is done by using an on-board laser range scanner and a vision system.

Andreopoulos et al. [1] try to solve the door opening problem using a robotics wheelchair. They used a computer vision approach based on Viola-Jones for door and handle recognition. However, they only study handle detection and grasping, without proposing a method for door opening.

Jain et al. [10] roughly estimate the handle position using a laser scan. After that, the robot haptically searches for the door handle over the surface of the door. After the handle unlatching, the door is pushed to be opened. They do not study the case of pulling door and they do not move the robot through the door.

Rusu et al. [28] present a laser-based approach for door and handle identification. The approach builds on a 3D perception pipeline to annotate doors and their handles solely from sensed laser data, without any a priori model learning. In particular, the authors segment the parts of interest using robust geometric estimators and statistical methods applied on geometric and intensity distribution variations in the scan.

Klingbeil et al. [15] combine a visual algorithm with laser data to locate the handle in the space. However, after handle unlatching, they do not tackle the problem of door opening.

Similar considerations can be made for Chitta et al. [5], where a planning algorithm is proposed for opening (pulling and pushing) doors, but the robot needs to know in advance if the target door is a pulling or a pushing one.

Meeussen et al. [21] propose a framework that integrates autonomous navigation and door opening. For door detection, they use a point cloud representation, while for handle recognition, they combine laser scans and a computer vision approach. Although they analyzed the entire navigation and door opening problem, their approach requires the knowledge of several details on the environment, such as the door width and the door type.

Kim et al. [14] detect doors using a context-based object recognition. The authors use the robotic context, such as the robot's viewpoint and the average height of doorknobs, to enhance the efficiency of object recognition. Robotic context is applied in the pre-processing step of object recognition to speed up the process and to reduce the false-positive rate by restricting the search space in the captured image. This approach, albeit applying for the first time both robotic context and shape-based object recognition to door detection, has a limited applicability due to the necessity to known the environment.

Gray et al. [8] present a framework that handles non-spring and spring-loaded doors, in cluttered or confined work-spaces, planning the approach to the door, pushing or pulling it open, and passing through. These task remain challenging as spring-loaded doors require making and breaking contacts with the door and preventing the door from closing while passing through. In order to plan a door-opening procedure quickly and reliably, the author start the planning using a low-dimensional, graph-based representation of the problem. However, the author do not analyze the entire problem flow. Moreover, their opening strategy requires to store additional information about the doors.

Shalaby et al. [30] build a navigation assisting tool for visually impaired people. Their based this tool on an inexpensive digital camera, such as the one used by tablets or mobile devices, able to gather information from the surrounding environment. The author also present a technique for reliable and robust door identification pairing visual information and door geometric description seen as a 4-side polygons. They implement and test the algorithm using MATLAB and its large image processing library. However, the approach requires a prior knowledge of doors details (such as the height of the handle), limiting the method applicability to only well-known scenarios.

Vertical edges have long been used by the robotics community as a first step for door detection. Fernández et al. [7] concentrate on high-level features, like doors and corridors, which are considered as key elements in urban buildings to achieve a localization with a high semantic or symbolic processing capabilities. The authors evaluate the position of the surrounding doors by fusing the information from a monocular web-cam and a 2D laser rangefinder. By considering a real-world environment, the authors demonstrate that their technique may perform the door detection task very reliably with a computational cost that allows the procedure to be used with light on-board computers and end-user cameras.

Lee et al. [18] develop a motion planning algorithm to enable humanoids to remove an object that is blocking its path. To remove an object in its path, a humanoid must be able to reach it. Unfortunately, stretching the arms (which are shorter than the body and the legs) is not sufficient to reach an object located at some distance away or on the ground. Therefore, the authors ensured reachability by a combination of motions that include kneeling and orienting the pelvis. Indeed, they focus on the optimization of the posture of a humanoid that is reaching toward a point, which depends on the initial posture, the location of the point, and the desired manipulability of the humanoid's arms.

The Defense Advanced Research Projects Agency (DARPA) Robotics Challenge (DRC) [17] was motivated by the 2011 nuclear disaster at Fukushima, in Japan. This event illuminated society's vulnerability to natural and man-made disasters and the inability of existing robot technology to help avert or ameliorate the damage. Given this framework, Johnson et al. [11] discus the challenges they faced in transitioning from simulation to hardware. They also illustrate the lessons learned both during the training period and the competition, addressing the value of reliable hardware and solid software practices. Given the same framework, Jeongsoo et al. [19] run experiments on robots performing tasks in a nuclear disaster situation. The authors concentrate on a humanoid robot platform (i.e., the DRC-HUBO+) able to solve complex tasks under restricted communication conditions, as the ones in a region filled with radiation. They presented a survey of their platform including the overall hardware configuration, software architecture, various control methods for operating the robot, and the vision system. They also provide details on the task-oriented vision algorithms that were used to solve the given tasks.

Boston Dynamics [3] presented a solution based on the cooperation of two SpotMini robots. However, given the robot structure (i.e., a four-legged robot), it is hard to transfer the approach to common service robots. Moreover, their approach is not public.

3   Configuration

3.1   Hardware Platform

As our development platform, we used the Toyota *Human Support Robot* (HSR). The robot is aimed at helping elderly people and people with disabilities. Given its design, HSR is optimal for operating in home settings without any modification that facilitates its tasks (e.g., automatic doors). Toyota also provides some primitives and some basic software routine for controlling the robot.

The HSR body is cylindrical with a set of wheels that makes the robot movable in all directions. It is equipped with a folding arm capable of grabbing objects, manipulating handles and even grasping paper sheets from the floor. Thanks to its microphone array and its speakers, HSR is able to receive voice commands and communicate with the user. Several sensors allow the robot interacting with the surrounding environment. The HSR head is equipped with a stereo video camera and a depth camera. The robot base is equipped with a collision detector. The Robot Operating System (ROS)[2] is installed on the robot, allowing communicating with the hardware layer. This way, writing low level controlling algorithms is not necessary.

3.2   Software Architecture

Figure 1 shows our software architecture. We designed it to implement the robot's functionality, and it is the backbone of the entire system. It allows managing several basic tasks, the human-robot interaction, and easily adding new functionality on-demand (e.g., replacing voice commands with visual QR-code inputs). This improves system versatility, but it is not essential for the paper's goal.

---

[2] http://www.ros.org.

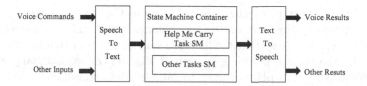

Fig. 1. Our robot software architecture consists of three layers: A speech to text layer for command processing, a state machine container layer that activates state machines according to the task, and a text to speech layer for result conveying.

We defined three different layers:

- A command processing layer (speech-to-text). We use the HSR's microphone array to capture the user command, and then we internally process it.
- A container (state machine container). State machines are deployed to solve different tasks.
- A user-friendly communication layer (text-to-speech). This is used to convey the operation results to the user.

The first layer processes the user's voice command, and it forwards the result to the second layer. To interpret the voice command, and generate a command, we used the Google Cloud Speech-to-Text API[3]. This tool allows developers to convert speech into text exploiting the power of neural networks and using the Google Cloud suite. Depending on the given command, the second layer activates the proper state machine to execute the task required by the user. The third layer receives the results of the state machines, which are interpreted and communicated to the user in a user-friendly fashion. The state machine container is the element that provides flexibility to the entire architecture. It is possible, in fact, to embed new state machines for executing tasks. We implement all state machines using SMACH[4].

3.3 Semantic Navigation Framework

For the path planning we rely on the ROS global and local path planners. These modules receive the desired coordinates in the space, and they convert these coordinates into commands to move the robot. Using the ROS navigation stack built-in Hector-SLAM algorithm [16] we can create a map describing the environment and the obstacles. This map allows the robot to receive coordinates and reach specific locations by automatically choosing an optimal path free of obstacles. However, semantic navigation requires a richer description of the environment to convert human understandable locations (e.g., *the kitchen table*) into suitable coordinates for the robot. As a consequence, additional information needs to be

---

[3] https://cloud.google.com/speech-to-text.
[4] SMACH is a ROS-independent Python library for building hierarchical state machines.

added to the map to improve the knowledge about the environment. We propose a framework for creating and managing semantic maps. This framework works as an interface layer, converting the location sent by the user to a location understandable by the motion planning module. Using RVIZ[5] we manually associate coordinates in the path planner map to human understandable locations. The association among coordinates and locations are stored as meta-data into an *xml*, and a *csv* files.

We manage two different types of entities in the environment: *Rooms* and *locations*. A room is a portion of the map identified by walls or boundaries. Locations are places inside rooms. Each room can contain multiple locations. A room entity is identified by its name and it is represented by a list of corners, arranged as a polygon, plus a room center. To manage polygons and coordinates we use the python package *matplotlib.path*. A location, on the other hand, is represented by a location name, its coordinates in the map and some attributes describing the place (e.g., "isStorage" is a Boolean attribute stating if the location is a storage area). The hierarchical relationship between rooms and locations are stored in *xml* format while the room and location names with their respective coordinates are stored in *csv* format.

Figure 2 reports an example of the files we use to store the semantic information (left and middle) and a graphical representation of a possible environment map (on the right). The hierarchical relationship between rooms and locations are stored in *xml* format while the room and location names with their respective coordinates are stored in *csv* format. In the graphical representation of a possible environment map, R1–R5 designate rooms and D1–D4 indicate doors. R3 and R5 are not separated by a wall. The position of elements in the map is retrieved with respect a fixed reference system as represented in the figure. The origin of the Cartesian system is the robot initial position, from where the entire process starts. Even though the location of the doors is indicated, the robot keeps checking for the door while approaching it, to calibrate its position and

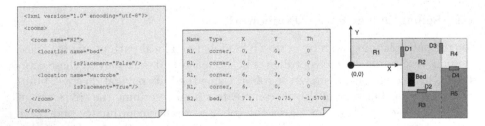

Fig. 2. The file on the left (in xml format) is an example of the rooms-to-locations relationship. The file in the middle (in csv format) is an example of the associations between rooms and locations and coordinates in the map. The map on the right, is the one for the navigation environment, with rooms (R), doors (D), and locations (Bed).

---

[5] RVIZ is a tool for displaying sensor data using ROS.

its state (open/closed, etc.). The semantic navigation framework is also used for completing other tasks, such as localizing a person or an object.

To gain planning stage flexibility, we also developed a way-points based navigation approach. In this way, to move the robot between two locations in the map, we can force it to follow intermediate points not belonging to a specific or optimal path. This is particularly useful to test motion features in specific parts of the scenario, or to reach specific places during the trajectory (e.g., to force the robot to pass through a specific door). The path between intermediate points is computed by the ROS path planner. A dictionary data structure is used to represent way-points paths: The keys are entity pairs (i.e., the source and the destination in the map), and the values are the list of places reached along the path. The way-points dictionary is stored as a *json* file. The way-points based navigation is activated if the pair source-destination is present in the dictionary. Figure 3 is an example of dictionary to reach each room in Fig. 2, starting from room R1 and using doors as way-points.

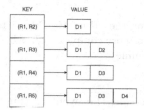

Fig. 3. Dictionary representing paths based on way-points.

3.4 The "Help Me Carry" Context

As a realistic scenario for door opening, we based our study on the "Help Me Carry" task included in *Robocup 2018*. To complete it, the robot has to memorize locations, move following user commands, avoid obstacles, and open doors. The task description is as follows. The user went shopping, and needs the robot's help for bringing inside all the bags. To complete the task the robot will:

1. Follow the owner to the bags.
2. Memorize the bags location.
3. Understand the owner's command to bring the bags to a specific different location.
4. Bring all bags to that desired specified location.

The automaton designed to perform the task is shown in Fig. 4. Blue circles indicate operational states, green ones are initial states, and yellow ones represent ending states. The red color represents error recovery states. Black and red dashed arrows indicate transitions between states and transitions between a state and the error recovery state, respectively. The red lines are bi-directional because after the error handling the control may be given back to the calling state.

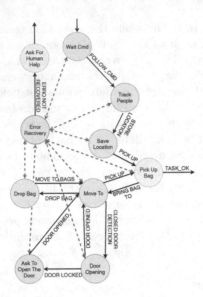

Fig. 4. Automaton representing the "Help Me Carry" task. It shows the problem of door opening in the context of a more complex task, which involves human interaction and navigation. (Color figure online)

The text on the arrows represent the event causing the transition. Each state is implemented as an automaton, hence the overall architecture is a hierarchical state machine. For the sake of readability, we did not used the often used "double border" notation to identify nested state machines. This structure is quite flexible and it is easy to maintain.

As an example of behavior, the robot is activated in the state named "Wait Cmd" (wait for command). In this state the robot simply waits for commands coming from the user. If the command for following the user is received, the state machine transit to the "Track People" state. Otherwise, if the command cannot be correctly interpreted, the state machine transits to the "Error Recovery" state. The general policy of the "Error Recovery" state is that, if the error is rectified, the control is given back to the incoming state. If the error cannot be rectified, the state returns the control to a higher level state machine or directly interacts with the user asking for help.

4   Nesting Automata

Detecting, opening and navigating through doors is a complex problem that involves many algorithms. In our approach, we decomposed the problem into different stages. The flowchart in Fig. 5 (left-hand side) describes the algorithmic approach we followed.

Each block involves different technologies and techniques. The top part represents the overall door/handle detection, and the door parameters estimation.

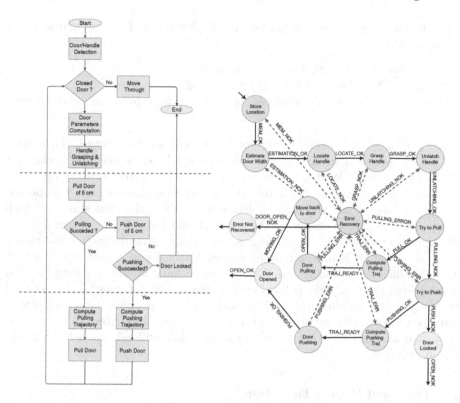

Fig. 5. On the left, we report the operational flowchart for door opening. It includes the entire flow from the moment if which the robot detects a door to the one in which it crosses the door or it understands that the door is locked. On the right, we illustrate our automaton for door opening. The names over the red dashed lines indicate the type of transition between a state and the "Error Recovery" state. (Color figure online)

The door type (pulling or pushing) is checked in the central part, whereas the opening phase is executed at the bottom part. In summary, the robot autonomously recognizes the door, it localizes the handle for grasping, and it decides the opening action (i.e., pulling or pushing). To open the door, the robot needs to know two parameters, i.e., the opening direction (pushing or pulling), and the door width. Following many other approaches, these characteristics could be annotated in advance in the environment description. However, we want to achieve a flexible and completely autonomous interaction with the door. Therefore, our robot computes the door width and the opening direction at run-time. The automaton implementing our door opening approach is shown on the right-hand side of Fig. 5. Notice that this state machine is nested in the automaton designed for the overall "Help Me Carry" task and previously described in Fig. 4. The door opening state machine is launched when the robot detects a closed door. In the first state the current location is memorized. The following states complete the entire process described in the flowchart. The automaton has 3 ending states:

- "Door Opened": Reached when the door is open.
- "Door Locked": Reached if the door is locked.
- "Error Not Recovered": Reached if an error that prevents door opening occurs.

If the "Door Locked" or the "Error Not Recovered" states are reached, the door can not be opened. This situation is managed by the state machine working at a higher hierarchical level (i.e., the one in Fig. 4). Our error recovery approach plays an essential role to reach robustness and flexibility against unexpected situations. First of all, the error is handled locally within the state in which occurs. For the sake of usability, the robot should not rely on human help for solving minor issues. Thus, in our framework, each state stores enough knowledge of the situation to handle minor problems. Examples of minor errors are: A wrong handle recognition in the 3D space, a grasping failure, a wrong location spelling from the user, etc. If local error correction is not possible, the control flow jumps to the previous (higher) hierarchical level, in which the error recovery state tries more drastic error rectification procedures. Only after the system has attempted all error recovery procedures, the robot will ask for help from the human operator.

4.1   Door and Handle Detection

For the door and handle detection we use a deep learning approach. Several deep neural networks have been proposed for object detection, and more specifically for door and handle recognition. Among state-of-the-art networks, we decided to exploit the Single Shot MultiBox Detector (SSD) neural network [20]. Authors proved that this network outperforms other well know networks, like Yolo and Faster R-CNN in terms of speed and accuracy. Moreover, since SSD performs better on embedded systems, the network can work correctly at run-time, and it guarantees a fast interaction with the environment. Compared to other single shot methods, SSD provides a much better accuracy, even with a smaller input image size. The input to SSD is a monocular color image, and the output is a list of bounding boxes containing the detected objects in the image, namely, the top left angle of each detected object plus its height and width (*object detection* part). Each detected object has an associated label indicating which class the object belongs to (*object recognition* part).

In our version of SSD, the object recognition part is based on the VGG16 model pre-trained on the ILSVRC CLS-LOC data-set [27]. Then, we trained the object detection part, and fine-tuned the object recognition part, by constructing our own data-set, the "MIL-door" data-set. The "MIL-door" data-set consists of images of "doors" and "handles" crawled from Google Images. After filtering the erroneous results, MIL-door contains 462 images of doors and 318 images of handles, for a total of 780 images. The height and width of the images range from 400 to 1200 pixels. For each image, we manually annotated bounding boxes delimiting the area corresponding to doors and handles. Annotations are not inserted on top of the images, but stored in a separate text file. Figure 6 shows three example images extracted from our annotated data-set.

When training our SSD network with the MIL-door data-set, we performed data augmentation on the training data, namely, 90° rotations and horizontal flips. This increases the size of our data-set eight times, for a total of 6240 images. Considering that the object detection part of the original SSD was trained with 9963 images for 20 object classes, we believe our data size is reasonable for our 2 object class detection problem.

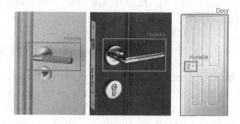

Fig. 6. Sample images from the "MIL-door" data-set.

As training parameters, we used the following configuration (please refer to [20] for more details on the meaning of these parameters): Batch size 32, maximum iterations 120, 000, learning rate 0.001 (the original learning rate is decayed by 10 at iterations 80, 000, 100, 000 and 120, 000), weight decay 0.0005, γ 0.1, momentum 0.9.

We used a low learning rate to assure convergence during training and we selected it empirically. We evaluated our door and handle detection with our MIL-door data-set using a 10-fold cross-validation setting. We consider that the door (or handle) has been correctly detected if the intersection over union (IoU) between the estimated bounding box and the annotation is greater than 85%. The detection accuracy in this controlled setting is of 94.7% for doors, and 86.3% for handles. However, during the evaluation in a real setting, the IoU recognition accuracy was slightly lower than using the data-set images. This was mainly due to three factors: The large diversity of doors that exist in the real world, the small size of some handles, and sporadic image quality loss due to poor lighting conditions.

Since there are cases in which the door is detected but the handle is not, we designed an error recovery algorithm to add robustness. When a door is detected but the handle is not, the robot moves slightly forward, backwards, and laterally to change the perspective until the recognition succeeds. If the handle is not detected after a certain number of trials (5 in our case), the error is passed to the above error recovery state in the state machine hierarchy.

4.2   Door Width Computation

The door width is an important parameter to correctly estimate the robot's trajectory. To compute it, we combine the door size in the image, taken from the robot camera, and the door to robot distance computed using the depth camera. Assuming that the object width on the image is $width_{image}$, and the detected distance is d, we can obtain the relative size in the real world using the following formula:

$$width_{real\ [pixel]} = width_{image} \cdot d. \tag{1}$$

However, Eq. 1 measures the door size using the pixels as measurement unit. To transform the computed value from pixel into centimeters, we empirically calibrated our camera and we computed a conversion factor $conversion_{coeff}$. The door width, expressed in length units (centimeters), is thus given by:

$$width_{real\ [cm]} = d \cdot conversion_{coeff} \cdot width_{image}. \tag{2}$$

We measured the quality of our method by comparing our estimated widths against ground truth values, on four different types of doors. These doors differ in terms of color, surface material, and shape. We also varied the distance of the robot from the door from 1 m to 3 m, measures that are somehow reasonable in a home environment. We used the root mean square error to evaluate the error. Our results show that we reached an average error of $\pm$ 6 cm. As observed in our experiments, this value does not affect the door opening noticeably.

4.3   Opening Direction

To open the door, the robot should move backward from left to right if the hinges are on the right, and vice-versa. Anyway recognizing the hinge position is not robust enough, since hinges are often undefined or barely visible. However, our handle and door detector provides the handle location with respect to the door, and thus, inferring the opening direction is straightforward. The opening direction is used to compute the opening trajectory for both pulling and pushing doors (see Sects. 4.7 and 4.8, respectively).

4.4   Closed Door

The door detected in the door recognition phase may be already open. To check this, we use the HSR's RGB-D sensor, the Xtion PRO LIVE. First, we obtain the depth image corresponding to the frame where the door has been located. Then, we take two horizontal rows (e.g., one in the lower half and one in the upper). Finally, we compute the Sobel derivative along the horizontal direction of these lines, and we check if it contains values above a certain threshold t. This allows our method to detect if there are edges where the depth suddenly increases, which translates into the door being open.

We experimentally established that the door can be considered open if the log_{10} of the derivatives exceed a threshold $t = 3.5$.

4.5   Handle Grasping and Unlatching

Once the door opening direction has been established, and the distance from the door d evaluated, the robot can approach the handle enough to get a more precise measure of its location with the depth sensor. If some error occurs while evaluating the handle position, we retrieve a new depth measurement from the sensor to get the right location. The robot, with its grip open, gets in front of the door, and when it reaches the handle location, the grip closes and the robot grasps the handle. To unlatch the handle, we combine the robot hand rotation with a downward movement. We rotate the hand 20°, and we move it downwards 10 cm. We empirically found that HSR does not have a strong grip and a rotation plus a downward movement can improve the pressure that the hand can apply to the handle. This allows a robust unlatching even if the handle is not grasped perfectly at its end, or the surface of the handle is slippery (e.g., metallic).

4.6   Door Type Checking

Before computing the opening trajectory the robot has to understand the door type, i.e., whether the door is a pulling or a pushing door. To discriminate between the two categories, after the grasping and the unlatching, the robot tries to move backwards and forward to test the opening type. First, it attempts to pull the door back 5 cm while monitoring the force acting on the wrist torque sensor. The measure of 5 cm has been heuristically selected as a good compromise among several requirements. If during this movement, the torque on the wrist sensor grows continuously, the door cannot be pulled. In this case, the HSR attempts to push the door by moving forward and it checks the force acting on the wrist sensor as before. In case the torque force does not increase in one of these two attempts, the robots start the opening phase (see Sects. 4.7 and 4.8). On the other hand, if the door cannot be pulled or pushed, the robot assumes that the door is locked. The "Error Recovery" state handles this case by calling for human help.

We also considered other approaches for testing the door type. One of those involves monitoring movement of the robot's base while performing the test. This approach did not succeed mainly because, to measure a significant movement of the base, we have to move the robot more than 5 cm. This in turn can damage both the robot and the door (e.g., by pulling a pushing door too hard). Another approach implies the classification of the door type using a computer vision approach. However, this solution depends largely on the size of the training data-set, which should contain a wide variety of doors and annotations indicating their type. Unfortunately, many available images are not annotated, and manually create a large data-set is very time consuming.

Notice that all checks performed by our approach are done to assure robustness and to minimize the number of errors. We emphasize the importance of robustness in such a complicated scenario, since an error in door type recognition could lead to hard-to-manage situations or risks for the robot or the handle and the door integrity.

Fig. 7. A visual example of our door opening approach. The HSR first grasps the handle and then it unlatches it. After that, HSR tries to move back for 5 cm to pull the door. If the door cannot be pulled, the robot moves the handle back to its neutral position, and the door is opened by moving backwards and drawing an angle with respect to the door closing position. During the entire process the door-to-robot distance is maintained constant.

4.7 Door Pulling

Figure 7 shows the entire flow for opening a pulling door, from the moment the robot must grasp the handle to the one in which the door is open. Figure 8 shows the corresponding code flow.

Fig. 8. Schematic code flow for opening a pulling door (left), and opening a pushing door (right). The code flows are encoded as SMACH state machines, and they are fully integrated in our software framework.

When the robot stands in front of the door, and before starting the door pulling phase, the application stores the current robot position. These coordinates will be used when the door is open, as the robot will move back to the stored position to pass through the door. The first three images, from left to right, are part of the door type understanding process described in Sect. 4.6. In the latter phase, the robots moves backward 5 cm to check whether the door is a pulling one. In the affirmative case, the robot moves the handle back to its neutral position. A visual representation is given in the forth picture. This action emulates typical human behavior, and it effectively reduces the load on the robot wrist that does not need to hold the handle down. At this point, the robot computes the pulling trajectory as shown in the fifth image. The final trajectory is an arc-shaped sequence of map coordinates that form an angle of 80° with respect to the door hinges. In this way, the door is opened wide enough for the robot to pass through it.

Because the HSR's arm has less than six degrees-of-freedom (DoF), we have to move the base and the arm together, keeping the robot hand in a fixed position. As a consequence, the door-to-robot distance remains constant. In this way, we do not need to continuously check for collision between the robot and the door. This situation is shown in Fig. 7(e). Once the robot completes the trajectory, it releases the handle, and it moves back in front of the door to continue the navigation toward the final goal. The robot position saved in the first state is used as a target position to cross the door.

4.8 Door Pushing

Following the flowchart of Fig. 5, if the robot detects that the door cannot be pulled, it checks whether it can be pushed, and, in this latter case, the pushing process starts. The pushing door action flow is detailed on the left-hand side image of Fig. 8. As in the pulling door case, our robot attempts to push the door to check the opening type. After the handle releasing phase, the robot moves in front of the door at a fixed distance of 50 cm. Once this position is reached, the robot first extends its arm to reach the door, which is already open a few centimeters after pushing it to check its type. As the robot is going to move forward, reaching the door is not strictly necessary. At the same time, we also monitor the wrist sensor to assure that no unexpected collision occurs. During the pushing phase, the HSR moves forward, and when the phase finishes, the robot is on the other side of the door. The last action executed by the robot before restarting the normal navigation, is to retract its arm into its original and safer position.

To succeed in the pushing action, the handle position is an important parameter. When unlatching the handle, the robot faces it, but during the pushing action, some collisions may occur. Since HSR is a left-handed robot, the most unfavorable scenario is when the handle is on the right side. A schematic top-view of this situation is given in Fig. 9. Since HSR is a left-handed robot, the most unfavorable scenario is when the handle is on the right side of the door.

While pushing the door, a collision check is performed in the robot base to prevent HSR from hitting the door frame. If a potential collision situation is detected, the robot is moved slightly to the left with respect to the handle. If a collision is detected, the "Error Recovery" state stops the robot and moves it back to the beginning of the pushing stage. These strategies were validated empirically, and allowed for a safe and robust navigation through doors, as described in the next section.

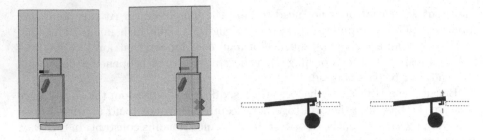

Fig. 9. The figure shows two ways of pushing a door and passing through it, depending on the handle position (left or right-hand side). Since HSR is a left-handed robot, the most unfavorable scenario is when the handle is on the right side of the door. In this case the HSR may suffer a collision. To avoid hitting the door frame, the sensor on the robot base is activated. If HSR detects a possible collision, its position is slightly shifted to the left.

5   Experimental Analysis

We evaluated our unified framework by means of two set of experiments. These experiments were designed to verify two main aspects: 1) Our framework's robustness in a real navigation scenario, and 2) The quality of the entire door opening process with different doors, handles, materials, etc.

First, we evaluated the door opening process in a realistic navigation scenario by using a simplified version of the "Help Me Carry" task previously described. In this task, the user instructs the robot to fetch an object in a specific location in a different room, and he awaits for the robot to return. We also imposed way-points during navigation, i.e., we force the robot to follow a different path on the way back. To run this scenario, we arranged a house environment similar to the one in Fig. 2. Initially, the HSR robot is in a location within room R1. The robot is supposed to reach room R4 by passing through doors D1, D2, and D4. Then, it should go back to the initial position by passing through doors D3 and D1. The doors in this task have different characteristics. When moving from R1 to R2, door D1 is a pushing door with the handle on the left. Door D2 is open. When moving from R5 to R4, and door D4 is a pulling door with its handle on the left. On the way back, when moving from R4 to R2, door D3 is a pulling door with its handle on the left. Finally, when the robot moves back from R2 to R1, D1 is still open. The robot detected the doors during navigation, following a route determined by the ROS path planner. Since the experiment does not involve any obstacles, we did not employed the way-points navigation approach. Notice that the door type and handle position affects the door opening process in terms of the selected trajectories and the final success rate. In order to show the robustness of our framework, the door and handle attributes are unknown by the robot.

We commanded the robot to execute the task 50 times. In all cases, the robot reached R4 without navigation errors, and it successfully detected and discriminated between closed and opened doors. The accuracy of the door and the handle detection in the real scenario does not vary significantly with respect to the detection accuracy reported for our MIL-door data-set. Whenever a handle was not initially recognized, the error recovery procedure forced the robot to move slightly forward, backwards, and laterally to change the perspective until the recognition was successful. This procedure provided a recognition success rate up to 95%. In the remaining 5%, the error persisted so the higher hierarchical automata level dealt with it. Moreover, even if initially the location of the detected handle was not aligned perfectly, the location was refined when approaching the handle and using depth images. Regarding the handle grasping, every time the HSR could not hold the grip on a handle, the error recovery procedure reactivated the detection phase and the "door opening" phase restarted from the beginning.

In light of these results, we designed a second experiment with an emphasis on the handle grasping sub-task. In this experiment, the HSR had to deal with a variety of doors and handles, which differ in terms of door type (pushing or pulling), handle position (left or right), and material (slippery or non-slippery). We commanded the robot to move from room R1 to room R2 while modifying the configuration of D1. The robot starts in front of the door ready to grasp the handle, and it stops after the door is open (passing through is not required). As above, the robot does not know the door and handle attributes. We conducted 20 runs for each door and handle configuration. Notice that the door type influences the robot trajectory, whereas the handle material influences the quality of the handle grasp and its holding process. Moreover, some metallic handles may cause noise in the depth image due to reflections. We separate the door opening results for slippery handles (metallic), and non-slippery handles (wood or plastic-like material), and their location with respect to the door (i.e., left or right). Similarly, we also consider spring loaded doors, that is, doors that close by themselves after they are open. We do not evaluate opening pushing spring loaded doors since, once the robot arm releases the handle after the unlatching, the door closes again before the HSR has the chance to push it.

Table 1 summarizes the results for this second experiment. The handle localization using depth images proved to be robust with different handle shapes and materials. After the handle grasping, our approach recognized in 100% of the cases the door type, i.e., whether the HSR had to pull or push the door. As the HSR grip did not have enough strength to hold slippery handles (in particular, those in spring loaded doors) the door opening did not always succeed. However, when an error arose, the robot was able to retry the task by itself by following the error recovery procedure previously described. The robot asked for human help only in a total of 3 occasions. This results are very promising for a practical application, as the recovery procedure is able to rectify errors in most cases. However, for the sake of fairness, Table 1 considers runs as failed whenever an error arose, even if the robot recovered from the error autonomously. Overall, we reached a 98% of success rate for non-slippery handles, and 94% for slippery metal-like handles. Notice that these results are influenced not only by the robot's grasping ability, but also by the handle detection under different types of light reflection on the handle surface. Regarding pulling spring loaded doors, holding the handle when opening was quite challenging for the robot, specially in the case of slippery handles. This is due to the limited strength of the HSR's grip. Moreover, handles on the right side of pushing doors are more challenging due to the reasons explained in Sect. 4.8.

Table 1. Results of our door opening approach. The table presents the number of successes out of 20 opening attempts, with 4 different handle types. T_1: Slippery handle on the door left side. T_2: Slippery handle on the door right side. T_3: Non-slippery handle on the door left side. T_4: Non-slippery handle on the door right side.

Action type	Handle type			
	T_1	T_2	T_3	T_4
Pulling non-spring loaded door	16	18	18	19
Pulling spring loaded door	16	18	19	19
Pushing non-spring loaded door	20	18	20	17

5.1 Final Considerations

As seen in the evaluation, the door opening task takes advantage of the proposed framework in multiple ways:

- The benefit of our unified structure: The proposed framework encompasses the entire task of opening a door, from the start of the navigation to the goal after the door is traversed. It provides a comprehensive view of the task and the connection between subtasks, and the modules that implements them.
- The benefit of our door detection module: Our deep learning-based door detection module trained with our MIL door dataset allows recognizing a more variety of doors than rule-based methods. Moreover, it is possible to fine-tune it for adaptation to other environments if necessary.
- The benefit of the error recovery module: Our error recovery procedure is adapted to the layered structure of our state machine implementation. This allows recovering from multiple errors in different parts of the framework, making it possible to return to an upper layer if there is a problem in the current subtask that cannot be overcome.
- The benefit of using a standard platform: To solve the door opening scenario, we leverage the functionalities (e.g., sensors, navigation, etc.) of Toyota's HSR, so our proposed solution can be easily reproduced for researchers using the same or a similar platform. There is also a community for HSR[6] that supports developers and provides useful software.

Most importantly, by evaluating the framework in an end-to-end manner, we came across several errors and situations that cannot be observed when evaluating individual parts of the problem. For example, readjusting the door position

---

[6] https://newsroom.toyota.co.jp/jp/detail/8709536.

while approaching the door, collisions during door traversing, etc. Therefore, this work is a valuable contribution to the community of software developers for robots, in particular, those participating in robot competitions (e.g., Robocup), who value practical application over theoretical discussion.

6 Conclusions

In this paper we present a unified robotic framework for approaching, opening, and navigating through doors. The paper covers the analysis, design, and synthesis of such a system and our experiments on a real scenario. To the best of our knowledge, this is one of the first attempts to solve the door opening problem in a navigation scenario.

Our unified framework integrates an automata model and its state machine hierarchy. The state machine includes techniques for error recovery, enabling a robust door opening framework. We propose a deep learning-based method for door and handle detection. To appropriately train our neural network, we create, and we made publicly available, a large door and handle image dataset. To facilitate the reproducibility of our work, we implement our framework on a standard platform, i.e., the Toyota Human Support Robot (HSR). Handle grasping, door type checking, door unlatching and opening have been performed with techniques optimized for our HSR framework, but they are extrapolable to similar off-the-shelf platforms with moderate effort.

We evaluate our application in a challenging realistic scenario, named the "Help Me Carry" task within the RoboCup 2018 challenge. To complete its task, the robot was required to memorize locations, move around in an unknown environment, follow user commands, avoid obstacles, and open doors. We tested our platform against different types of doors, different types of handles, and both door opening directions (inward and outward). The robot successfully identifies the door state, distinguishing between totally open, widely open, slightly open and closed doors. The robot is also able to judge if the doorway is suitable for crossing and it is capable to drive itself across the door. Our results show the robustness and flexibility of our approach and its high reproducibility on standard service robotic platforms.

7 Future Works

Among the possible extensions of this work, we report the following.

Our current framework relies on all HSR features, such as the depth camera, the base sensor, and the wrist torque sensor. Currently, a robot missing any of these devices may not be able to perform its duty. We are working on some specific steps of the overall framework to make the application even more flexible in terms of hardware requirements.

As approaches that adapt well to changing environments are increasingly important, we plan to improve the robustness and the flexibility of our application against greater environment modifications, such as recognizing and opening a wider variety of doors and handles. Within this framework, we also have to improve our robot's ability to recognize and adapt its behavior to moving obstacles. A recognition algorithm with the ability to identify removable obstacles and determine the positions of grasping points is required to develop a fully autonomous system. Crowded environments are also a potential target, as occasional passersby cause small unmodeled effects which become more frequent in highly crowded or cluttered environments.

Acknowledgments. We would like to thank Yusuke Kurose, Yujin Tang, Jen-Yen Chang, James Borg, Takayoshi Takayanagi, Yingy Wen and Reza Motallebi for their help implementing this research. This work was partially supported by JST CREST Grant Number JPMJCR1403, Japan. The authors have been part of the HSR developer community (see footnote 6), and they made use of HSR hardware and software platforms.

References

1. Andreopoulos, J.A., Tsotsos, J.K.: A framework for door localization and door opening using a robotic wheelchair for people living with mobility impairments. In: Robotics: Science and Systems, Workshop: Robot Manipulation: Sensing and Adapting to the Real World (2007)
2. Aude, E.P.L., Lopes, E.P., Aguiar, C.S., Martins, M.F.: Door crossing and state identification using robotic vision. In: 8th IFAC Symposium on Robot Control IFAC Proceedings, vol. 39(15), 659–664 (2006). https://doi.org/10.3182/20060906-3-IT-2910.00110, http://www.sciencedirect.com/science/article/pii/S1474667016385895
3. Boston Dynamics: Robots: SPOT. https://www.bostondynamics.com/spot-mini (2019). Accessed 10 Nov 2019
4. Burgard, W., et al.: The interactive museum tour-guide robot. In: Conference on Artificial Intelligence/Innovative Applications of Artificial Intelligence, pp. 11–18. AAAI 1998/IAAI 1998, American Association for Artificial Intelligence, Menlo Park, CA, USA (1998) http://dl.acm.org/citation.cfm?id=295240.295249
5. Chitta, S., Cohen, B., Likhachev, M.: Planning for autonomous door opening with a mobile manipulator. In: IEEE International Conference on Robotics and Automation, pp. 1799–1806, May 2010. https://doi.org/10.1109/ROBOT.2010.5509475
6. Kim, D., Kang, J.-H., Hwang, C.-S., Park, G.-T.: Mobile robot for door opening in a house. In: Negoita, M.G., Howlett, R.J., Jain, L.C. (eds.) KES 2004. LNCS (LNAI), vol. 3215, pp. 596–602. Springer, Heidelberg (2004). https://doi.org/10.1007/978-3-540-30134-9_80
7. Fernández-Caramés, C., Moreno, V., Curto, B., Rodríguez-Aragón, J.F., Serrano, F.: A real-time door detection system for domestic robotic navigation. J. Intell. Robot. Syst. **76**(1), 119–136 (2014). https://doi.org/10.1007/s10846-013-9984-6
8. Gray, S., Chitta, S., Kumar, V., Likhachev, M.: A single planner for a composite task of approaching, opening and navigating through non-spring and spring-loaded doors. In: IEEE International Conference on Robotics and Automation, pp. 3839–3846, May 2013
9. Hernandez, K., Bacca, B., Posso, B.: Multi-goal path planning autonomous system for picking up and delivery tasks in mobile robotics. IEEE Latin Am. Trans. **15**(2), 232–238 (2017)

10. Jain, A., Kemp, C.C.: Behaviors for robust door opening and doorway traversal with a force-sensing mobile manipulator. In: RSS Workshop on Robot Manipulation: Intelligence in Human Environments (2008)
11. Johnson, M., et al.: Team IHMC's lessons learned from the DARPA robotics challenge trials. J. Field Robot. **32**(2), 192–208 (2015). https://doi.org/10.1002/rob. 21571. https://onlinelibrary.wiley.com/doi/abs/10.1002/rob.21571
12. Khatib, O.: Mobile manipulation: the robotic assistant. Robot. Autonomous Syst. **26**(2), 175–183 (1999). https://doi.org/10.1016/S0921-8890(98)00067-0. http://www.sciencedirect.com/science/article/pii/S0921889098000670, field and Service Robotics
13. Kim, G., Chung, W., Kim, K.R., Kim, M., Han, S., Shinn, R.: The autonomous tour-guide robot Jinny. In: IEEE/RSJ International Conference on Intelligent Robots and Systems (IROS). vol. 4, pp. 3450–3455, January 2004. https://doi. org/10.1109/IROS.2004.1389950
14. Kim, S., Cheong, H., Kim, D.H., Park, S.: Context-based object recognition for door detection. In: 15th International Conference on Advanced Robotics (ICAR), pp. 155–160, June 2011
15. Klingbeil, E., Saxena, A., Ng, A.Y.: Learning to open new doors. In: IEEE/RSJ International Conference on Intelligent Robots and Systems, pp. 2751–2757, October 2010. https://doi.org/10.1109/IROS.2010.5649847
16. Kohlbrecher, S., von Stryk, O., Meyer, J., Klingauf, U.: A flexible and scalable SLAM system with full 3D motion estimation. In: IEEE International Symposium on Safety, Security, and Rescue Robotics, pp. 155–160, November 2011. https:// doi.org/10.1109/SSRR.2011.6106777
17. Krotkov, E., et al.: The DARPA robotics challenge finals: results and perspectives. J. Field Robot. **34**(2), 229–240 (2017). https://doi.org/10.1002/rob.21683
18. Lee, I., Oh, J.H.: Humanoid posture selection for reaching motion and a cooperative balancing controller. J. Intell. Robot. Syst. **81**(3), 301–316 (2016). https://doi.org/ 10.1007/s10846-015-0225-z
19. Lim, J., et al.: Robot system of DRC-HUBO+ and control strategy of team KAIST in DARPA robotics challenge finals. J. Field Robot. **34**(4), 802–829 (2017). https:// doi.org/10.1002/rob.21673
20. Liu, W., et al.: SSD: single shot multibox detector. In: Leibe, B., Matas, J., Sebe, N., Welling, M. (eds.) ECCV 2016. LNCS, vol. 9905, pp. 21–37. Springer, Cham (2016). https://doi.org/10.1007/978-3-319-46448-0_2
21. Meeussen, W., et al.: Autonomous door opening and plugging in with a personal robot. In: IEEE International Conference on Robotics and Automation, pp. 729–736. Anchorage, Alaska, USA (2010)
22. Ott, C., Bäuml, B., Borst, C., Hirzinger, G.: Autonomous opening of a door with a mobile manipulator: a case study. In: 6th IFAC PSymposium on Intelligent Autonomous Vehicles, vol. 40, no. 15, pp. 349–354 (2007). https://doi.org/10. 3182/20070903-3-FR-2921.00060, http://www.sciencedirect.com/science/article/ pii/S1474667016346857
23. Peterson, L., Austin, D., Kragic, D.: High-level control of a mobile manipulator for door opening. In: IEEE/RSJ International Conference on Intelligent Robots and Systems (IROS). vol. 3, pp. 2333–2338 (2000). https://doi.org/10.1109/IROS. 2000.895316

24. Petrovskaya, A., Ng, A.Y.: Probabilistic mobile manipulation in dynamic environments, with application to opening doors. In: Proceedings of the 20th International Joint Conference on Artifical Intelligence, pp. 2178–2184. IJCAI 2007, Morgan Kaufmann Publishers Inc., San Francisco, CA, USA (2007). http://dl.acm.org/citation.cfm?id=1625275.1625627

25. Rhee, C., Chung, W., Kim, M., Shim, Y., Lee, H.: Door opening control using the multi-fingered robotic hand for the indoor service robot. In: Proceedings IEEE International Conference on Robotics and Automation, vol. 4, pp. 4011–4016. IEEE, January 2004. https://doi.org/10.1109/ROBOT.2004.1308898

26. RoboCup 2018: http://www.robocup2018.com (2018). Accessed 10 Nov 2019

27. Russakovsky, O., et al.: ImageNet large scale visual recognition challenge. Int. J. Comput. Vis. **115**(3), 211–252 (2015). https://doi.org/10.1007/s11263-015-0816-y

28. Rusu, R.B., Meeussen, W., Chitta, S., Beetz, M.: Laser-based perception for door and handle identification. In: International Conference on Advanced Robotics, pp. 1–8, June 2009

29. Savarese, F., Tejero-de-Pablos, A., Quer, S., Harada, T.: Detecting, opening and navigating through doors: a unified framework for human service robots. In: 14th International Conference on Software Technologies (ICSOFT 2019), pp. 416–427, January 2019. https://doi.org/10.5220/0007947604160427

30. Shalaby, M.M., Salem, M.A., Khamis, A., Melgani, F.: Geometric model for vision-based door detection. In: 9th International Conference on Computer Engineering Systems, pp. 41–46, December 2014. https://doi.org/10.1109/ICCES.2014.7030925

31. Sunspiral, V., Kunz, C., Nourbakhsh, I.: The History of the Mobot Museum Robot Series: An Evolutionary Study. pp. 514–518, January 2001

32. Thrun, S., et al.: MINERVA: a second-generation museum tour-guide robot. IEEE Int. Conf. Robot. Automat. **3**, 1999–2005 (1999)

33. Toyota: Partner Robot. https://www.toyota-global.com/in-no-va-tion/partner_robot/ro-bot/#link02 (2019). Accessed 10 Nov 2019

Two-Stage Game Theoretic Approach for Energy Management in Networked Microgrids

Ilyes Naidji[1,2]([✉])[iD], Olfa Mosbahi[2][iD], Mohamed Khalgui[2][iD], and Abdelmalik Bachir[3][iD]

[1] University of Tunis El Manar, Tunis, Tunisia
ilyesnaidji@gmail.com
[2] National Institute of Applied Sciences and Technology (INSAT), University of Carthage, 1080 Tunis, Tunisia
[3] LESIA Laboratory, University of Mohamed Khider, Biskra, Algeria

Abstract. The architecture of smart distribution systems is becoming more and more complex after the appearance of networked microgrids. Maintaining the power balance between demand and supply in a cost effective way is turning into a very challenging task. Due to the intermittent nature of renewable energy and distributed architecture of microgrids (MGs), the energy management in networked microgrids requires a smart coordinated control. This paper presents an optimal energy management system (EMS) for networked microgrids in a smart distribution system. The problem is formulated with a two-stage game theoretic approach. In the first stage, a non-cooperative demand response (DR) game is designed between MGs and distribution system operator (DSO) to find the optimal power consumption of MGs. In the second stage, a coalition formation game among networked microgrids is designed to self-organize into structured coalitions that maximize the profits from energy exchange. We develop an algorithm based on merge and split rules to form coalitions between MGs. Then, we design an energy transfer algorithm for energy exchange between MGs within the same coalition to minimize the power loss. The simulation results demonstrate a satisfactory performance in terms of profit maximization that exceeds 21% and in terms of loss reduction in distribution system that exceeds 51%, thanks to the proposed cooperative scheme.

Keywords: Microgrid · Energy management · Demand response · Coalition game theory

1 Introduction

From the perspective of the smart grid, the improvement of the power system performance is one of the main objectives behind the development of the traditional power grid [10,12,15,18]. After the appearance of microgrids that consists

© Springer Nature Switzerland AG 2020
M. van Sinderen and L. A. Maciaszek (Eds.): ICSOFT 2019, CCIS 1250, pp. 205–228, 2020.
https://doi.org/10.1007/978-3-030-52991-8_10

of renewable energy sources, the operation and control of the power system is significantly evolved. This evolution is due to the deregulation of the system caused by the intermittent nature of renewable energy. These changes impose challenges to smart grid development in both research and operational levels [11, 19, 25, 31]. The smart power distribution networks are composed of multiple microgrids, which include distributed energy resources (DERs) such as renewable energy sources (e.g., photovoltaics panels, wind turbines...etc), end users, and the control components for the microgrid operation [7]. The microgrid should provide stable and sufficient power supply for the end users either by cooperating with the main power grid, i.e., "on-line" mode [24] or by autonomously supplying the users disconnected from the main power grid, i.e., "off-line" mode [13].

Recently, with the increasing integration of DERs especially renewable energy into the smart grid, manifold microgrids may emerge within the distribution system, which generates the problem of networked MGs operation and control [20]. Due to the high complexity of the MGs energy management problem, some studies apply the bio-inspired metaheuristics such as simulated annealing [26] and bacterial foraging [16]. Hierarchical control is also used as a solution for microgrid EMS [27]. Robust optimization approaches are a popular choice to address the uncertainty of renewable energy sources and load demand [8]. Linear programming (LP) is another popular choice for microgrid EMS [23]. Unfortunately, LP involves the assumption of linearity that cannot be the optimal choice of multi-microgrid systems.

A double auction with hidden user information has been recently examined to energy transactions in microgrids [6]. The authors in [21] propose a method for microgrid EMS with stochastic load where the problem is decomposed into two optimization levels. In [22], a model predictive control (MPC)-based power dispatch is proposed for distribution systems considering the parking electric vehicle (PEV) uncertainty. In [1], a multi-agent system (MAS) architecture is proposed for forecasting-based control strategy with load priority for microgrids in islanded mode. The MAS uses a master-slave model where the communication and negotiation between agents are performed by the concept of tokens. However, these studies only consider a single MG, and the interactions between MGs and distribution system (DS) are not explicitly investigated.

The studies in [4, 9, 14, 28–30] demonstrate that the interconnection of multiple MGs can improve the system operation and control. The authors in [28] propose a coordinated EMS strategy of networked MGs. The coordinated operation between MGs is formulated as a stochastic bi-level problem with the distribution system operator in the first level and MGs in the second level. In [30], a voltage and frequency control algorithm is designed using multi-layer architecture in Networked Microgrids. In [9], a priority-based energy scheduling operation is designed for multiple MGs. A noncooperative energy competition game is designed to solve the problem.

However, the interactions among the networked MGs is not considered and only interactions between MGs and the DS is taken into account.

In [4], a novel bidding behavior and an auction architecture are proposed for networked MGs. The authors in [14] propose an online EMS for the DSO to control the energy scheduling of networked MGs using regret minimization and online ADMM. In [29], the optimal control problem of networked MGs is modeled with decentralized partially observable Markov decision process. A dynamic programming solution is proposed to minimize the MG operation cost. In [5], a cooperative operation model is proposed for multiple MGs where the whole network is considered as the grand coalition to achieve higher operation economy.

However, in most of the above existing literature, the coordinated control of networked MGs as well as their interaction have not been efficiently investigated. Furthermore, the behavior of microgrids has not been explicitly modeled. Specifically, these studies consider the interactions between MGs and DSO without taking into account the cooperative behavior that can exists between MGs. The limitation of the interaction to only the distribution system can reduce the gain of MGs due to the unprofitable energy transfers between MGs and DSO. In addition, the energy transfer between MGs and DSO increases the power loss due to the long transferring distances.

In this respect, this paper addresses the coordinated control of networked MGs by explicitly modeling the cooperative behavior of the networked MGs and considering the different interactions between MGs and DSO. We solve the MGs energy management problem in a distributed manner where the network is autonomously self-organized into multiple sub-networks, i.e., coalitions to achieve an efficient and economic energy sharing.

This research work is an extension of the work reported in [17]. The added value here is to propose an efficient energy management for networked MGs in two stage approach. In the first stage, a non cooperative demand response game is designed between MGs and DSO. The DR game aims to find the optimal energy consumption of microgrids by considering the real-time electricity prices and the available power supply. A significant reduction in peak load is reached thanks to the designed DR scheme. After that, the result of the first stage is used by the second one in a coalition formation game. This game allows the microgrids to self-organize into structured coalitions in order to maximize their profits. We propose a coalition formation algorithm based on coalitional game theory and merge and split rules. The algorithm aims to find the possible coalition structures for microgrids that maximize the profit for each microgrid. Then, an energy transfer algorithm is proposed to transfer energy between microgrids that are in the same coalition. The energy transfer algorithm aims to minimize the power loss resulting from transferring energy in long distances.

A significant gains are found with the proposed two-stage approach in terms of energy saving, thanks to the demand response game and energy transfer scheme that reduces the energy cost and power loss, respectively. Furthermore, a notable gains are found in terms of profit maximization, thanks to the designed cooperative energy exchange scheme between microgrids. The originality of this paper is threefold:

- The management of the load demand is addressed with a demand response scheme to modify the usage of energy for reducing the peak load and energy cost.
- The formation of stable coalitions that allows the MGs to exchange energy in order to maximize their benefits and minimize power loss.
- The control of complexity of the energy management problem in networked microgrids.

This paper is organized as follows: Sect. 2 gives the system model, Sect. 3 formulates the problem of energy management of networked MGs with the proposed two-stage approach; Sect. 4 gives the proposed methodology for solving the energy management problem, Sect. 5 shows the simulation results and finally Sect. 6 concludes this paper.

2   System Model

This section describes the networked MGs system architecture, the pricing scheme that allows to apply the Coalition formation and the coalition formation preliminaries.

2.1   Networked Microgrids Architecture

Consider a smart distribution system consisting of N networked microgrids with distributed energy resources (DER) units including conventional generators, renewable generators such as photovoltaics (PV) panels and wind turbines (WT) and energy storage systems (ESS). We assume that each microgrid has loads to serve. The distributed energy resources (DERs), including renewables and energy storages are responsible for the power supply of the microgrid. We assume also that each microgrid has an energy management system (EMS) that is responsible for the optimization of the power consumption and the usage of DERs.

Let Θ_i^j denotes the ith microgrid belonging to the jth group (i.e., coalition). Let $P_D(\Theta_i^j)$ be the total power demand of Θ_i^j and $P_S^i(\Theta_i^j)$ its total power supply. The energy status $E(\Theta_i^j)$ of Θ_i^j is given by the difference of its power supply and its power demand, i.e.,

$$E(\Theta_i^j) = P_S(\Theta_i^j) - P_D(\Theta_i^j) \tag{1}$$

A positive value of the energy status denotes that Θ_i^j can sell $E(\Theta_i^j)$ amount of energy while a negative value denotes that Θ_i^j needs to purchase $E(\Theta_i^j)$ amount of energy from the distribution system.

Conventionally, the energy transfer is carried out between MGs and DS. Consequently, this transfer results in more power loss due to the existence of transformers and the transmission loss due to the I^2R effect if the distribution system operator is located within long distances to the microgrid. Furthermore,

the energy transfer between MGs and DSO is unprofitable to MGs due to operator policy that imposes disadvantageous energy prices (e.g., the operator buy in
low prices and sell in high prices). Figure 1 shows the architecture of microgrid
that consists of DERs such as wind and photovoltaic generators, energy storage
systems and electrical loads such as smart homes.

An interesting alternative to achieve a cost effective energy management and
minimize the power loss is the cooperation between MGs by forming coalitions.
The MGs inside the same coalition can exchange energy with an appreciable
energy price and interact with the distribution system operator as a last resort
to minimize the power loss and reduce the energy cost. The networked MGs system is described in Fig. 2. Each microgrid consists of distributed energy resources

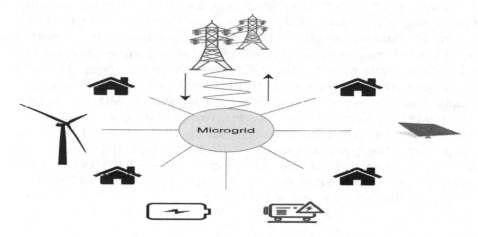

Fig. 1. Microgrid architecture.

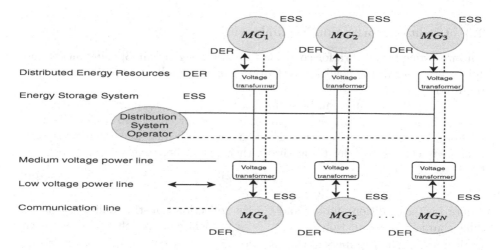

Fig. 2. Networked microgrids system.

(DERs) and energy storage systems (ESSs). Furthermore, each microgrid is connected with the distribution system through a voltage transformer while each microgrid is connected with the other MGs via a low voltage power line. Consequently, the power transfer between MG and DS is performed through the transformer which involves the power loss. With this architecture, a MG can exchange power with another MG if there is a transmission line between them, i.e., a low voltage power line. The minimization of the power exchange with the distribution system operator brings more profit to the MGs since the power exchange within MGs in a coalition is cheaper and more efficient.

2.2 Pricing Scheme for Coalition Formation

The pricing scheme is influential factor to perform cooperation between MGs. Particularly, the coalition formation process should justify the preference of MGs over the DSO in energy exchange. The design of inappropriate pricing scheme will result in disadvantageous outcome. The designed pricing scheme must motivate a MG to cooperate with the other MGs by exchanging the energy surplus. In this respect, we have designed a motivating pricing scheme that ensures that forming coalition between MGs is always prioritized than DSO. For instance, let $\alpha = 0.2\$$/kwh denotes the price of selling energy to the DSO, $\beta = 0.4\$$/kwh denotes the price for purchasing energy from the DSO and $\gamma = 0.25\$$/kwh is the price of selling/purchasing between MGs. Such that, a MG always prefers to exchange energy with the other MGs since it can save 0.05\$/kwh in selling and 0.2\$/kwh in purchasing by exchanging energy to MGs instead of DSO. Such that, the pricing scheme is designed as follows:

$$\beta \gg \gamma > \alpha \tag{2}$$

where $(\gamma - \alpha) \le \sigma$ is a predefined threshold.

2.3 Coalition Formation Preliminaries

An interesting framework for coalition formation is given in [3] using merge and split rules. To run the coalition formation game, the following preliminaries are required.

The coalitional game can be defined with the following pair (N, v) that consists of a finite set of players N (microgrids in our case) and a characteristic function or value v. A coalition Ξ_j^k is a set of players, i.e., microgrids that exchange services in order to maximize their profit, i.e.,

$$\Xi_j^k = \{\Theta_1^j, ..., \Theta_{|\Xi_j^k|}^j\} \tag{3}$$

where j is the coalition number and k is the collection that the coalition belongs. The characteristic function $v : 2^N \rightarrow \mathbb{R}$ associates a payoff $v(\Xi_j^k)$ for each coalition Ξ_j^k. The members of the coalition Ξ_j^k can distribute this payoff among themselves. Thus, the carachteristic function quantifies the payoff that can gain a set of players in coalition.

Let Ω_k denotes a collection of coalitions k that are disjoint, i.e.,

$$\Omega_k = \{\Xi_1^k, ..., \Xi_{|\Omega_k|}^k\} \tag{4}$$

A preference operator $\triangleright$ is an order defined for comparing two collections $\Omega_k = \{\Xi_1^k, ..., \Xi_{|\Omega_k|}^k\}$ and $\Omega_l = \{\Xi_1^l, ..., \Xi_{|\Omega_l|}^l\}$.

We assume that we have a subset $A \subseteq N$. This subset has two different partitions as a choice that are Ω_k and Ω_l. Therefore, $\Omega_k \triangleright \Omega_l$ denotes that Ω_k is prefered than Ω_l in partitioning A.

Various criteria exist in the literature to compare between collections or partitions [2]. These criteria are referred to orders which can be divided in two main categories that are coalition value orders and individual value orders. The first category compare two collections using the value of coalitions that belong to these collections. The second category compares collections using the players utilities instead of coalition value. As example, the Pareto order is one of the main individual value orders. The pareto order is used in our case which is given as follows:

In a collection Ω_k, each player, i.e., microgrid $\Theta_i^j \in \Xi_j^k$ has a utility function $\Phi(\Theta_i^j)$ which defines the payoff of the player in a coalition Ξ_j^k. Here in our case, as more as the microgrid Θ_i^j exchanges energy in a coalition Ξ_j^k, the energy profit increases thus, the utility function is at its best (max) when the energy status of a microgrid $E(\Theta_i^j)$ in the coalition Ξ_j^k approaches to zero, i.e.,

$$\Phi(\Theta_i^j) = \begin{cases} max, & \text{if } E(\Theta_i^j) = 0, \\ \frac{1}{E(\Theta_i^j)}, & \text{otherwise} \end{cases} \tag{5}$$

$\Omega_k \triangleright \Omega_l$, i.e., Ω_k is preferred over Ω_l by Pareto order, if

$$\Phi(\Theta_i^j) \geq \Phi(\Theta_i^g) \quad \forall i \in \Xi_j^k, \Xi_g^l \tag{6}$$

with at least one strict inequality, i.e., a collection is preferred by the players over another collection, if at least one player is able to improve its utility without decreasing the utility of the other players. Thus, the merge and split rules for coalition formation can be defined as follows:

Merge Rule. Merge any set of coalitions $\{\Xi_1^k\}, ..., \{\Xi_{|\Omega_k|}^k\}$ if $\bigcup_{j=1}^{|\Omega_k|} \Xi_j^k \triangleright$ $\{\Xi_1^k\}, ..., \{\Xi_{|\Omega_k|}^k\}$.

Split Rule. Split any coalition $\bigcup_{j=1}^{|\Omega_k|} \Xi_j^k$ if $\{\Xi_1^k\}, ..., \{\Xi_{|\Omega_k|}^k\} \triangleright \bigcup_{j=1}^{|\Omega_k|} \Xi_j^k$

A distributed coalition formation game is given by specifying a value for each coalition. The set of the formed coalitions form the coalition structure CS, i.e,

$$CS = \sum_{j=1}^{|\Omega_k|} \Xi_j^k \tag{7}$$

The coalition structure payoff $\rho(CS)$ is the sum of the coalition payoffs in it, i.e.,

$$\rho(CS) = \sum_{j=1}^{|\Omega_k|} v(\Xi_j^k) \tag{8}$$

Running Example. Suppose we have a set of four microgrids. Each microgrid has the following energy status from 1 to 4, respectively, $E = \{25, -15, -10, 5\}$. As example, we take two different collections that partition the set of microgrids for comparison. The first collection $\Omega_1 = \{\Xi_1^1, \Xi_2^1\}$ partitions the set of microgrids in two coalitions that are $\Xi_1^1 = \{25, -15, -10\}$, $\Xi_1^2 = \{5\}$. The second collection $\Omega_2 = \{\Xi_1^2, \Xi_2^2\}$ partitions the set of microgrids in two coalitions, $\Xi_1^2 = \{25, -15\}$, $\Xi_2^2 = \{-10, 5\}$. It is clear that $\Omega_1 \triangleright \Omega_2$. This is because, the utility function Φ for each player in Ω_1 is $\{max, max, max, \frac{1}{5}\}$ which is greater than Φ in $\Omega_2 = \{\frac{1}{10}, max, -\frac{1}{5}, max\}$, thus, the energy exchange between microgrids in Ω_1 is greater than Ω_2, consequently, the profit in Ω_1 is greater.

3   Problem Formulation

This section gives the formulation of the energy management problem in networked MGs. Here the problem is formulated in two stage approach. In the first stage, a non-cooperative demand response game between MGs and DSO is designed to find the optimal power consumption for the MGs. In the second stage, a coalition formation game is designed for MGs cooperation to optimally exchange the power surplus among MGs instead of selling or purchasing power from the DSO.

3.1   First Stage

Challenge. We emphasize here that the first stage mainly focuses on finding the optimal energy consumption of MGs by limiting the interaction with the DSO in a day-ahead manner. In particular, the first stage allows the microgrid to search for the quantity of energy to sell/purchase. After that, instead of selling/purchasing this quantity of energy to/from the DSO, a coalition formation game is designed in the second stage to share the energy surplus/shortage between MGs. Finally, if an amount of energy remains unbalanced, it can be purchased/sold from/to the DSO as a last resort.

Formalization. We design a demand response game G which is a non-cooperative game between N players. These players are the set of networked MGs and the distribution system operator (DSO). Note that in the first stage, each microgrid Θ_i^j does not belong to any coalition, i.e., $j = 0$. Each player of the demand response game has its utility function U_i and selects an action a_i from its action space $a_i \in A_i$. The action space of the microgrids consists of the quantity of selling or purchasing energy while the action space of the DSO consists of the energy price interval. The vector of actions of all players $a = (a_1, a_2, ..., a_N)$ is called action profile. Note that $A = \overset{N}{\underset{i=1}{\cup}} A_i$ and $U = \overset{N}{\underset{i=1}{\cup}} U_i$. Thus the DR game can be defined by the following 3-tuple:

$$G = (N, A, U) \tag{9}$$

The utility function $U_i : A_i \rightarrow \mathbb{R}$ of the player i in case of i is a microgrid is defined as follows:

$$U_i(a_i) = E(\Theta_i^j) = P_S(\Theta_i^j) - P_D(\Theta_i^j) \tag{10}$$

and in case of i is the distribution system operator

$$U_i(a_i) = \phi_{SUP} - \delta_{GEN} \tag{11}$$

where ϕ_{SUP} is the utility function of power supply and δ_{GEN} is the generation cost function of the distribution system operator. If $U_i > 0$, the player earns money, i.e., U_i is the profit. If $U_i < 0$, the player pays money, i.e., U_i is the cost. As a result, three types of MGs will appear. First, balanced MGs that have a generation capacity equal to load. Second, MGs with surplus of power that have a generation capacity more than load. Finally, MGs with shortage that have generation capacity less than load.

3.2   Second Stage

Challenge. Instead of sharing the power surplus with the DSO, MGs can cooperate with others by forming several coalitions to exchange their power surplus. Unbalanced power of each MG is purchased or sold within coalition. After performing the energy transfer within coalition, the rest of energy surplus or shortage can be balanced by the DSO as a last resort.

Formalization. The characteristic function v of a coalition Ξ_j^k is defined by the aggregated energy status in the coalition. The characteristic function $v(\Xi_j^k)$ has its best value when the difference between the total power demand and supply is minimized, i.e.,

$$v(\Xi_j^k) = \min |P_S(\Xi_j^k) - P_D(\Xi_j^k)| \tag{12}$$

Thus, as less as the microgrid exchanges power with the distribution system operator, the microgrid receives more utility. The objective is to maximize the profits of the MGs by forming the best coalition structure

$$CS = arg \max \rho(CS) \tag{13}$$

The energy transfer (ET) among MGs in a coalition should have a minimum power loss $P_L^{\Xi_j^k}$. The overall power loss $P_L^{\Xi_j^k}$ of a coalition Ξ_j^k while transferring power among MGs is given by

$$P_L^{\Xi_j^k} = -\sum_{i,e \in \Xi_j^k} P_L(i, e) \tag{14}$$

where $P_L(i, e)$ is the power loss resulting from transferring energy over transmission lines between Θ_i^j and Θ_e^j. Note that, the power loss is defined as a characteristic function of a coalition Ξ_j^k instead of microgrid Θ_i^j, this is because loss occurs during power transfer between MGs in the same coalition. Technically, the power loss function is given by

$$P_L(i, e) = I^2 R = \left[\frac{P(E)}{\Psi}\right]^2 \cdot \alpha \cdot d(i, e) \tag{15}$$

where $P(E)$ is the power required for energy transfer, Ψ is the carrying voltage on the transmission line, α is the line resistance and $d(i, e)$ is the distance between Θ_i^j and Θ_e^j. The characteristic function of the coalition formation game is designed to consider a tradeoff between power supply and loss. In the coalition formation process, the aggregated energy status is the characteristic function and in the energy transfer process, the power loss is the characteristic function.

Overall, the energy management problem of networked MGs can be formulated with the following equations:

$$a = arg\max\left(U(a)\right) \tag{16}$$

$$CS = arg\max \rho(CS) \tag{17}$$

$$ET = arg\min \sum_{\Xi_j^k \in CS} P_L^{\Xi_j^k} \tag{18}$$

4   Methodology

This section gives the solution of the energy management problem formulated in the previous section. The proposed methodology is globally illustrated in Fig. 3 and detailed in the next subsections.

The first stage starts with a demand response scheme designed between MGs and DSO. The result of the DR game appears with two kinds of MGs that are balanced or unbalanced MGs. Unbalanced MGs participate in the coalition formation game to self-organize into structured coalitions in order to maximize their profits from energy exchange. After that, MGs that are in the same coalitions, execute the energy transfer with the objective to minimize the power loss.

Here, the energy management problem in networked MGs is entirely solved where we address the optimal management of load demands at first in a non cooperative way. After that, the management of power surplus is addressed in a cooperative way to maximize the profits of microgrids and finally, the management of energy transfer is solved with the objective to minimize the power loss in each coalition.

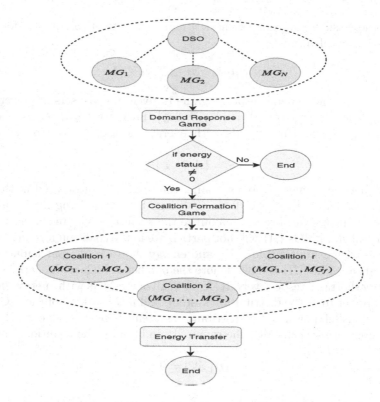

Fig. 3. Flowchart of the proposed two stage approach.

4.1 Stage I: Demand Response Game

Motivation. The power consumption has a significant impact on the energy cost of a microgrid. For this reason, it is important to have an optimal power consumption to reduce the energy cost and the peak consumed power. In this respect, we propose a demand response game between MGs and DSO to find the optimal power consumption for each microgrid where a non cooperative game is designed to model the DR game.

Formalization. Solving the demand response game consists of finding the Nash Equilibrium for each player in the non cooperative game. In non cooperative games, the utility function of each player U_i depends on the selected action of the player a_i^* and the action profile of the other players $\overline{a_i^*}$, i.e.,

$$U_i(a) = U_i(a_i^*, \overline{a_i^*}) \tag{19}$$

The vector $a = (a_1^*, a_2^*, ..., a_n^*)$ is a Nash equilibrium for the energy management game $G = (N, A, U)$ if the following constraint is valid:

$$\forall i \in N, \forall a_i \in A_i, \quad U_i(a_i^*, \overline{a_i^*}) \geq U_i(a_i, \overline{a_i^*}) \tag{20}$$

Finding the Nash equilibrium of the DR game consists of solving the following optimization problem:

$$\max U_i(a), \quad \forall i \in N, \forall a \in A \tag{21}$$

The result S of the demand response game is given in three sets of players that are the balanced microgrids $\Lambda = \{\lambda_1, ..., \lambda_{|\Lambda|}\}$, microgrids with energy surplus $\Pi = \{\pi, ..., \pi_{|\Pi|}\}$ and microgrids with energy shortage $\Psi = \{\psi, ..., \psi_{|\Psi|}\}$ as follows:

$$S = \{\Lambda, \Pi, \Psi\} \tag{22}$$

After solving the demand response game, the result S will be used in the next stage in a cooperative game to form coalitions between microgrids in order to exchange the power surplus and maximize the profit of MGs. In the next stage, the set of balanced MGs $\{\Lambda\}$ will not participate in the coalition formation game while MGs with energy surplus $\{\Pi\}$ and energy shortage $\{\Psi\}$ participate in the coalitional game. Let $|\Pi|$ and $|\Psi|$ denote the number of MGs with energy surplus and energy shortage, respectively. If $|\Pi| = 0$, all of the MGs with energy shortage purchase power from the distribution system, and if $|\Psi| = 0$, all of the MGs with energy surplus sell power to the distribution system. Thus, in such case, the MGs cannot cooperate. Specifically, the required condition of the coalitional game is given by

$$|\Pi| \cdot |\Psi| \neq 0 \tag{23}$$

Running Example. Consider a network with a set of six networked microgrids $N = \{\Theta_1^0, \Theta_2^0, \Theta_3^0, \Theta_4^0, \Theta_5^0, \Theta_6^0, \}$. These microgrids have the following power demand and supply capacity from 1 to 6, respectively,

Microgrid	Θ_1^0	Θ_2^0	Θ_3^0	Θ_4^0	Θ_5^0	Θ_6^0
Power supply (P_S)	12	15	13	13	25	30
Power demand (P_D)	-12	-18	-15	-15	-18	-20

Thus the energy status of the microgrids is $E = \{0, -3, -2, -2, 7, 10\}$. After running the demand response game and finding the Nash equilibrium, the microgrids manage their loads and change their power demand, i.e., action as follows: $a = P_D = \{-10, -15, -14, -14, -16, -19\}$, such that, the utility function (which is equal to energy status) becomes $U = E = \{2, 0, -1, -1, 9, 11\}$. As a result, $\Lambda = \{\Theta_2^0\}$, $\Pi = \{\Theta_1^0, \Theta_5^0, \Theta_6^0\}$ and $\Psi = \{\Theta_3^0, \Theta_4^0\}$.

We notice that the utility of each microgrid is improved compared with the utility before the demand response game, thus, a notable gains are found, furthermore, a significant reduction of the peak consumed power is reached which exceeds 10%, thanks to the DR scheme that allows to find the optimal power consumption.

4.2   Stage II: Coalition Formation Game

Motivation. As some MGs might fail to generate/consume the predicted amount of energy, they are required to exchange energy with other MGs at more beneficial prices than the distribution system operator. For this reason, a coalition formation game is designed to form the best coalition structure in order to have an optimal energy management between networked microgrids. The coalition formation game is executed in two consecutive steps: adaptive coalition formation and then energy transfer. A merge and split based algorithm can be developed for coalition formation in networked MGs. The network is self-organized into coalitions that are formed with merge and split rules. After that, the energy transfer process takes place in each coalition.

Formalization. The result of the first stage, i.e., $S = \{\Lambda, \Pi, \Psi\}$ is used in the coalition formation process. The coalition formation process aims to find the best coalitions that maximize the profit from energy exchange, i.e.,

$$\forall \pi \in \Pi, \forall \psi \in \Psi, find \; \Xi_j^k \tag{24}$$

where

$$\Xi_j^k = \{\pi_1, \pi_2, ...\} \bigcup \{\psi_1, \psi_2, ...\} \tag{25}$$

to find the best collection Ω_k

$$\Omega_k = \arg \max \sum_{j-1}^{|\Omega_k|} v(\Xi_j^k) \tag{26}$$

Implementation. Algorithm 1 gives the proposed merge-and-split coalition formation algorithm (MSCF). The algorithm can be executed by a trusted third party that coordinates between coalitions and MGs. The algorithm assumes that MGs report their energy status to this party.

The first collection Ω_k is initialized with every singleton microgrid $\Theta_i^j \in N$ as a coalition $\Xi_j^k \in \Omega_k$. Based on the distribution of MGs, the MSCF algorithm starts with the initialized Ω_k and checks the energy surplus/shortage that can be shared with the other MGs to calculate $v(\Xi_j^k)$. A *visited* matrix is used to memorize all pairs of the visited coalitions for merge process. Initially, the *visited* matrix is set to false for all coalitions, after that, the merge process starts. A random pair of coalitions (Ξ_j^k, Ξ_l^k) is chosen from Ω_k to check if $\Xi_j^k \bigcup \Xi_l^k \; \triangleright$ $\{\{\Xi_j^k\}, \{\Xi_l^k\}\}$, then coalitions Ξ_j^k and Ξ_l^k decide to merge. $\Xi_j^k \bigcup \Xi_l^k$ is saved in Ξ_j^k, and Ξ_l^k is removed from Ω_k, then Ξ_j^k enters in the next merge step. So, the *visited* matrix is reinitialized again to false, i.e., $\forall \; \Xi_m^k \in \Omega_k, m \neq j$, visited $[\Xi_j^k][\Xi_m^k]$ = false. Ω_k continues for merging by searching non-visited coalitions after the test of all the combinations, if there is no merge, the merge process ends.

The resulted Ω_k is then passed to split process. Every coalition $\Xi_j^k \in \Omega_k$ having more than one member, i.e., microgrid, is subject to splitting. The algorithm tries to split Ξ_j^k into two disjoint coalitions Ξ_l^k and Ξ_m^k where $\Xi_l^k \bigcup \Xi_m^k = \Xi_j^k$. The splitting occurs only if one of the microgrids belonging the coalition can improve its individual payoff, without hurting the payoff of the other microgrids.

Algorithm 1: Merge and Split Coalition Formation (MGCF).

---

1 **Input:** $\Theta_1^0, \Theta_2^0, ..., \Theta_N^0$ (set of microgrids)
2 **Output:** $CS\{$coalition structure$\}$
3 **for** $j \leftarrow 1$ **to** N **do**
4 $\quad$ $\Xi_j^k = \Theta_j^j$;
5 **end**
6 initialization $\Omega_k = \{\Xi_1^k, \Xi_2^k, ..., \Xi_N^k\}$
7 **repeat**
8 $\quad$ $finish \leftarrow True$
9 $\quad$ **forall the** $\Xi_j^k, \Xi_l^k \in \Omega_k, j \neq l$ **do**
10 $\quad\quad$ visited $[\Xi_j^k][\Xi_l^k] \leftarrow$ False
11 $\quad$ **end**
12 $\quad$ {Merge process}
13 $\quad$ **repeat**
14 $\quad\quad$ $exit \leftarrow True$
15 $\quad\quad$ Randomly select $\Xi_j^k, \Xi_l^k \in \Omega_k, j \neq l$ for which visited $[\Xi_j^k][\Xi_l^k] =$ False
16 $\quad\quad$ visited$[\Xi_j^k][\Xi_l^k] \leftarrow True$
17 $\quad\quad$ **if** $\Xi_j^k \bigcup \Xi_l^k \rhd \{\{\Xi_j^k\}, \{\Xi_l^k\}\}$ **then**
18 $\quad\quad\quad$ $\Xi_j^k \leftarrow \Xi_j^k \bigcup \Xi_l^k$
19 $\quad\quad\quad$ $\Xi_l^k \leftarrow \emptyset$
20 $\quad\quad\quad$ **forall the** $\Xi_m^k \in \Omega_k, m \neq j$ **do**
21 $\quad\quad\quad\quad$ visited$[\Xi_j^k][\Xi_m^k] \leftarrow False$
22 $\quad\quad\quad$ **end**
23 $\quad\quad$ **end**
24 $\quad\quad$ **forall the** $\Xi_j^k, \Xi_l^k \in \Omega_k, j \neq l$ **do**
25 $\quad\quad\quad$ **if** $not\ visited[\Xi_j^k][\Xi_l^k]$ **then**
26 $\quad\quad\quad\quad$ $exit \leftarrow False$
27 $\quad\quad\quad$ **end**
28 $\quad\quad$ **end**
29 $\quad$ **until** $(exit = True)$ or $(|\ \Omega_k\ |= 1)$;
30 $\quad$ {Split process}
31 $\quad$ **forall the** $\Xi_j^k \in \Omega_k$ $where\ |\ \Xi_j^k\ |> 1$ **do**
32 $\quad\quad$ **forall the** $partitions\ \{\Xi_l^k, \Xi_m^k\}$ $of\ \Xi_j^k,$ $where\ \Xi_j^k = \Xi_l^k \bigcup \Xi_m^k, \Xi_l^k \bigcap \Xi_m^k = \emptyset$ **do**
33 $\quad\quad\quad$ **if** $\{\{\Xi_l^k\}, \{\Xi_m^k\}\} \rhd \Xi_j^k$ **then**
34 $\quad\quad\quad\quad$ $\Xi_j^k \leftarrow \Xi_l^k$
35 $\quad\quad\quad\quad$ $\Omega_k = \Omega_k \bigcup \Xi_m^k$
36 $\quad\quad\quad\quad$ $finish \leftarrow False$
37 $\quad\quad\quad\quad$ Break
38 $\quad\quad\quad$ **end**
39 $\quad\quad$ **end**
40 $\quad$ **end**
41 **until** $finish = True$;
42 $CS = \Omega_k$;

Running Example. In order to clarify the proposed algorithm, let us consider a simple example with three MGs with the following energy status $E = \{20, -5, -10\}$. Ω_k is initialized with every microgrid as a coalition Ξ_j^k, i.e., $\Omega_k = \{\Xi_1^k, \Xi_2^k, \Xi_3^k\}$. Ξ_2^k and Ξ_3^k cannot form coalition because they cannot improve their payoff since E is negative for both of them. Consider that Ξ_1^k communicates with Ξ_2^k in order to merge. Based on the values of E, $\{\Xi_1^k, \Xi_2^k\} \vartriangleright \{\{\Xi_1^k\}, \{\Xi_2^k\}\}$ since $\{\frac{1}{15}, max\} \vartriangleright \{\{\frac{1}{20}\}, \{-\frac{1}{5}\}\}$, such that both of Ξ_1^k and Ξ_2^k improve their payoff.

Now, there are two coalitions $\{\Xi_3^k\}$ and $\{\Xi_1^k, \Xi_2^k\}$. $\{\Xi_3^k\}$ communicates with $\{\Xi_1^k, \Xi_2^k\}$ in order to merge. $\{\Xi_1^k, \Xi_2^k, \Xi_3^k\} \vartriangleright \{\{\Xi_1^k, \Xi_2^k\}, \{\Xi_3^k\}\}$ since $\{\frac{1}{5}, max, max\} \vartriangleright \{\{\frac{1}{15}, max\}, \{-\frac{1}{10}\}\}$, so the merge occurs. This is because, Ξ_1^k and Ξ_3^k improve their payoff while Ξ_2^k keeps its previous payoff. Now $\{\Xi_1^k, \Xi_2^k, \Xi_3^k\}$ tries to split. Ξ_1^k will not split to from a coalition with Ξ_2^k or even with Ξ_3^k. Thus, there are no coalitions to be able to merge or split any further. As a result, the final coalition structure $CS = \Omega_k = \{\Xi_1^k, \Xi_2^k, \Xi_3^k\}$.

As we notice, the final coalition structure CS gives the maximum utility to each microgrid by finding the optimal coalitions that maximize the energy exchange in order to have the best profit. The proposed algorithm is repeated periodically, i.e., each day, enabling the MGs to autonomously self-organize and adapt the network topology depending on their energy needs.

MSCF Algorithm Complexity. The complexity of the proposed MSCF algorithm is determined by the number of merge and split attempts. To find this complexity, the complexity of a single iteration of the main loop should be analyzed.

Initially, every singleton microgrid Θ_i^j is considered as a coalition Ξ_j^k, therefore, there are N coalitions. In the worst case of merge process, each coalition attempts to merge with all the other coalitions in Ω_k. Thus, the first merge process occurs after $\frac{N(N-1)}{2}$ attempts, the second after $\frac{(N-1)(N-2)}{2}$ attempts and so on. In such case, the complexity is $O(N^3)$. However, the merge process significantly requires less number of attempts since a merge of two coalitions occurs, it does not need to search for other merge attempts. Splitting a coalition Ξ_j^k in the worst case is $O(2^{|\Xi_j^k|})$ involving to find all the possible partitions of the considered coalition. The split rule is restricted to the coalitions with size greater or equal to two, i.e., $|\Xi_j^k| \geq 2$ in Ω_k. In addition, it is not executed for all MGs. So, the complexity of the split process depends on the size of the formed coalitions and not on the total number of MGs. Furthermore, once a split occurs, there is no need to search for another split. In the worst case, no split occurs for a coalition Ξ_j^k which involve to check all the possible two partitions of the coalition Ξ_j^k. To avoid this scenario, one of the two partitions of size $|\Xi_j^k - 1|$ and 1, respectively, should be feasible. If none of them is feasible, the split process stops. As a result, in some cases the complexity of the split process is reduced to $O(|\Xi_j^k|)$. Therefore, the complexity of the proposed MSCF algorithm can be reduced by limiting the size of the formed coalitions, thus allowing to control the complexity of the proposed algorithm.

Energy Transfer. After the coalition formation process, the energy transfer among coalitions members is executed. The energy transfer process is given in Algorithm 2. This algorithm aims to find the optimal energy transfer between

---

Algorithm 2: Energy Transfer.

1 **Input:** Coalition Ξ_j^k, distance matrix $dist$
2 **Output:** Energy transfer matrix ET
3 Π = set of energy seller within Ξ_j^k;
4 Ψ = set of energy buyer within Ξ_j^k in decreasing order;
5 **foreach** $\psi \in \Psi$ **do**
6 | $\pi = \text{argmin } dist(\psi, \pi)$; %nearest MG seller %
7 | **if** ψ *is None* **then**
8 | | $ET(0, \psi) = \psi.energy$;
9 | | break;
10 | **end**
11 | $dif = \min(\pi.energy, |\psi.energy|)$;
12 | $\psi.energy \mathrel{-}= dif$;
13 | $\pi.energy \mathrel{-}= dif$;
14 | $ET(\pi, \psi) = dif$;
15 **end**
16 **foreach** $\pi \in \Pi$ **do**
17 | **if** $\pi.energy > 0$ **then**
18 | | $ET(\pi, 0) = \pi.energy$;
19 | **end**
20 **end**

---

microgrids in the same coalition by transferring energy between the closest microgrids in order to minimize the power loss. Initially, for each microgrid buyer, we search for the nearest microgrid seller. After that, we subtract the given amount of energy from the energy buyer and seller and the energy transfer matrix ET is filled with the energy sellers in rows and with energy buyers in columns and so on until we supply all the microgrids that have energy shortage. Finally, if an amount of energy rests, it is saved in ET indexed with energy sellers in rows and zero in columns. We notice that we save a significant amounts of energy thanks to the energy transfer algorithm. Since energy transfer is carried within very short distances instead of transferring energy from/to the distribution system operator which is located far from microgrids. The gains in terms of energy saving are given in the next section.

5   Simulation Results

This section shows the case study and gives the simulation results of the proposed two-stage approach. In order to investigate the effectiveness of the proposed two stage approach, a set of simulation experiments are performed.

5.1   Simulation Setup

The networked MGs system is modeled with a mesh structure which guarantees a high level of service. We assume that the distribution network covers an area of $100\,\mathrm{km}^2$ and consists of N microgrids. We assume that MGs are randomly located around the distribution system operator (DSO) which is located in the center of the network. We have randomly scatter $16\,\mathrm{MGs}$ which is a reasonable number of MGs in real smart grids (Fig. 4).

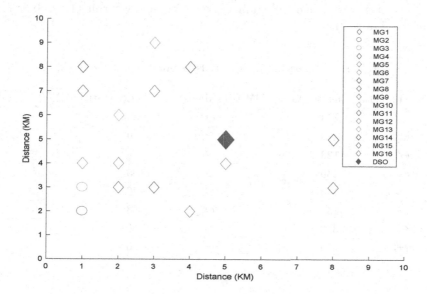

Fig. 4. Networked microgrids system.

5.2 Problematique

As some microgrids can fail to have balance between power demand and supply, their unbalanced energy can be wasted or traded punitively with the distribution system operator. The problem here is how to manage the networked microgrids system in order to balance energy in a cost effective way, i.c., manage the energy consumption and coordinate the energy supply. For this reason, we treat the problem in different manner from the literature where we search for the optimal energy consumption in the first stage, then in the second stage, we coordinate the energy supply between microgrids by forming the best coalitions to exchange energy and maximize the profits from energy exchange.

5.3 First Stage

Each player in the non cooperative game, i.e., microgrid gets the information about time-differentiated electricity price from the distribution system operator (DSO) to adjust its energy consumption. Table 1 gives the energy status of MGs before applying the demand response game. After running the demand response game, the MGs adjust their energy consumption by shifting their manageable loads (applying load shedding or shifting) to minimize their energy cost, thus a new energy consumption profile is resulted as follows:

We notice that a significant minimization in the peak consumed power is occurred for each microgrid. For example Θ_6^0 reduced the power consumption from 134 MW/h to 120 MW/h which is more than 10%. This results in a reduction of the energy shortage and an increase of the energy surplus for unbalanced microgrids (Table 2).

Table 1. Microgrids energy needs before demand response.

Microgrid	Energy status (MW/h)	Microgrid	Energy status (MW/h)
Θ_1^0	273	Θ_9^0	−45
Θ_2^0	30	Θ_{10}^0	−129
Θ_3^0	−123	Θ_{11}^0	68
Θ_4^0	230	Θ_{12}^0	−105
Θ_5^0	−110	Θ_{13}^0	−46
Θ_6^0	−134	Θ_{14}^0	−3
Θ_7^0	340	Θ_{15}^0	−60
Θ_8^0	−45	Θ_{16}^0	−20

Table 2. Microgrids energy needs after demand response.

Microgrid	Energy status (MW/h)	Microgrid	Energy status (MW/h)
Θ_1^0	295	Θ_9^0	−35
Θ_2^0	40	Θ_{10}^0	−119
Θ_3^0	−103	Θ_{11}^0	78
Θ_4^0	240	Θ_{12}^0	−90
Θ_5^0	−89	Θ_{13}^0	−40
Θ_6^0	−120	Θ_{14}^0	0
Θ_7^0	201	Θ_{15}^0	−55
Θ_8^0	−35	Θ_{16}^0	−17

5.4   Second Stage

Figure 5 shows the coalition structure of the proposed MSCF algorithm that is applied in the case of 16 networked MGs. We compare the performance of our Merge and Split Coalition Formation (MSCF) algorithm, with that of three other algorithms: Grand Coalition Formation (GCF), Random Coalition Formation (RCF), and Same-Size Coalition Formation (SSCF). The GOF algorithm consider that the grand coalition as an optimal solution for the coalitional game

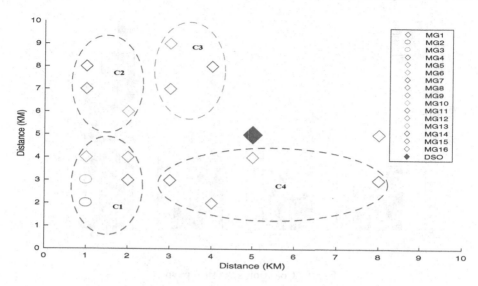

Fig. 5. Coalition structure.

to perform the energy exchange between MGs. The RCF algorithm forms a random size of coalitions, where the members of that coalitions are randomly selected. The SSCF algorithm forms coalitions with the same size where the members of that coalitions are also randomly selected. Table 3 gives the MGs belonging each formed coalition. Since Θ_{14}^0 is a balanced microgrid, it does not participate in the coalition formation game.

Table 3. Stable coalitions.

Coalition	Members	Exchanged power with DSO
Ξ_1^k	$\{\Theta_1^1, \Theta_2^1, \Theta_3^1, \Theta_5^1, \Theta_6^1\}$	23
Ξ_2^k	$\{\Theta_7^2, \Theta_8^2, \Theta_{10}^2\}$	47
Ξ_3^k	$\{\Theta_9^3, \Theta_{11}^3, \Theta_{13}^3\}$	3
Ξ_4^k	$\{\theta_4^4, \Theta_{12}^4, \Theta_{15}^4, \Theta_{16}^4\}$	78

In Fig. 6, we show the performance of the coalition structures (CS) payoff with different size of the networked MGs. The payoff consists of the earned money for exchanging power among MGs. The figure shows that the MSCF gives the highest global payoff for MGs compared with the other algorithms. This is because the less power exchange with the DSO, the more profit from power exchange. The proposed MSCF algorithm creates a stable coalitions that minimize the power exchange with the DSO. The significant difference between the MSCF and the SSCF is in the decision making in coalition formation process. The proposed MSCF algorithm forms coalitions based on merge-and-split rules.

224   I. Naidji et al.

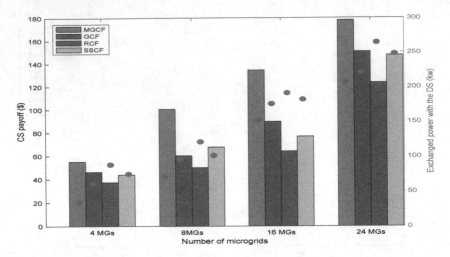

Fig. 6. Coalition structure payoffs.

The decision making in SSCF and RCF is random which yields to a very high standard deviation. As a result, the formed coalitions are unable to perform energy exchange efficiently and the coalition members receive less payoff. In addition, the proposed MSCF algorithm outperforms the GCF algorithm which considers the grand coalition as an optimal solution. This is because, the grand coalition will result in more power loss which is non optimal. On average, the global CS payoff of MSCF exceeds the payoff of the RCF, GCF and SSCF about 18.24%, 21.33% and 17.15%, respectively.

Figure 7 shows the average power loss for individual microgrids with non cooperative approach as in [9], i.e., the power is only exchanged between MG and DSO, and with a cooperative approach, i.e., the power is exchanged between MGs. In the cooperative approach, the GCF algorithm as in [5] and the proposed MSCF algorithm are compared. In the non-cooperative approach, a high level of power loss is observed due to the long distances between MGs and DS and the existence of power transformers resulting in more power loss. A significant decrease in power loss is observed with the cooperative approach in the case of GCF algorithm where MGs inter-exchange power. The power transfer between MGs, i.e., short distances which reduces the power loss caused by transporting power which is the case of distribution system that transfers power to long distances. Unlike the traditional power exchange which is performed between MGs and DS, the cooperative approach allows the MGs to inter exchange the power locally taking the advantage of the cost of power while reducing the power loss in long distances. However, with the proposed MSCF algorithm, the power loss is less than the GCF algorithm. The proposed MSCF algorithm forms many small size coalitions resulting in short distances of power transfer which reduce the power loss compared with the GCF algorithm that forms the grand coalition resulting in long distances of power transfer, so, more power loss. Figure 8 shows

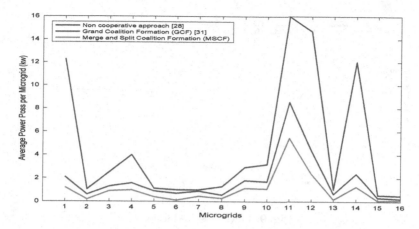

Fig. 7. Power loss per microgrid.

the total power loss of MGs when the number of MGs is up to 100. The result is obtained after executing a non-cooperative and cooperative energy exchange (GCF and MSCF). The loss is significantly reduced with the cooperative approach. Furthermore, the reduction rate is about to 72%.

In order to demonstrate the scalability of the MSCF algorithm, Fig. 9 is presented. This figure shows the percentage of power loss reduction after running the MSCF and GCF algorithms for different sized networked MG systems. As more as the network size increases, the MSCF algorithm further reduces the power loss (about 72%) and the reduction is significantly high compared with the GCF algorithm (about 51%).

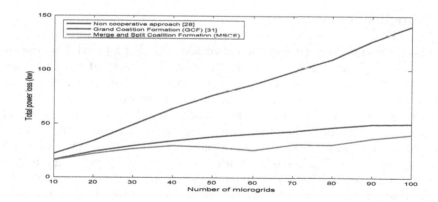

Fig. 8. Total power loss.

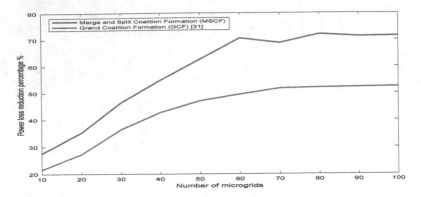

Fig. 9. Power loss reduction.

5.5 Discussion

The difference between the proposed two stage approach and the existing literature for MG EMS is that the existing studies do not regroup the load management with the electricity supply problem resulting in biased solutions in sometimes. In addition, the cooperation between MGs is rarely explored. Therefore our approach has twofold advantages. The first advantage is the load management scheme that design the optimal energy consumption for reducing the peak load and energy cost, thanks to the proposed demand response game. The second advantage is the cooperation among networked MGs that offers a significant profits to MGs in the same coalition benefiting from energy exchange and minimizing the power loss of the distribution system.

6 Conclusion

An efficient energy management for networked MGs is proposed. The optimal energy consumption of MGs is designed in first via a demand response game. After that, the result of the demand response game is used in a coalition formation game. A motivating pricing scheme is designed to encourage the MGs for cooperation by forming several stable coalitions. This cooperation is beneficial from the economic and technic point of view. We design a scalable merge and split based coalition formation algorithm that performs better in over sized systems where the power loss reduction is greater and the payoff is more. After the coalition formation, the energy transfer is executed with the proposed algorithm by searching the nearest MGs within a coalition to minimize the power loss which occurs during energy transfer. The importance of the proposed MSCF algorithm is demonstrated by the reduction of the energy burden from the distribution system and reduction of the technical loss while maximizing the profits of the MGs from energy exchange. Furthermore, we control the complexity of the proposed MSCF algorithm by limiting the size of the formed coalitions.

References

1. Abidi, M.G., Smida, M.B., Khalgui, M., Li, Z., Wu, N.: Multi-agent oriented solution for forecasting-based control strategy with load priority of microgrids in an island mode-case study: Tunisian petroleum platform. Electr. Power Syst. Res. **152**, 411–423 (2017)
2. Apt, K., Witzel, A.: A generic approach to coalition formation. In: Proceedings of the International Workshop on Computational Social Choice (COMSOC), Amsterdam, The Netherlands, December 2006
3. Apt, K., Witzel, A.: A generic approach to coalition formation. Int. Game Theory Rev. **11**(03), 347–367 (2009)
4. Cintuglu, M.H., Mohammed, O.A.: Behavior modeling and auction architecture of networked microgrids for frequency support. IEEE Trans. Industr. Inf. **13**(4), 1772–1782 (2017)
5. Du, Y., et al.: A cooperative game approach for coordinating multi-microgrid operation within distribution systems. Appl. Energy **222**, 383–395 (2018)
6. Faqiry, M.N., Das, S.: Double auction with hidden user information: application to energy transaction in microgrid. IEEE Trans. Syst. Man Cybern.: Syst., 1–14 (2018). https://doi.org/10.1109/TSMC.2018.2800006
7. Han, Y., Zhang, K., Li, H., Coelho, E.A.A., Guerrero, J.M.: MAS-based distributed coordinated control and optimization in microgrid and microgrid clusters: a comprehensive overview. IEEE Trans. Power Electron. **33**(8), 6488–6508 (2018)
8. Hu, W., Wang, P., Gooi, H.B.: Toward optimal energy management of microgrids via robust two-stage optimization. IEEE Trans. Smart Grid **9**(2), 1161–1174 (2018). https://doi.org/10.1109/TSG.2016.2580575
9. Jadhav, A.M., Patne, N.R.: Priority-based energy scheduling in a smart distributed network with multiple microgrids. IEEE Trans. Industr. Inf. **13**(6), 3134–3143 (2017)
10. Karoui, O., Khalgui, M., Koubâa, A., Guerfala, E., Li, Z., Tovar, E.: Dual mode for vehicular platoon safety: simulation and formal verification. Inf. Sci. **402**, 216–232 (2017)
11. Khalgui, M., Carpanzano, E., Hanisch, H.M.: An optimised simulation of component-based embedded systems in manufacturing industry. Int. J. Simul. Process Model. **4**(2), 148–162 (2008)
12. Khalgui, M., Mosbahi, O.: Intelligent distributed control systems. Inf. Softw. Technol. **52**(12), 1259–1271 (2010)
13. Li, Y., Yang, Z., Li, G., Zhao, D., Tian, W.: Optimal scheduling of an isolated microgrid with battery storage considering load and renewable generation uncertainties. IEEE Trans. Industr. Electron. **66**(2), 1565–1575 (2019). https://doi.org/10.1109/TIE.2018.2840498
14. Ma, W.J., Wang, J., Gupta, V., Chen, C.: Distributed energy management for networked microgrids using online ADMM with regret. IEEE Trans. Smart Grid **9**(2), 847–856 (2018)
15. Meskina, S.B., Doggaz, N., Khalgui, M., Li, Z.: Multiagent framework for smart grids recovery. IEEE Trans. Syst. Man Cybern.: Syst. **47**(7), 1284–1300 (2017)
16. Motevasel, M., Seifi, A.R.: Expert energy management of a micro-grid considering wind energy uncertainty. Energy Convers. Manag. **83**, 58–72 (2014)
17. Naidji, I., Mosbahi, O., Khalgui, M., Bachir, A.: Cooperative energy management software for networked microgrids. In: Proceedings of the 14th International Conference on Software Technologies: ICSOFT, vol. 1, pp. 428–438. INSTICC, SciTePress (2019). https://doi.org/10.5220/0007965604280438

18. Naidji, I., Smida, M.B., Khalgui, M., Bachir., A.: Non cooperative game theoretic approach for residential energy management in smart grid. In: Proceedings of the the 32nd Annual European Simulation and Modelling Conference, pp. 164–170. ETI, EUROSIS (2018)

19. Naidji, I., Smida, M.B., Khalgui, M., Bachir, A.: Multi agent system-based approach for enhancing cyber-physical security in smart grids. In: Proceedings of the the 33rd Annual European Simulation and Modelling Conference, pp. 177–182. ETI, EUROSIS (2019)

20. Samet, H., Azhdari, E., Ghanbari, T.: Comprehensive study on different possible operations of multiple grid connected microgrids. IEEE Trans. Smart Grid 9(2), 1434–1441 (2018)

21. Silani, A., Yazdanpanah, M.J.: Distributed optimal microgrid energy management with considering stochastic load. IEEE Trans. Sustain. Energy, 1 (2018). https://doi.org/10.1109/TSTE.2018.2846279

22. Su, W., Wang, J., Zhang, K., Huang, A.Q.: Model predictive control-based power dispatch for distribution system considering plug-in electric vehicle uncertainty. Electr. Power Syst. Res. 106, 29–35 (2014)

23. Sukumar, S., Mokhlis, H., Mekhilef, S., Naidu, K., Karimi, M.: Mix-mode energy management strategy and battery sizing for economic operation of grid-tied microgrid. Energy 118, 1322–1333 (2017)

24. Tan, Z., Zhang, X., Xie, B., Wang, D., Liu, B., Yu, T.: Fast learning optimiser for real-time optimal energy management of a grid-connected microgrid. IET Gener. Transm. Distrib. 12(12), 2977–2987 (2018). https://doi.org/10.1049/iet-gtd.2017.1983

25. Tuballa, M.L., Abundo, M.L.: A review of the development of smart grid technologies. Renew. Sustain. Energy Rev. 59, 710–725 (2016)

26. Velik, R., Nicolay, P.: Grid-price-dependent energy management in microgrids using a modified simulated annealing triple-optimizer. Appl. Energy 130, 384–395 (2014)

27. Wang, C., Liu, Y., Li, X., Guo, L., Qiao, L., Lu, H.: Energy management system for stand-alone diesel-wind-biomass microgrid with energy storage system. Energy 97, 90–104 (2016)

28. Wang, Z., Chen, B., Wang, J., Begovic, M.M., Chen, C.: Coordinated energy management of networked microgrids in distribution systems. IEEE Trans. Smart Grid 6(1), 45–53 (2015)

29. Wu, J., Guan, X.: Coordinated multi-microgrids optimal control algorithm for smart distribution management system. IEEE Trans. Smart Grid 4(4), 2174–2181 (2013)

30. Zamora, R., Srivastava, A.K.: Multi-layer architecture for voltage and frequency control in networked microgrids. IEEE Trans. Smart Grid 9(3), 2076–2085 (2018). https://doi.org/10.1109/TSG.2016.2606460

31. Zhang, J., et al.: Modeling and verification of reconfigurable and energy-efficient manufacturing systems. Discrete Dyn. Nat. Soc. 2015, 14 (2015)

Author Index

Printed in the United States
By Bookmasters